ECO-PHENOMENOLOGY

SUNY Series in Environmental Philosophy and Ethics
J. Baird Callicott and John van Buren, editors

ECO-PHENOMENOLOGY

Back to the Earth Itself

Edited by
Charles S. Brown
and
Ted Toadvine

STATE UNIVERSITY OF NEW YORK PRESS

Published by
State University of New York Press, Albany

For information, address State University of New York Press,
194 Washington Avenue, Suite 305, Albany, NY 12210-2384

Production by Christine L. Hamel
Marketing by Michael Campochiaro

Library of Congress Cataloging in Publication Data

Eco-phenomenology : back to the earth itself / edited by Charles S. Brown
    and Ted Toadvine.
        p. cm. — (SUNY series in environmental philosophy and ethics)
    Includes bibliographical references and index.
    ISBN-13: 978-0-7914-5621-7 (hc : alk. paper) — 978-0-7914-5622-4 (pbk. : alk. paper)
    ISBN-10: 0-7914-5621-8 (hc : alk. paper) — 0-7914-5622-6 (pbk. : alk. paper)
    1. Environmentalism—Philosophy. 2. Ecology—Philosophy. 3. Phenomen-
ology. I. Brown, Charles S., 1950– II. Toadvine, Ted, 1968– III. Series.

GE195.E23 2003
363.7'001—dc21

                                                                2002075850

                                    10 9 8 7 6 5 4 3 2 1

Contents

Acknowledgments

In the fall of 1999, we invited Wes Jackson and Ed Casey to speak at Emporia State University as part of the First Annual Flint Hills Regional Environmental Colloquium. Our interaction with Wes and Ed at this conference spurred the thinking that led to this volume, and we would like to thank them for this inspiration. We are also grateful to Jane Bunker of the State University of New York Press for her immediate enthusiasm for our proposal and continued support throughout its development, and to the anonymous reviewers of the volume, whose suggestions resulted in numerous improvements. The Social Sciences Department at Emporia State University, under the leadership of Chair Phil Kelly, provided invaluable support for this work on many levels. We thank Nathan Hall and Jacque Fehr for their proofreading assistance. We would also like to thank our partners, Dianne Brown and Elizabeth Locey, for their support and encouragement. And, of course, we are indebted to our contributors, whose work here has confirmed our confidence in eco-phenomenology as a new direction for philosophy.

Eco-Phenomenology

An Introduction

CHARLES S. BROWN AND TED TOADVINE

In one of the oldest stories in the history of philosophy, a witty Thracian maid was said to have mocked Thales as he fell into a hole while watching the sky. Later we learn that Thales, through his sky watching, foresaw a bountiful olive harvest, rented the presses while the prices were cheap, and sold access to the presses for a handsome profit. According to Aristotle, who recounts this tale, Thales intended to demonstrate that philosophers can use their wisdom for practical affairs when they wish. But this demonstration of the practical application of philosophy, as impressive as it is, has not greatly enhanced the reputations of philosophers as practical problem solvers. Today, faced with serious environmental concerns, both local and global, as well as with the growing realization that our current mode of life as humans on this planet is not sustainable, we look to science and technology for solutions. Biologists, earth scientists, and meteorologists offer us increasingly technical solutions to our problems. But is there, perhaps, a role for philosophy to play in responding to our current problems?

Although a few voices can be heard calling for philosophical examination of our predicament, they are a small minority. For the most part, we are living through a massive cultural propaganda exercise dedicated to the task of convincing ourselves that the dominant cultural forces have identified the problem and are working steadily toward appropriate solutions. While we may not yet be walking the green walk, we are well on our way to mastering the green talk. Apart from a few hardened reactionary voices, the entire American mainstream from Disney to the White

House now sings a green song. Environmental slogans that were heard only among a dedicated core of "treehuggers" a generation ago have become today's accepted clichés. Political spin doctors and corporate public relations departments, having mastered the art of "green speak," reassure us that our environmental concerns, as real as they are, are being handled attentively. We may continue to drive our SUV's to fast-food franchises in support of the global beef market without any need for alarm or personal sacrifice.

Although the world rarely looks to them for help in analyzing such practical matters, philosophers have nevertheless been busy reevaluating our relation with nature and its underlying assumptions. Even in the ivory-tower discipline of academic philosophy, environmental ethics has become a legitimate topic of study. Treated at best as a fringe interest only a generation ago, the philosophical examination of the environment is gaining respect as a desirable area of academic teaching and research. But while philosophers have begun to talk among themselves about the current state of nature, difficulties persist in establishing serious dialogue with other academic disciplines, much less with the public outside the academy. Philosophy has yet to find an effective voice in our struggle with the environmental crisis or a clear role in our quest for a sustainable human presence on the earth.

If philosophy does have a contribution to make in today's practical decision making, this contribution will likely begin with steady and insightful clarification of our ethical and metaphysical assumptions about ourselves and the world around us. These basic assumptions— about the relation between individual and society, human nature, the nature of nature, and the nature of the Good—underlie all of our current behavior, both individually and culturally. But the assumptions that have guided our past behavior reveal their limitations as we think about, imagine, and live through the events and consequences of what we call the environmental crisis. When confronted with the consequences of our actions—mass extinctions, climate change, global pollution, dwindling resources—we inevitably experience a moral unease over what has been done, what we have done, to nature. We cannot help but ask about the root of this deep-seated moral reaction, and the changes it calls for in our current practices. To answer these questions, we need the help of philosophy.

The suggestion that philosophy should play a role in reorienting our relation with the natural world will no doubt come as a surprise to many. It may be even more surprising that the present volume is dedicated to the role phenomenology can play in developing this new relation with nature, given its reputation as a highly abstract theoretical inquiry into "consciousness" or "being." In fact, one of the basic themes of the present collection of essays is that phenomenology, as a contemporary method in philosophy, is particularly well suited to working through some of the dilemmas that have faced environmental ethicists and philosophers of nature.

Originating in the work of Edmund Husserl and developed and enriched by thinkers such as Max Scheler, Martin Heidegger, Jean-Paul Sartre, Maurice Merleau-Ponty, and Emmanuel Levinas, phenomenology has won a worldwide following, not only among philosophers, but also among scholars in fields ranging from anthropology and architecture to geography and nursing.[1] While there have been methodological divergences over the course of phenomenology's first century, phenomenologists have continued to share the rallying cry first introduced by Husserl himself: "To the things themselves!" Phenomenology takes its starting point in a return to the "things" or "matters" themselves, that is, the world as we experience it. In other words, for phenomenologists, experience must be treated as the starting point and ultimate court of appeal for all philosophical evidence.

Although phenomenologists do not all agree on the best manner of characterizing or describing experience, or on the nature of the subject that experiences, this general tendency to start from experience—here taking this term in a broad sense—already demonstrates a basic convergence of the phenomenological method with the concerns of contemporary environmental thought. Our conviction that nature has value, that it deserves or demands a certain proper treatment from us, must have its roots in an *experience* of nature. As Neil Evernden has argued, those approaches to nature that strip it of all experienced qualities leave us with an unrecognizable abstraction, and certainly not with any version of nature that could have inspired our initial appreciation.[2]

From the beginning, phenomenologists have taken an interest in this process of abstraction by which the world as we experience it is gradually transformed into the naturalistic conception of the world taken for granted by contemporary science. One point of agreement among phenomenologists is their criticism and rejection of the tendency of scientific naturalism to forget its own roots in experience. The consequence of this forgetting is that our experienced reality is supplanted by an abstract model of reality—a model that, for all of its usefulness, cannot claim epistemological or metaphysical priority over the world as experienced. The return to "things themselves" and the critique of scientific naturalism both point in the direction of much contemporary environmental thought.

Throughout its development, phenomenology has seemed to promise a methodological route toward the disclosure of an "alternative" conception of nature—one that would avoid the reductionism of scientific naturalism as well as the excesses of speculative metaphysics. It should not surprise us, then, that today's environmentalists see promise in the methods of phenomenology. Phenomenology is set apart from other theoretical methods by its unique capacity for bringing to expression, rather than silencing, our relation with nature and the experience of value rooted in this relation. For environmental philosophers, phenomenology suggests alternatives to many of the ingrained tendencies that limit our inherited perspectives: our myopic obsession with objectivity, our anthropocentric conceptions of value, and other legacies of Cartesian dualism. Phenomenology opens a space for the interdisciplinary examination of our relation with nature, for a scrutiny of the historical and institutional construction of the "natural," and even of the role this concept plays in the formation of our cultural and self-identities. From its starting point in experience, phenomenology provides an open horizon for the exploration of all facets of our relation with nature outside of narrowly prescribed disciplinary boundaries. By doing so, phenomenology makes it possible, perhaps for the first time, for philosophical thinking to express and respond to the full range of our natural experiences.

Even as environmental thinkers have begun to gravitate toward phenomenology, phenomenological philosophers have found the momentum of their own field always returning them to the question of nature. A careful examination of the history and development of the phenomenological tradition throughout the twentieth century reveals numerous interwoven strands that lead, through their own internal tensions, toward the emergence of ecological reflection—from Husserl's critique of naturalism to Heidegger's disclosure of *Dasein* as *Being-in-the-world*, from Merleau-Ponty's descriptions of the lived body's perceptual dialogue to Levinas's attestation of the singularity of the face. Admittedly, each of these "classic" phenomenological authors stops short of developing an "environmental" philosophy. And yet, there is the growing conviction, evident among the authors collected here, that the fulfillment of these classic phenomenological truths points us in the direction of ecological investigation. Of course, after Hegel's tutelage in the historical nature of concepts, we should not be surprised to find the concept of phenomenology unfold in novel ways at the dawn of its second century, especially as it draws on its task of exploring and disclosing the complexities and novelties of our experience of the world.

The intersection of ecological thinking with phenomenology, the momentum that drives each toward the other, begets a new cross-disciplinary inquiry: eco-phenomenology. Eco-phenomenology is based on a double claim: first, that an adequate account of our ecological situation requires the methods and insights of phenomenology; and, second, that phenomenology, led by its own momentum, becomes a philosophical ecology, that is, a study of the interrelationship between organism and world in its metaphysical and axiological dimensions. Of course, this cross-disciplinary inquiry is still in its infancy; how the dialectical exchange between ecological thinking and phenomenology will operate is a matter that only future work can determine. Nevertheless, the essays we have collected here provide a first sketch of the contribution eco-phenomenology can make for us today.

The first three chapters in this volume demonstrate the relevance of Husserl's phenomenology to the themes and issues comprising environmental philosophy. These authors see in Husserl's method and in his critique of naturalism the beginnings of an understanding of nature, rationality, and knowledge that would overcome the nihilism of uncritical scientism and instrumental rationality. New phenomenological approaches to the study of nature and culture follow from this beginning, approaches that are friendly to the projects of ecological philosophy.

In the opening chapter, "The Real and the Good: Phenomenology and the Possibility of an Axiological Rationality," Charles S. Brown argues that Husserl's critique of naturalism makes him a clear but unnoticed ally of the Radical Ecologists—those who claim that environmental destruction and crisis are caused by core beliefs within our worldview that sanction, legitimate, and even encourage the domination and technological control of nature. Brown, however, finds in Husserl's theory of intentionality the possibility of the development of an axiological rationality. This axiological rationality, in contrast with our current conceptions of rationality, would begin with the articulation of goodness and value within nonhuman nature, leading us to an experiential, if not ontological, grounding of an ecological ethics.

In the second chapter, "An Understanding Heart: Reason, Value, and Transcendental Phenomenology," Erazim Kohák argues that an alternative conception of rationality developed from Husserl's transcendental phenomenology is necessary for two reasons: first, to fulfill the European dream of a commitment to reason as the arbiter of good and evil; and, second, to provide a vision of the world and our place in it that makes possible our long range sustainable coexistence with the community of life. Both Brown and Kohák agree that phenomenology offers ecological philosophy an alternative point of departure that begins with descriptions of our essentially value-laden and meaning-structured lifeworld.

The last of the Husserlian-inspired chapters, Lester Embree's "The Possibility of a Constitutive Phenomenology of the Environment," extends the possibilities of the phenomenological method by locating the "encountered environment" within the cultural lifeworld, thereby rendering this environment available for phenomenological exploration from the perspectives of ethnology, sociology, and history. Focusing on valuational and volitional encounterings of nature, be they aesthetic, practical, or political, as directly experienced lifeworldly nature, Embree argues that such descriptions of encountering nature and nature as encountered, in addition to aiding in the clarification of the justification of environmental action, also demonstrate the plausibility of applying the phenomenological method to the concerns of ecological philosophy.

While Husserl's phenomenological method may suggest an alternative and eco-friendly vision of nature and reason, his approach is not without its difficulties. One of the initial worries of Husserl's philosophy concerned the tension between his claims of radicality and the uncompromising Cartesian cast of his thinking. For Husserl, phenomenological reflection reveals the constitution of meaning through the intentional acts of a transcendental ego. To many of Husserl's critics and admirers, his phenomenology is a reduction of the world to meaning and of meaning to subjectivity. This worry about an excessive idealism in Husserl's method reappears in our context as a worry about the inevitable anthropocentrism in such an approach. Husserl, on the other hand, would certainly argue that the perspective of a transcendental ego has already been freed from human entanglements.

In the next chapter, "Prolegomena to Any Future Phenomenological Ecology," John Llewelyn examines Husserl's description of transcendental subjectivity and Heidegger's analysis of Dasein as potential points of departure for a phenomenological ecology. Llewelyn finds that the eco-philosophical possibilities of both are limited by the anthropocentrism latent in their work: for Husserl, this anthropocentrism comes to the fore in his account of intersubjectivity, while it surfaces for Heidegger in his claim that the everyday world of Dasein unfolds as a totality of utilities. This worry is mitigated, for Llewelyn, by the recognition of the historical unfolding of phenomenology's self-understanding, which brings with it increasingly rich notions of phenomenological description. Llewelyn suggests a fusion of Heidegger's later thinking of the Fourfold (earth, sky, gods, and mortals) with Levinas's insight that the ethical imperative rests on the singularity of the face. This "deep" eco-phenomenological framework would replace the "shallow" anthropocentrism of earlier phenomenology.

The suggestion that Heidegger's later philosophy may contribute to a new eco-phenomenology is scrutinized in Michael E. Zimmerman's "Heidegger, Phenomenology, and Contemporary Environmentalism." Zimmerman frames his chapter with the question of whether Heidegger's thinking offers us any real hope for an escape from the nihilism of technological modernity. After exploring the ecological implications of Heidegger's earlier phenomenological ontology, especially his appropriation of Aristotle's account of *physis*, Zimmerman confronts the criticism that Heidegger offers no alternative to the nihilism of technological modernity. Any desire to "escape" from this nihilism is inconsistent, some commentators hold, with Heidegger's own position concerning Dasein's disclosive character. Zimmerman explores responses to this critique, but he also points out other difficulties with reading Hedegger in an eco-friendly fashion, for example, his failure to appreciate the validity of traditional ethical norms, and the lack of any true reciprocity between ontological wisdom and ethical compassion in his thought. As an alternative, Zimmerman suggests a panentheism within which Spirit is gradually fulfilled through the evolution of disclosive and creative powers within nature and humanity. This conception, Zimmerman concludes, provides a basis for compassion, progressive political action, and dialogue between traditions that had remained lacking in Hedidegger's account.

Monika Langer's chapter, "Nietzsche, Heidegger, and Merleau-Ponty: Some of Their Contributions and Limitations for 'Environmentalism'," continues this examination of Heidegger, but now within a larger historical context that places Nietzsche and Merleau-Ponty along the same axis of thought. Langer finds Heidegger's critique of values to be inherently subjectivistic, but she suggests that his distinction between meditative and calculative thinking may provide resources for a deeper ecological approach. Reading Nietzsche as a phenomenologist, she finds in his work a significant critique of the dominant, dualistic ontology underlying the ecological crisis. As a corrective to the excessive rationalism and scientism of traditional thinking, Nietzsche's Zarathustra commands us to remain "true to the earth." Other motifs in Nietzsche's thinking, however, especially his maintenance of traditional human/animal and male/female hierarchies, seem to block the development of his ecological insights. Lastly, it is in Merleau-Ponty's descriptions of corporeality and the flesh of the world that Langer places most of her hope for a nondualistic ontology that respects the alterity of Being. Even so, Merleau-Ponty's account is also limited by his ahistorical and gender-neutral description, and Langer suggests that his account may benefit from an encounter with the insights of recent eco-feminism. In conclusion, she finds in the critical engagement of phenomenology and environmentalism the possibility for an "open-ended, mutually enriching dialogue."

The discussion of Merleau-Ponty is continued in the last of the volume's historically oriented chapters, Don E. Marietta, Jr.'s "Back to Earth with Reflection and Ecology." In Merleau-Ponty's conception of phenomenology as "concrete reflection," Marietta finds the path to a critical holism, one that reveals no sharp distinction between the self and the environment or between values and facts. Although he rejects any attempt at a logical derivation of the normative from the descriptive, Marietta holds that phenomenological reflection directly reveals values in the experienced world, thereby overcoming the is/ought impasse of traditional value thinking. These immediately apprehended values lend support for a minimal metaphysical holism that undergirds a commitment to an environmentally sound ethics without being wedded to any particular biological model. The success of Merleau-Ponty's method here suggests that his approach preserves the eco-friendly aspects of the phenomenological tradition while overcoming some of its Cartesian or anthropocentric limitations.

The preceding chapters have explored the ecological potential of figures in the phenomenological tradition, and despite the differences in their points of departure, each aims for a similar destination: the development of a phenomenological mode of access to a value-laden domain of experience, an experience that can help us understand and justify alternative, eco-friendly conceptions of rationality and ethical action. In the next group of chapters, the concern with the method and interpretation of classic phenomenological philosophers recedes while the phenomenological descriptions themselves take center stage. This gradual turn away from methodological issues and toward concrete descriptions reflects the traditional practice of phenomenological philosophy itself. In fact, the lifeblood of phenomenology lies in its concrete descriptions, the "return to the things themselves." By following the description of experience wherever it may lead, phenomenology discovers new horizons for exploration. But it is also forced to constantly reexamine its own methodological presuppositions, and this possibility for methodological revitalization is at the heart of its longevity as a vibrant philosophical method. The following chapters push the descriptive powers of phenomenology to new levels, while at the same time renewing the methodological self-examination that our exploration of the tradition has already begun.

In "The Primacy of Desire and Its Ecological Consequences," Ted Toadvine argues that the recent tendency of environmental thinkers to stress the "kinship" between humanity and nature runs the risk of collapsing humanity and nature into a predictable, continuous, and homogenous unity. Our idiosyncratic experience of nature, Toadvine suggests, is not reducible to this predictable unity, and an ethical response to nature requires our recognition of its unpredictable, nonhomogenous, and noncontinuous character. Drawing on analyses of corporeality, desire, and flesh in Schopenhauer, Sartre, and Merleau-Ponty, Toadvine explores how such an "idiosyncratic" experience of nature might be approached without lapsing into noumenality. He concludes by suggesting that the radical exteriority of nature requires an "impossible" phenomenology—that is, an opening onto the unnameable opacity or resistance to perception and thought that nature discloses. According to Toadvine, the ultimate ground of an ethical response to nature lies in the im-possible experience of this opacity and resistance.

In "Phenomenology on the Rocks," Irene J. Klaver argues that the recent phenomenon of globalization, and with it our increasing recognition of the fragility of the natural world, brings us face to face with the coconstitution of nature and culture. This interdependency requires a new philosophical perspective on the natural world. For the first time in history, we are beginning to experience nature itself as a significant presence, intertwined with our own history and politics. Klaver's descriptions of this politicized and coconstituted nature—from crashing boulders in the Montana mountains to stone relicts from Jesse James's grave—reveal an ontology of im/permanence, incompatibility, and boundary, as well as the insight that meaning and materiality are phenomenologically inseparable. With this recognition, Klaver argues, traditional phenomenology finds itself "on the rocks." Klaver concludes by reminding us of the power of stones, the black boulders at Buchenwald in particular, to express silently a horror that outstrips all sense—the meaningless and mass suffering of the holocaust.

Of course, it is Levinas, more than any other, who has taught us to hear the call memorialized in such stones, stones that bear witness to our disastrous "humanity." In the next two chapters, Christian Diehm and Edward S. Casey explore the possibilities for extending Levinas's insight concerning the ethical singularity of the face to the realm of the nonhuman. In "Natural Disasters," Diehm inquires whether the suffering and mortality—that is, the "disastrousness"—experienced on the human face can be found on faces other-than-human. By raising the question of "natural disasters" Diehm asks, in part, if it is proper to apply moral (or perhaps protomoral) predicates to nature. Answering in the affirmative, Diehm writes that there are countless natural disasters. Drawing on Hans Jonas's existential interpretation of biological facts, Diehm concludes that "every body is the other," both in the sense of forming an other center of awareness that I cannot occupy, and of manifesting the vulnerability characteristic of naked flesh. Despite Levinas's own hesitations, Diehm argues that his philosophy may sensitize us to the "tenderness of all flesh" in a world teeming with natural disasters.

Edward S. Casey, in "Taking a Glance at the Environment: Preliminary Thoughts on a Promising Topic," is also concerned with the location of an "equivalent of the face" in the nonhuman world. As Casey points out, an ethic of the environment must begin with the sheer and simple fact of being struck by something wrong happening in the environment. Casey locates the first moment of ethical responsiveness in the glance, the "first moment of noticing" that is indispensable for later ethical reflection, judgment, and action. Extending the "face" as the locus of ethical obligation into the domain of ecological ethics, he finds that place-world shows itself in its surfaces either as existing within its own normative parameters, or else as exceeding or undermining these parameters, that is, as "ill at ease" with itself. Just as we notice, in a glance, the vulnerability and distress of a person assaulted on a city street, we see straightaway the nakedness, fragility, and distress of a deforested mountainside—and the imperative to respond. Casey admits that not all—indeed, perhaps very few—will feel the force of an ethical imperative in the landscape, but this fact is, in his view, a measure of our "massive cultural disconnection" from the natural world.

As we have seen above, phenomenology in general, and eco-phenomenology in particular, take their start from a critique of naturalism and the attempt to break with its reductive mode of thinking. But in our final chapter, "What Is Eco-Phenomenology?" David Wood seeks a certain rapprochement between phenomenology and naturalism. Phenomenology has an essential role to play in describing our involvement with the natural world, Wood notes, but the traditional conception of intentionality fails to uncover the deeper "relationalities" of our engagement with the world. These relationalities form a "middle ground" irreducible either to simple intentionality or simple causality, and our pursuit of them must therefore take both modes of involvement into account. Offering the plexity of time and the boundaries of thinghood as examples, Wood demonstrates the integration of intentionality with embodied existence and the world. Intentionality's embodiment and essential link to our human needs and desires—and through them to the larger milieu—closes the gap between phenomenology and naturalism, leading to a "naturalization" of consciousness as well as an "expansion of our sense of the natural." This nonreductive eco-phenomenology offers us new resources, Wood suggests in conclusion, for understanding the complex logics and boundary relations that have been a stumbling block for Deep Ecology and other environmental approaches.

We find in Wood's chapter several points that are worth emphasizing as we consider the possible future of eco-phenomenology. The first is phenomenology's need for reconciliation with naturalism, even if this convergence reforges both—phenomenology as well as naturalism—into forms as yet unrecognizable. Although it is true that nature cannot adequately be reduced to purely extensional categories, it is also true that phenomenology must reconsider its own dependence on the natural world. A true eco-phenomenology must become a naturalized phenomenology, although perhaps in a sense of "nature" that has yet to be adequately described.

Perhaps we can offer several suggestions about this alternative conception of nature on the basis of the contributions included here: First, it will avoid the dualism of classical Cartesian thought, the separation of consciousness from matter that has infected philosophy, including phenomenology, up to our present century. But the "alternative" to classical dualism cannot be a homogenous monism either. Rather, an adequate account of nature must find better ways of expressing our complex relationship with it—a relation reducible neither to the causality of meaningless matter in motion, nor to the meanings arrayed before a pure subject. It must articulate meaning's embeddedness within nature in a way that avoids positing a metaphysical discontinuity between the two, while also resisting the countertemptation of reducing either one to the other.

Second, by making possible the rediscovery of our natural experiences as value laden, eco-phenomenology would recognize nature's axiological qualities as both inherent and ineliminable. In addition to displacing our culture's nihilistic conception of the natural world, this insight also paves the way for a new conception of rationality; namely, of a reason that encounters and enters into dialogue with the immediately apprehended values, human and nonhuman, of our experienced world. With the head and heart reunited, reason can find its place once again in moral, social, and political discourse. True rationality, then, is found as far as possible from "instrumental" reason or scientific "objectivity"; it lies, rather, in the pursuit of *phronēsis* and of the good life for humanity and the earth.

But perhaps this new vision of nature sounds more than a little utopian. What can phenomenology show us that has not already been demonstrated by other radical ecology movements? What genuine hope can it bring for healing the rift at our culture's heart, our recoil from the nature both outside us and within us? With other radical ecology movements, eco-phenomenology shares the conviction that our cultural detachment from our natural roots rests on the very structure of our current modes of thought, that we are weighted down by the ballast of tradition, by the assumptions and commitments carried forward from Platonism, Christianity, capitalism, Cartesian dualism, patriarchy, and the like. Part of the solution to our current situation must lie in tracking down these philosophical land mines, scattered through the landscape of our cultural history, in order to diffuse them. This process is necessarily a slow one, and other radical ecology movements are playing an essential role in this endeavor. But what is lacking in other contemporary approaches to the natural world is the positive project that must complement this critical effort; they lack a way in, an approach to nature on its own terms that nevertheless leaves our connection with our own world intact. Eco-phenomenology offers a methodological bridge between the natural world and our own, or rather the rediscovery of the bridge that we are and have always been but—thanks to our collective amnesia—have forgotten, almost irretrievably. It is not enough to diagnose our forgetting; there is also a matter of remembering—remembering the earth.

The alternative experience and account of nature to which eco-phenomenology gives us access is potentially revolutionary. The rediscovery of a natural world that is inherently and primordially meaningful and worthy of respect might help us to overcome our cultural estrangement from the world around us. This new vision of nature might also allow us, once freed from our nihilistic attitudes toward the natural world, to develop an appropriate philosophy of nature, a "phenomenological naturalism," that circumvents intractable puzzles concerning intrinsic value and anthropocentrism. For far too long, humanity has envisioned itself as an alien presence in nature, thus steering many of the world's religions and moral codes toward a rebellion against our own natural being. Having constituted ourselves in opposition to nature, we adopt values and purposes that threaten the earth itself. Only a reconceptualization of our place and role in nature can work against this tragic disconnection from ourselves and from the wellspring of our being. To begin this task by reconnecting us with our most basic and primordial experiences of the natural world—such is the power and promise of eco-phenomenology.

One final point about the aims and scope of eco-phenomenology deserves mention, namely, its transcendence of disciplinary boundaries. Although phenomenology as a contemporary movement began among philosophers and has persisted within the academic discipline of philosophy, academic philosophers are quite probably a minority among phenomenologists today. This is simply because the insights originally developed within the context of philosophy have quickly proven themselves adaptable to a range of concerns, theoretical and applied, across the boundaries of discipline, language, and nationality. In parallel, eco-phenomenology is now coming to awareness of itself as a theoretical movement among philosophers and ecologists. But, like phenomenology before it, eco-phenomenology may also bear valuable fruit in cross-pollination with other academic disciplines and with fields outside the academy. In time, the insights of eco-phenomenology hold the promise of bringing about a dramatic shift in our current understanding of ourselves and of our place in the natural world. For us today, such an end would be an incomparably greater harvest than all of the olives of Miletus.

Notes

1. For some sense of the international and disciplinary range of phenomenology, peruse the entries in *The Encyclopedia of Phenomenology*, ed. Lester Embree et al. (Dordrecht: Kluwer Academic Publishers, 1997).
2. Neil Evernden, *The Natural Alien: Humankind and Environment*, 2d ed. (Toronto: University of Toronto Press, 1993), especially chapter 1.

I

Ecological Philosophy and the Phenomenological Tradition

CHAPTER 1

The Real and the Good

Phenomenology and the Possibility
of an Axiological Rationality

CHARLES S. BROWN

In what ways can an encounter, conversation, or dialogue between eco-logical philosophy and phenomenology be fruitful? The issues driving ecological philosophy concern the ontological status of human and non-human nature, intrinsic value and humanity's axiological relation to nature, and the boundaries and limits of the moral community. Although such questions seem to lie beyond the methodological restrictions of phe-nomenology's commitment to describe experience within an attitude of normative and ontological abstention, even a phenomenology that remains close to Husserl's has much to offer ecological philosophy.

To begin to discover the possibilities in such an encounter, we will first examine Husserl's critique of naturalism.[1] His critique helps us to see that the modern enframing of nature results in a conception of nature con-sisting entirely of extensional properties related to each other within a causal matrix. Such an enframing leads to moral, social, and political crisis as the value-free conceptions of rationality and objectivity support-ing such naturalism dismiss the Good as subjective preference and thus remove questions of value from rational discourse. In reducing all reality to extension and causality, naturalism separates the Good from the Real, ultimately making moral philosophy impossible. The recognition of such an impossibility is apparent in the early-twentieth-century move away from normative ethics to metaethics.

Husserl's critique of naturalism helps us to see that a great deal of modern moral philosophy, including some aspects that make the development of an ecological ethics difficult, is based on an uncritical appropriation of the account of objectivity developed to epistemically support naturalistic metaphysics. As we will see in the last part of the chapter, some aspects of Husserl's theory of intentionality can be adapted to provide new directions for developing an account of an axiological rationality that would be open to the claim that there is goodness and value within nonhuman nature. Such a form of rationality, based in the dialectics of empty and filled intentions, would begin to provide a discourse in which the goodness and value of nonhuman nature could be registered, expressed, and articulated in a rational manner, thus providing an experiential, if not a metaphysical, grounding of an ecological ethics.

Husserl's rather passionate critique of the evils of naturalism make him a clear but unnoticed ally of contemporary ecological philosophers who have argued that there are important and largely unnoticed connections between our worldviews, metaphysical systems, and forms of rationality, on the one hand, and social and environmental domination, on the other. Such philosophers, often known as Radical Ecologists, typically are social ecologists, deep ecologists, or eco-feminists.[2] According to their specific diagnoses, each offers suggested cures involving some kind of revolution in thinking that would produce the kind of spiritual metanoia needed to develop and sustain socially just and environmentally benign practices. Radical Ecologists share the conviction that the massive ecological damage we are witnessing today, as well as inequitable and unjust social arrangements, are the inevitable products of those ways of thinking that separate and privilege humanity over nature. The Radical Ecologists' call to overcome this kind of thinking and replace it with a new understanding of the humanity-nature relation that would result in the emergence and maintenance of environmentally benign practices requires a rethinking of both the meaning of humanity and the meaning of nature in which normative and ontological issues are at stake. Such questions lie in the very interesting crossroads of metaphysics and value theory but also intersect with a Green political agenda and (forgive the term) a "spiritual" quest for the cultivation of a new state of *humanitas*[3] that transcends the relative barbarism of *homo centrus centrus*.[4]

The Radical Ecologists see this damage as symptomatic of a deeper disorder embedded within the humanity-nature relation. It is embedded within the way nature and humanity are experienced in daily life, in myth, in literature, and in abstract thought. To the extent that the ecological devastation we witness today is the result of anthropocentrism, androcentrism, or a dualistic value-hierarchical worldview (as many have claimed), the ecological crisis is a crisis of meaning. It is ultimately the meaning of nature and humanity that is at stake. As such it can be managed, solved, or perhaps overcome by new myths or improvements in thinking that would reconceptualize the boundaries, as well as the content, of our understanding of humanity and nature.

For the existential philosopher, the roots of the ecological crisis may be much deeper than the Radical Ecologists realize. The humanity-nature disorder is perhaps best conceived as a manifestation of the tendency toward alienation inherent in the human condition, one that operates prior to any particular meaning system. This tendency toward alienation, leading to war and oppression in the past, has now been coupled with the technological power to sustain a massive *homo centrus centrus* population explosion, the by-products of which are poisoning and dismantling the Earth's bio-web. There is a certain irony here as the realization of massive ecological destruction occurs just when we had thought that our science and technology would save us from the ravages of the organic world. Instead we find ourselves hurtling toward or perhaps through an irrevocable tear in the fabric of the planetary biotic web (and perhaps beyond). Dreams of technological Utopia have been replaced overnight by nightmares of ecological holocaust. The existential philosophers remind us that the replacement of one conceptual system for another is not enough unless there occurs with it a corresponding shift or lifestyle change that actually ushers in a new mode of being for humanity. Such thinking reinforces the claim of radicality within the projects of Radical Ecology.

Phenomenology's specific contribution to ecological philosophy begins in the attitude of respect for experience that it shares with ecological philosophy and many environmentalists. Just as Thoreau, Muir, and Leopold describe the world in such a way that the experiencing of the world is an integral part of it, and in doing so show us broader possibilities of experience, phenomenology as a philosophical method begins with a respect for experience and ultimately grounds all meaning in experience. Phenomenology is a method of philosophical research that describes the forms and structures of experience as well as a critique of those ways of doing philosophy that operate from a naïve standpoint. The description of experience is an attempt to return to the "things-themselves"[5] rather than simply taking for granted higher-level, culturally sedimented idealizations and abstractions that often pass for ahistorical metaphysical discoveries. Phenomenology seeks to describe the meaning within experience and to uncover the experiential phenomena on which categories of higher-level philosophical discourse are founded and in which those experiential phenomena are embedded. A phenomenological approach to moral philosophy[6] begins with descriptions of moral experience, while a phenomenological natural philosophy begins with descriptions of encounters with life-worldly nature, that is, the nature we experience prior to theoretical abstraction.

The naïve standpoint, which is simply our natural taken-for-granted involvement with the world, is initially undermined by the uniquely phenomenological method of epochē, which requires a philosophical abstention[7] from everyday metaphysical and normative commitments. From this perspective, theories, ideologies, traditions, and discourses are revealed as historically and intentionally constituted. From the phenomenological perspective, there is no one correct tradition, theory, or discourse, although from this perspective we do see that there are many worlds, traditions, and theories that claim to be privileged.[8] The phenomenological reduction helps to free thinking from its natural ideological naiveté by adopting such a position of ontological neutrality. By a "bracketing" of the realistic assumptions of everyday consciousness, we are in a position to see that the world and the things in it are only given to us through the interpretative and meaning-bestowing function of our intentional acts. Husserl's steady development of this method eventually led to the discovery of the everyday world of pretheoretical experience, viz., the lifeworld, which serves as the sense foundation for the idealized and historically constituted typifications of the human and social sciences. It is within this lifeworld of direct and immediate experience that we may begin to find an experiential grounding of an ecological ethics.

Phenomenology exemplifies an attitude of respect for lived experience. Unlike naturalism, phenomenology does not seek to dismiss experience as subjective, nor does it wish to replace or reduce experience with or to a more fundamental or more basic mode of being. A phenomenological philosophy is one that remains close to our original experience, respects that experience, and seeks to find within experience a measure of rationality and truth. To this extent all phenomenology begins with a critique and rejection of metaphysical naturalism, which disrespects and seeks to eliminate, reduce, or replace experience.

Husserl's Critique of Naturalism

Husserl argued that the naturalistic metaphysics of his day, which he believed dominated philosophical thinking, was naïve in that it took the idealized and abstract objects of a mathematized physics to be not only a faithful representation of reality itself but the only such possible one. He argued that, by the double identification of extensional properties as "the Real" and reason as "scientific method," rationality had become trapped in the success of its own natural sciences, and that, by the interpretation of rationality as value free, reason had lost the ability to confront problems of value. Husserl thus blames the irrationalism and slide toward barbarism that he witnessed throughout his life on such a nihilistic conception of reason.[9] Husserl and phenomenologists in general, I believe, should be initially sympathetic to the Radical Ecologists' diagnosis that metaphysically distorted worldviews and forms of rationality are responsible for the crisis of the environment and sympathetic to the proposal that new forms of rationality and new worldviews are needed to halt environmental destruction and forge new ways of coexisting with the natural world.

Both the Radical Ecologists and Husserl argue that the very idea of nature is deeply historical, in that the founding metaphors we use to construct a concept of nature are neither universal nor necessary but rather are historical achievements of particular cultural life forms. Husserl, like many Radical Ecologists, complains that the monistic materialism of contemporary naturalism offers us a view of the world in which only extensional properties are real. On this view not only is our traditional spiritual and mentalistic conception of ourselves relegated to the status of myth and superstition or, at best, conceived of as a folk psychology that awaits replacement by a mature materialistic science, but nature itself is constructed as devoid of meaning and value. In this way the Good has been so conceptually severed from the Real that goodness itself is often dismissed as an empty concept reflecting only personal preference.

It was, of course, part of Descartes's genius to so sharply separate the natural from the spiritual and the mental that each had its own autonomous sphere. In this way, the autonomy of the realm of mind, spirit, and value was to be preserved in the face of the rising scientific-materialist conception of the world. Such a metaphysical *détente* proved unstable in the history of modern philosophy. By the end of the nineteenth century, the whole collection of mental attributes was being dismissed as mere appearance or epiphenomenon.

Such a version of materialistic metaphysical naturalism clearly rejects Cartesian Dualism but has not succeeded in overcoming dualistic thinking or Cartesian ontological categories. Such thinking accepts the Cartesian distinction of *res cogitans* and *res extensa* but then denies the reality of mind, spirit, value, and meaning—leaving only a world of value-free physical entities, viz., *res extensa*. Here Cartesian Dualism becomes Cartesian Monism. *Res extensa* becomes objective and real while *res cogitans* becomes subjective and unreal. Although Descartes could clearly see the difference between the phenomenon of subjectivity and the phenomenon of objectivity, he misinterprets that difference within the categories of thinking available to him. He interprets objectivity in terms consistent with the new mathematized Galilean science, and he interprets what has been exorcized from nature by Galilean science—subjectivity, meaning, value, and transcendence—according to the standard religious categories of the day, that is, as outside of nature.

The naturalism that Husserl feared, as well as the naïve faith that natural science presents to us the one true picture of the world, have always sought to justify themselves by appeal to the so-called objectivity of these sciences as their metaphysical guarantor. But the notion of objectivity itself is a highly idealized and abstract construction. An intentional analysis of the phenomenon of objectivity reveals that the sense of "objectivity" results from an encounter between the possibilities of understanding and that which is understood. We experience objectivity, for example, when we view an object from conflicting perspectives, take another look, and resolve the conflict. In this way the achievement of objectivity emerges from the dialectic of empty and filled intentions.

The modern sense of objectivity contains both the sense of that achievement in our pretheoretical lives and complex intersubjective sedimented meanings such as "emotional detachment," "empirical reliability," and "procedural correctness," as well as the sense of "absolute truth." The modern sense of objectivity has further been shaped by Descartes's interpretation of the phenomenon in terms consistent with the objects of a mathematized Galilean science. The modern sense of objectivity has thus been interpreted within the discourse of extensional realism and has come to include as core moments the senses of

1. something that admits of a single correct description;
2. something wholly determinable with fixed properties; and
3. mind-independent reality.

As the modern notion of objectivity is conceived within the theoretical discourse of extensional realism, it is, of course, irreducibly circular to ground extensional realism on such a notion of objectivity.

Husserl's return, in the *Crisis*, to the originary experiences of the lifeworld reveals that the metaphysical privileging of *res extensa* mistakes what is a complex multileveled historical abstraction for the nature of reality. The intentional analysis that reveals *res extensa* as an historical achievement does not invalidate the claim of the ontological priority of *res extensa*, but it does undermine such a claim. Similarly, an examination of lifeworldly moral experience reveals that moral phenomena are often vague and indeterminate, pluralistic, and never without a subjective component. And yet, as we shall see, modern moral theory relies on a notion of "moral objectivity" that dismisses vagueness, indeterminacy, plurality, and subjectivity as unreal. Moral theories are also highly idealized abstractions from lived moral experience and are historical and social constructions. This phenomenological insight undermines but does not overturn their metaphysical claim to being the one correct moral theory.

Phenomenology and Moral Theory

Despite the considerable differences among the various types of modern moral theories (Kantianism, Utilitarianism, Egoism, Contractarianism), all share an underlying and unexamined metaphysical view concerning the nature of moral phenomena that parallels naturalistic assumptions about physical phenomena. These moral theories share a conception of moral objectivity that incorporates the three "core moments" of physical objectivity listed above. Each tacitly assumes that all moral phenomena share a single underlying essence. Based on the allegedly single essential character of moral phenomena, each theory is able determinately to specify duties and obligations as well as determinately to specify the rightness or wrongness of real and possible actions. These wholly determinable fixed obligations are independent of our desires and beliefs and are thus independent of subjectivity. Each of these theories is committed to an ideal of objectivity that clearly seems parasitic on the notion of objectivity developed to support the realistic metaphysical interpretation of *res extensa*. And we may wonder if relying on the concept of objectivity in this way is fitting for moral philosophy at all. Indeed it is easy to suspect that here the extensional interpretation of objectivity, developed to epistemically support the natural sciences, has silently colonized some key aspects of modern moral theory.

Relying on an extensional interpretation of objectivity, modern moral theory approaches issues of morality in a distinctly nonmoral manner. For modern theory, morality becomes effectively decidable as some sort of calculus is applied to so-called objective standards of right and wrong. When morality becomes governed by an external calculus, the good has become secondary to the right.[10] Each of the historically influential moral theories emerging from the Enlightenment admirably makes the case for the moral relevancy of the feature it picks out as the essential nature of moral phenomena. Kant does this for rational motive, the Utilitarians do this for consequences, and the Contractarians do this for shared decisions. And each fails to make the case that their chosen single feature explains, articulates, or gives coherence to all moral phenomena. Each moral theory does a better job than its rivals at explaining its carefully chosen set of core examples, but each does a poor job of making philosophical sense out of others. Each of these moral theories provides us with deep and rich insight into the nature of a limited set of moral phenomena but fails to provide the single, universal criterion of all moral phenomena as it claims. These theories are each instances of a Rule-Based Moral Monism that, by reducing all moral phenomena to a single criterion, generates a procedure for positing a set of rules to guide and judge behavior. Such a schema fits the projects of power and control better than the simple desire to gain insight and wisdom and to practice tolerance and compassion.

Traditional moral theory is also monistic in another way, as it assumes a monistic criterion for moral considerability or inclusion within the moral community. Whether it is rationality, or the ability to suffer, or being the subject of a life, or simply being human, the relevant criterion for moral considerability or being worthy of moral regard is monistic, determinately specifiable, and independent of our sentiments or beliefs. If moral theory could be freed from its "objectivistic" (and here "monistic") assumptions, the collection of currently competing moral theories could be reconceptualized as a collection of moral insights and moral tools. In everyday moral experience, we intuitively find that both the consequences of our actions and respect for the subjective integrity of the other are morally relevant, and we also find both humans and nonhumans to be worthy of moral regard. Everyday experience resists being forced into monistic models. Monistic models of moral essence and moral considerability have little basis in experience.

A phenomenological and critical approach to moral philosophy that begins with an attitude of respect for pretheoretical experience must also begin with an initial acceptance of the idea that the prospect of reducing all moral phenomena to a single criterion may be hopelessly flawed. Thus we must be open to a kind of moral pluralism in which, for example, a duty to tell the truth may be, in one case, grounded in utility and, in another case, grounded in respect for the person with whom I am speaking. Or, from another perspective, we may find that it is appropriate to have an attitude of moral regard and respect for some nonhuman others because they may be able to suffer and for others because they are components of the biosphere.

Phenomenology and Moral Experience:
Toward an Axiological Rationality

From a phenomenological point of view, we find moral experience to be one of the irreducible domains of lifeworldly experience. Within our prereflective experiences, we regularly find the world and the things within it to be infused with value. The sun, the rain, and all manner of others are regularly experienced as good. We continually find action and events in the world to be morally satisfying or morally frustrating. Our everyday life is filled with moral sentiments that appear from a phenomenological perspective as instances of a prereflective axiological consciousness—that is, as an intentional and evaluative aiming at objects and states of affairs. Value experiences may be analyzed as a form of intentional consciousness in which the phenomenon of valuing and something valued are given together. As phenomenology is a "return to the things themselves," it does not wish to break apart the primal unity of the act of valuing and thing valued, as theory often does, but rather to simply describe that primal unity.

Our various understandings of the Good are, however, subject to continual reassessment in light of subsequent experience, just as we continually reassess our previous understandings of the Real or the True. In this way, value experiences exhibit their own kind of objectivity and, as is the case with perception, any one experience is given as provisional and revisable in light of future experience. We may, for example, experience something as good and desirable from one perspective and later experience that same thing as evil or undesirable from another. In case of such conflicting experiences, we may, metaphorically speaking, "take another look" in an effort to resolve the inconsistency. Clear-cutting large tracks of old-growth forest may appear as good from the perspective of business and profit while appearing evil from the perspective of wildlife habitat preservation. Parties to disputes such as these are essentially arguing that future intersubjective experience will support their experience and conception of the good. In this fashion, moral consciousness exhibits its own kind of objectivity and its own kind of rationality, grounded within the dialectics of empty and filled intentions.

Simply to say that we find things in the world to be good is not to say that we like these things. Nor is it simply to say that others like them as well, thus producing an intersubjective verification for their goodness, although, like other forms of objectivity, personal and intersubjective agreement are essential to any lasting claims. When I say that I find the rain and the sun to be good, it is not simply that I enjoy them. The experience of finding something to be good and finding something to be pleasurable are not the same. Value experiences usually come with a pleasurable affect or a positive sentiment, although it is not clear to what extent a pleasurable feeling is an essential part of value experience. Pleasure is an immediate quality that does not refer beyond itself. But the good is different. When we experience friendship as good, we have a sense, even if unarticulated, of why or how what we experience as good is good. Even if we cannot express it, we know that friendship extends our sphere of concern while comforting us in ways that provide our lives with meaning. Value experiences bring with them their own procedure for confirmation. Within the intentional structure of experience, including axiological experience, lies a recipe or an inner logic that provides or denies justification of the lived sense of that experience. For example, to experience friendship as good is to interpret and impose the sense of good upon friendship, but it is also to expect to continue to find goodness in friendship and to have such expectations fulfilled. It is precisely at this point that we may begin to find a measure within experience for distinguishing between good and evil, and it is here that we may begin to understand more deeply what it means to "philosophically respect" experience.[11]

The empiricists attempted to ground morality in experience, and Hume's efforts along these lines were certainly the most perceptive, rightly pointing to the importance of moral sentiments. Without a theory of intentionality, however, and operating with an impoverished concept of intuition (the theory of ideas), he could not get beyond the subjectivism that later ended in emotivism, an emotivism generally thought to be grounded in that very form of naturalism that separates the Real from the Good. By the very separation of the Real and the Good, ordinary experience is disrespected, and our experience of the Good is judged to be subjective, personal, private, and reducible to a kind of nonrational preference for pleasure.

Unlike mere experiences of pleasure, value experiences have their own value horizon. When I experience something as good, I know what to expect of it. I experience rain, sun, and soil as good not simply because I enjoy them but because I appreciate their roles in sustaining the Earth's biotic web. Water is regularly experienced as a good not only for me and my fellow homosapiens but for many other organisms and species. Water is a shared good. When we hear of a herd of elephants walking many days over parched landscapes and at last finding water, and then stopping to drink, bathe, and play, we understand their satisfaction and their bodily appreciation of the goodness of water. When I quench my own thirst with a cool drink of fresh and clean water, my sophisticated or simple appreciations of water are fulfilled in a moment of bodily awareness of the goodness of water. We experience both sun and rain as good when we glimpse their roles in the fabric of the planet's biotic web. As we experience our own dependency on the planet's biotic web, we realize the massive and inescapable interdependency among other species and processes in a mutually sustaining web of life, and with it a constellation of shared goods.

One of the essential characteristics of any web of life (as far as we know, anyway) is that the web itself and the coevolvents within the web are subject to the possibility of death. Among the web's more self-conscious evolvents, the awareness of death has become quite an issue. We know from our own studied observations of the bioweb and from our own existential anxiety, as well as from the joy of living, that life is to be sought and cherished while death is to be shunned and avoided. Let us then follow Erazim Kohák in asserting that "good and evil does have an ontological justification: some things sustain life, others destroy it."[12] The experiential foundation of the claim that what sustains life is good and what hinders or destroys life is evil lies in the fact that "whatever is alive, wants to remain alive. . . . [L]ife is a value for itself."[13] As Kohák points out "Death, too, is a part of the order of good life." We understand this point completely, even if we rebel against it. It is the unwelcome death, the premature death that cuts off life's possibilities, that is tragic, not the death that comes anyway, at the end of life, especially at the end of a well-lived life.

It is within this context that the moral horizon emerges, within the context of the human situation, within the context of our experience. We are biological evolvents, existing within the biotic web and self-consciously moving forward toward our death while embracing and valuing the life we live. Our pretheoretical experience, infused with cognitive, evaluative, and volitional moments, is not the experience of an "objective world" (i.e., of a devalued world consisting of causal relations and extensional properties), but rather "the actual experienced world, value laden and meaningfully ordered by the presence of life."[14] It is this meaningful order, provided by the presence, activities, and function of life that provides the deep context for the emergence of moral experience. This meaningful order does not have the status of fact. It is not a "given" of experience, but rather, to use a Husserlian locution, it is "pregiven," or to use another phrase popularized by subsequent phenomenologists, it is "always already" there. This meaningful order of life, this ecology of bios within which we are experientially intertwined, is the experiential ground of our intuitions about holism, as well as a condition of the possibility of moral consciousness—that is, an axiological transcendental. This meaningful order of purpose and value is part of the unnoticed background of experience available for phenomenological reflection. There is every reason to believe that this meaningful background of purpose and value has existed long before the human species, and that our specifically human goods only exist within a larger system of good arising from the biotic and prehuman constitution of nature as good. The constitution arising from the experience of being a part of and dependent on that order is perhaps the source of age-old intuitions that Goodness itself is beyond humanity.

To the extent that we are experientially intertwined and embodied within the biotic web, the relationship between the human organism and its environment can be phenomenologically described. Such a phenomenology can be used in the service of an experiential grounding of ecological ethics, as I am attempting here (as well as working toward a uniquely phenomenological conception of nature), or it can be used to rethink the foundations of experience in general from an ecological perspective. The first option is phenomenology's contribution to ecological philosophy, and the second is ecological philosophy's contribution to phenomenology. By exposing the limits of traditional naturalism, phenomenology makes possible a new philosophy of nature respecting the integrity of everyday experience. At the same time phenomenologists may wish to rethink their conceptions of the foundations of experience from a point of view that recognizes that embodied existence is primordially and unavoidably experientially embedded within the planetary biotic web. Eco-phenomenologists will recognize that traditional phenomenological investigations into experience are incomplete until ecological and even Darwinian perspectives are incorporated into the description and interpretation of experience. Eco-phenomenologists will wish to investigate the ways that the structure of experience and meaning arise from the deep ecological context of self-conscious nature.

It is, of course, this meaningfully ordered and value-laden world of our direct experience that ultimately justifies all moral claims. Why are we so sure that dishonesty, fraud, rape, and murder are evil? Because they each, although in different ways, retard and inhibit the intrinsic purposes and desires of life, which as we have seen, presents itself as a value for itself in our most basic and world-constituting intuitions. Value experiences occur within a meaningfully ordered value horizon. It is this value horizon of life that supplies the final justification of our experiences of the good. It is within this value horizon of life that our experiences of good and evil are shown to be more than "mere subjective preferences."

To illustrate this point, suppose I have a square red box in front of me. My perception of this as a square red box is not arbitrary. Even though I might be able, for short periods of time, to see it as a blue round box, assuming my powers of concentration and will are strong enough, such a perception is not sustainable. My attempts to impose the sense of "round blue box" on the object of my experience will end in frustration, as those particular meaning intentions will lack the intuitive fullness necessary to sustain that interpretation. Similarly, we habitually find in friendship a positive value and in fraud a disvalue. If we initially find friendship to be an evil and fraud to be a good, an openness to further experience will almost always correct this. Finding value in friendship and disvalue in fraud is not arbitrary.

Such an insight is at the bottom of Kierkegaard's rejection of the aesthetic lifestyle. The aesthetic lifestyle, based on hedonistic preferences, is not rejected on theoretical but on practical grounds. While we may temporarily view pleasure as the Prime Good, such an interpretation cannot be sustained indefinitely. Social institutions such as racism and slavery may appear to us as Good from certain perspectives for certain periods of time, but ultimately such practices destroy community. They are not sustainable. Such institutions and practices depend on an internal logic that divides community into mutually exclusive dichotomies, privileging one over the other. Such practices ultimately destroy the very community they attempt to build. On the other hand, in our everyday experience of value, we regularly find food, clothing, shelter, community, and friendship as good. Rarely do these things disappoint us. Our experience continues to establish these as goods in an ever evolving process of being open to the Good. By grounding ecological philosophy in the evolving wisdom of our collective experience, we can avoid the twin evils of absolutism and relativism. We avoid dogmatic absolutism by understanding that our experience and conception of the Good is always open to revision, and we avoid relativism by recognizing that our experiences of the Good themselves demand their own confirmation in future experience.

It seems to be a fundamental possibility that humans can experience nature as infused with goodness and from within an attitude of concern and empathy. Carolyn Merchant, in her influential *The Death of Nature*, reminds us that we once saw nature as alive, sensitive, and female, and that such perceptions generate normative restraints against the abuse of the Earth.[15] Christopher Manes points out, in his "Nature and Silence," that animist cultures typically perceive plants, animals, stones, and rivers as "articulate and at times intelligible subjects."[16] Erazim Kohák has shown that the lifeworlds of the hunter-gatherer, the ploughman/shepherd, and the urban craftsmen all generate experiences in which nature is perceived to be good and intrinsically worthy of respect and concern.[17]

While our current configuration of technocentrism and consumerism may not encourage such experiences, growing numbers of people continue to experience the ecological crisis as an evil done to the goodness of nature and the Earth itself. This is simply to say that experiencing the events of planetary destruction and waste that comprise the ecological crisis is increasingly a morally charged experience for many people. Of course, such nonanthropocentric experiences could not and cannot be expressed within traditional anthropocentric moral discourse and with the instrumental value-free rationality that usually supports it. We can read a great deal of nature writing, from Thoreau and Muir through Leopold and on to today's Radical Ecologists, as attempting to establish a new mode of moral and aesthetic discourse in which experiences of the intrinsic goodness of nature can be registered, expressed, and rationally developed. Without such a vehicle of articulation, experiences remain mute and powerless and are dismissed to the margins of rationality.

Often we experience a certain kind of moral unease at practices and institutions widely deemed to be good and just within our prevailing social and historical circumstance. The very fact that both Plato and Aristotle defended the institution of Greek slavery shows that some moral unease was felt by the Greeks toward the practice. This moral unease remained mute and powerless until Enlightenment rhetoric and the ideologies and discourses of freedom and equality were developed. Now, a certain kind of axiological unease pervades a growing number of people's experience of ecological destruction and change. The environmental and ecological changes brought about by industry, mining, and overconsumption are no longer simply seen as necessary by-products of the conversion of raw material into consumables, but such changes are now regularly experienced as a moral harm to the nonhuman natural world. Sadly, such experiences are informed by a haunting vision of the earth's wounds and irrevocable tears in the biotic web as well as growing systems failures. The very idea of the earth's mortality helps to explain the urgency in the call for an ethical response that the experience, direct or otherwise, of the growing ecological disaster solicits.

With the discovery of the mortality of nature, the traditional imagery of earth as GAIA is transfigured from Goddess to fellow mortal. GAIA's identity shifts from primordial mother to enduring sibling. With the transition of our most significant other from Goddess and mother to mortal and sibling, a subtle restructuring of the home takes place, and with it emerges the possibility of a new vision of a *logos* of the home—that is, an *eco-logos*. Such an *eco-logos* begins with the rejection of a value-free conception of nature (typical of modernistic thinking), as well as fanciful mystifications of a divine nature (typical of premodern thinking), by returning to nature as experienced—that is, to nature perceived as worthy of our moral respect and admiration. Such experiences would be self-justifying,[18] not by a rationality that reunites the Real and the Good but by one that never separates them. Husserl's critique of naturalism not only points to the limitations and dangers of modern forms of naturalism but also toward directions for developing a new conception of nature not accessible to traditional naturalistic thinking. It is the destiny of eco-phenomenology to complete this critique with a phenomenology of nature.

Notes

1. See Edmund Husserl, *The Crisis of European Sciences and Transcendental Phenomenology*, trans. David Carr (Evanston: Northwestern University Press, 1970). Particularly relevant in this text is Husserl's "Vienna Lecture," published as Appendix I, "Philosophy and the Crisis of European Humanity," 269–99.

2. See Michael Zimmerman, *Contesting Earth's Future: Radical Ecology and Postmodernity* (Berkeley: University of California Press, 1994) for a thorough critical review of the varieties of Radical Ecological thought.

3. Martin Heidegger, "Letter on Humanism," trans. Frank A Capuzzi and J. Glenn Gray, in Heidegger, *Basic Writings*, rev. ed., ed. David Farrell Krell (New York: Harper & Row, 1993), 213–65.

4. "Homo centrus centrus" is my construction for naming that mode of human being that seeks to escape the anxiety of its own finitude by treating the Earth as though it would provide an infinite source of distraction from that anxiety.

5. Edmund Husserl, *Logical Investigations*, vol. 2, trans. J. N. Findlay (New York: Humanities Press, 1970), 252.

6. My interests in pursing an axiological rationality developed from the resources of Husserl's philosophy was largely motivated by conversations with the late Ludwig Grunberg and in particular his essay "The 'Life-World' and the Axiological Approach in Ethics" in *From Phenomenology to an Axiocentric Ontology of the Human Condition*, Analecta Husserliana, vol. 21, ed. A.-T. Tymieniecka (Dordrecht: D. Reidel, 1986), 249–93.

7. The language used here of "abstention from metaphysical and normative commitments" is borrowed from David Carr's "Husserl's World and Our Own," *The Journal of the History of Philosophy* 25 (January 1987): 151–67.

8. See Charles Brown, "Phenomenology, Universalism, and Dialogue," *Dialogue and Humanism* 3, no. 1 (1993): 53–59.

9. The horrors of World War I, along with the increasing persecution of Jews by the Nazi regime, are the most obvious manifestations of increasing irrationalism in Husserl's social and political experience.

10. See H. Peter Steeves, *Founding Community: A Phenomenological-Ethical Inquiry* (Dordrecht: Kluwer Academic Publishers, 1998) for an attempt to develop a phenomenological communitarianism that also establishes the Good as being prior to the right.

11. See Robert Sokolowski, *Moral Action: A Phenomenological Study* (Bloomington: Indiana University Press, 1985) and his *Pictures,*

Quotations, and Destinations (Notre Dame: University of Notre Dame Press, 1992) for a phenomenological analysis of moral experience consistent with the one offered here.

12. Erazim Kohák, "Knowing Good and Evil . . . (Genesis 3:5b)," *Husserl Studies* 10 (1993), 31.
13. Kohák, "Knowing Good and Evil . . . (Genesis 3:5b)," 36.
14. Kohák, "Knowing Good and Evil . . . (Genesis 3:5b)," 33.
15. Carolyn Merchant, *The Death of Nature: Women, Ecology, and the Scientific Revolution* (San Francisco: Harper & Row, 1980).
16. Christopher Manes, "Nature and Silence," *Environmental Ethics* 14 (Winter 1992), 340.
17. Erazim Kohák, *The Green Halo: A Bird's Eye View of Ecological Ethics* (Chicago: Open Court, 2000), 55–58.
18. To assert with finality, as I do here, that such experiences will be self-justifying is to make a statement without justification. Just as, on my view, it *may* turn out that friendship is not good after all, it *may* turn out that our experiences of the goodness and beauty of nature cannot be justified. However, the overwhelming evidence of our experience testifies to the contention that we are presently justified in expecting such experiences to continue to be reaffirmed.

CHAPTER 2

An Understanding Heart

Reason, Value, and Transcendental Phenomenology

ERAZIM KOHÁK

The purpose of this chapter is to inquire whether transcendental phenomenology in the spirit of Edmund Husserl can help resolve the cognitive dilemma of a culture guided by a heartless reason and an irrational heart.[1]

We can observe the practical impact of that dilemma all about us. Over the past three hundred years we have been duly fruitful, have multiplied and subdued the earth as we are bade in Genesis 1:28, dramatically endangering its ability to sustain our kind of life. Yet in spite of unmistakable warnings we seem driven on by the logic of "progress," writing off all compassion for its victims as mere sentimentality. It is as if we approached questions of fact with a *Space Odyssey* computer while leaving questions of value to a Ouija board. Not surprisingly, our civilization—originally European, then Euro-American, today global—appears to be well on its way to self-destruction.[2]

Unlike some contemporary thinkers, I do not think this the result of some fatal flaw in our collective unconscious or of a defect in our genetic code.[3] Rather, I shall suggest it is the result of certain identifiable decisions—wrong turns, if you will—that European thought took in the seventeenth century and bequeathed to its global heirs.[4]

In the briefest of anticipatory outlines, I believe the greatness of our European civilization lies in its commitment to reason rather than instinct or custom as the ultimate arbiter of good and evil. On that basis the Stoic lawyers were willing to reject something as natural and traditional as slavery. So, too, the gospels speak of equality of all humans before God in spite of centuries of hierarchical tradition. Reason, not instinct or tradition, opened the horizon of liberty, equality, and brotherhood and would offer an alternative to self-destruction were that indeed natural.

Seventeenth-century thinkers, however, reduced the reason they charged with so noble a task to dealing with mathematical and causal relations, leaving questions of value and meaning in a limbo of the non-rational. Unfortunately, but understandably so. Value and meaning are a function not only of subjectivity, but specifically of a subject activity. An immovable and unmoving subject is, after all, a *contradictio in adiecto*. Only when there is purposive activity, be it human, animal, or vegetable, can we speak of its subject and qualify what there is as meaningful in relation or as value endowed as it aids or hinders that activity. Activity, though, requires time, a sequence of moments remembered and anticipated. In the timeless world of mathematical rationality of the seventeenth and eighteenth centuries, judgments of meaning and value could only intrude from without. Reason, once charged with the task of reading the signs of changing times, was thus consigned to the study of the timeless regularity of the unchanging. We have, in effect, entered modernity with an impressive mastery of the mechanics of the universe but wholly at a loss as to the purpose or value of life's world.[5]

That reduction of rationality to instrumentality leaves us precious few options. We can, with some postmodernists, write off questions of value as a matter of whim and contingency—picnic or pogrom, whatever turns you on—while we turn to the serious business of making money.[6] Alternately, we can look to instinct or custom for guidance, extolling natural spontaneity one moment and time-honored family values the next. If, however, neither of those alternatives seems satisfactory, we need to seek a *more adequate conception of reason* that would subsume relations of value and meaning as well as those of cause and number. In place of the *heartless reason* and the *irrational heart* of modernity, we need to seek the *understanding heart* of 1 Kings 3:9, *that we may discern between good and bad.*[7]

It is the third option that I wish to explore here, starting with the question of what we actually mean when we speak of European civilization as based on a commitment to a life in reason. First of all, reason here is not an organ or a faculty which a given being can be said to have or to lack. Rather, it refers to a way of interacting with the world around us. It might actually be more adequate to speak of living in reason rather than of "having" it. Living in reason means most fundamentally seeking reasons rather than simply accepting the data of consciousness as brute givens. Living in reason means confronting experience not merely with the binary question Is it/isn't it? but also with open questions of Why?

and To what purpose? To reason means ultimately to integrate a given datum in a web of actual and possible relations. The irrational is that which cannot be so integrated. The rational is that which can be so integrated—not only acknowledged but also understood.[8]

For future reference, it might be useful to note that though Husserl stresses the role of quantification in the birth of reason,[9] nothing in our characterization of reason requires that relations that render a given event rational be quantitative or causal. They can equally well be relations of value and meaning. Even our emotions are not simply arbitrarily given but can be integrated in explanatory networks. That is also emphatically true of our value decisions. We choose not arbitrarily but for reasons. At this level, the idea that values and meanings might be intrinsically irrational is quite counterintuitive. Rational may but need not mean numerical. Its basic meaning is intelligible, understandable, in whatever way.

Thus when Europe committed itself to a life in reason, it committed itself not to living by the numbers, but to a life in understanding rather than in an unreflecting acceptance of sheer givens, whether brute or sublime.[10] Certainly, a life of brute or sublime fact, devoid of reflection, is at most a limiting idea whose empirical instantiations seldom conform to the ideal limit. Yet it is the limiting idea that matters. For human cultures worldwide it was typically *life in fact*—in the natural, in the traditional— that was normative and reflection that was suspect. Nature and tradition, pronounced in hushed tones, tend to serve as both the ideal and the norm the world over, familiar vices tend to appear as virtues, with novelty as the only real vice.

For Europe and its heirs, at least in their moments of glory, it was the opposite. In those moments Europe dared challenge the cold, clammy hand of tradition in the name of justice, obscure instinct in the name of critical reason. There is the socratic example and socratic insistence that the unexamined life is not worth living. There is Jesus [Mt 5:22ff] with his contrast between what *had been said to those of old* and his own clear *but I say unto you*. Thereafter, doin' what comes naturally is not enough. What we do must also be good and just, not simply natural and traditional.

That, finally, is what rationality means. No event is simply an irrational given, brute or sublime. It is also capable of being understood and judged. There is a reason for it and a meaning to it—and the West committed itself to understanding them, emblazoning its banners with the verse from John 8:32, *Ye shall know the truth and the truth shall set you free.*

That commitment to a life in truth is Europe's great contribution to human self-realization.[11] It has also become a snare and a stumbling block when, at the dawn of modernity, European thought reduced its conception of explanatory rationality to mathematical and causal relations only, writing off relations of value and meaning as subjective and so intrinsically irrational. To understand would henceforth be taken to mean to integrate in a network of quantifiable causal relations, rigorously excluding relations of meaning and value.

That shift, to be sure, was not an arbitrary whim of René Descartes or some other malevolent genie.[12] Mathematical and causal relations really do appear as "objectively" there in a world independent of the subject. Like it or not, two bob, thruppence, tuppence, hapenny, and two farthings do add up to a half-crown.[13] Once we accept that colorfully archaic notation, though a subject does the sum, the sum holds for any vendor or buyer.

Rather than risk contaminating the vaunted objectivity of its judgments with the alleged subjectivity of value, Western thought accepted a reality reduced to the quantifiable while consigning judgments of value and meaning to the outer darkness of the irrational, which respectable scholars could dismiss as unscientific, leaving questions of good and evil to prophets, poets, and postmodernists.

Yet relations of meaning and value, though qualitative and subject related, are utterly fundamental to human decision making. Ignoring them would be difficult—and dangerous. Some contemporary thinkers have attempted just that, claiming value decisions to be a matter of indifference. Others, while considering them no less irrational, have sought to treat the irrational—instinct, intuition, or custom—as a legitimate counterpart of reason for dealing with questions of value and meaning. Though they seldom stated it explicitly, they assumed that constructing a nuclear bomb is legitimately a question of reason while dropping it is a matter of personal preference.[14]

Having been on the receiving end of airborne ordnance, I find this most troublesome—and not only because of my generation's experience with the cult of *Blut und Boden*, blood and soil. More basically, the problem is that instinct grows over millennia and custom over centuries, while culturally induced changes require an effective response in a matter of years. Were we to wait for instinct and custom to catch up with such changes, we should be rather likely to destroy ourselves long before we developed an instinctive or a traditional fear of firearms or automobiles, not to mention genetically modified crops.[15]

A civilization basing itself on instrumental reason while leaving value decisions to an intuitive reliance on the irrational—as in the case of the Nazi attempt to entrust the direction of a technically rational civilization to an intuitive call of *Blut und Boden*[16]—is a highly unstable compound. Technical reason is not enough and supplementing it with a dose of irrationality will not make it so. Communing with Gaia, however salutary, does not render quantitative expansion any more benign.[17]

I believe that long-range, sustainable coexistence of humans with the community of all life requires more than an intuitive supplement to technical rationality, a peripheral Ouija board attached to our computers. Yet if quantification were the only form of rationality, that would indeed be the only way of modifying the supremacy of the quantitative. I believe the most provocative contribution of Edmund Husserl's project of transcendental phenomenology is his persistent quest for an alternative conception of rationality based on the world constituted by the activity of life, not theory, a value-laden world structured by meaning. That is what Husserl with his unerring knack for choosing the most unfortunate term possible called *transcendental subjectivity* and what I have called, hardly less misleadingly, *qualitative rationality*.[18] Thereof I would write, hoping to make those words a shade less obscure.

For reasons of time and tedium, I shall not attempt to trace the entire project of Husserl's *Ideen* cycle and *Krisis*. From the former, it might be useful to note one distinction, that between *Tatsache* and *Wesen* and, correspondingly, between empirical and eidetic levels of inquiry.[19] Conventional translations render the two terms as "fact" and "essence"—and there are some grounds for believing that at times Husserl really means no more than that.[20] Still, the translation contributes little to understanding. The relevant point, quite unambiguous in Husserl's later writings, is that in any functioning system there will be *functions* or *niches* or tasks that need be filled. Such tasks, for instance—in an example Husserl does *not* use—that of the provider in a family, can be defined independently of the individual who fills them. Individuals do not define the niche or role. It is individuals who become intelligible in terms of the niche they fill in the system, the role they play. That, rather than some Adam-like naming of the animals as in Gen 2:19, I take to be the meaning of the *Sinngebung* or meaning bestowal of *Ideen I*, §55. Any system can then be studied either empirically or in principle (*eidetically*) as a complex of relations, independently of the individuals who might come to fill them.

So even if the rules of soccer did not call for a goalie, and even if there were no individuals who considered themselves such, the undefended goal would still constitute a niche waiting to be filled. As the ball neared the goal, one of the eleven players would assume the role of the goalie, constituting himself a goalie-in-act. Yet it was the game that defined the niche and the niche of the goalie could be studied independently of him, simply in terms of the way the game is played.

In time-honored phenomenological terminology, that is called *eidetic* analysis. While we can forget the term, we should file away the concept for future use. Phenomenology can be a phenomenol*ogy* and not mere phenomenal*ism* precisely because it focuses not on individual empirical instantiations but rather on principles, on the eidetic structure of life's functioning. The move from empirical ways of knowing to phenomenology is in part a shift from the *naivete*[21] of approaching reality as a set of space-time objects in causal relations to approaching it as a system of interlocking roles.

For us a second shift is no less important, that from the world as an alleged set of space-time objects to the *world as experience*.[22] Normally, we do think of the world as "objective," a set of entities occurring in space-time and linked by causal and mathematical relations. However, while that is how we *think* the world, it is not how we in truth experience it. The world we experience is first of all *our* world, the playing field constituted by our being and doing, whether we are humans, woodchucks, or plants reaching for sun and moisture.[23] That is what gives it unity and intelligibility. Certainly, it is not "merely subjective" in the sense of being arbitrary or contingent on my whim. If this cup is empty, no amount of thinking will make it full. Yet while not subjective, our world is fundamentally subject related. This cup *is a cup* at all—or more exactly, fulfils the function of a cup—*only in a world structured by its relation to a subject.* Only in relation to a purposing subject does a network of relations arise in which this object can have that meaning or any meaning.[24]

This is where our earlier distinction can come in handy. This object does not contain some mysterious essence of cupness that would make it a cup. Rather, *my experiencing* contains a function or a niche of "something from which I can drink" in the absence of a proboscis. That niche is not there because I wish it so. It is a function of a system whose functioning includes drinking and upright beings without probosces but with prehensile paws.[25]

Now, figuratively speaking, a suitable object, which could have started in life as half a coconut shell or a thermos cap, comes along and stumbles into that niche, fulfilling that function. In that moment it acquires an identity and becomes intelligible—ah, it is a cup. My thirsty presence did not "create" a cup. *Creatio ex nihilo* is a privilege reserved for God and vainly arrogated by computer users. My thirsty presence, though, *constituted* this object as a meaningful entity, a cup, by constituting a function into which it could enter.

In that sense, the cup is irreducibly subject related but not viciously "subjective." The web of relations within which it acquires meaning is constituted by the presence of a subject, but it is independent of this particular subject's individual whim. Certainly, there can also be private meanings that I attribute to individual objects. That, though, is a private activity possible because I live in a world of preconstituted meanings which, though subject dependent, is independent of any particular subject.

What is true of cups is also true of relational realities such as beauty or goodness or, more prosaically, of value or significance. From the very start, from the moment I open my eyes, I encounter the world as value laden and as meaning structured, not because I wish it so but simply because *I am*—or, more precisely, because *I do*.[26] The putative "objective" world is one at which I arrive by a process of abstraction from the value-laden world I actually experience. Nor is the value and meaning structure that makes my world intelligible one I invent. It is one I find, constituted by the presence of purposive life, including my own, prior to my reflecting upon it.

That is the playing field of phenomenology—the world as experienced, described as a complex of structural (or *ideal*) possibilities constituted by the presence of purposive activity. The project of phenomenology as Husserl presents it in *Ideen I, Ideen II,* and *Krisis* is one of description, not fantasy[27]—in his words, of *seeing clearly and articulating faithfully*—though with that double difference.

First of all, it takes as its initial datum world "in phenomenological brackets," that is, the world as experience, as it actually presents itself to us, not the world as a theoretical construct of scientific inquiry. What has been set aside or "bracketed" is world considered as a theoretical index to a putative transcendent reality. What remains is life's world in its immediacy, world as constituted by living, which is the starting point for phenomenological inquiry.

Secondly, what phenomenology seeks to describe are not fortuitous empirical occurrences but rather the necessary eidetic structure of niches that Husserl called *ideale Möglichkeit*. It is not this vessel which happens to serve me as a cup which concerns it, but rather the idea, the function of being-a-vessel which my thirsty presence constitutes and which the cup fortuitously fills as it becomes the content of an empty intention—or, in the language of another tradition, the function of a variable.[28]

That, then, is what it means to approach the world phenomenologically—to see and describe its functional structure clearly as it is constituted by the presence of life. Well and good, but what difference does that make?

For our purposes, quite literally, all the difference *in the world*. The problem of our usual conception of rationality, we said, is that it does not include the dimension of value and meaning. Necessarily so: there are no meanings or values in the world reconstructed in theoretical reflection as "objective." If we start out from that reconstructed world, meaning and value can enter in only as irrational intrusions, which [mathematical] reason must needs leave to instinct, custom, or whim.[29]

By contrast, *lifeworld*, the world constituted as a meaningful whole by the presence of life, *is neither value free nor meaningless*. As we have emphasized throughout, by its very constitution as the world of purposeful activity, it is *ab initio* and *per essentiam* value laden and meaning structured. It is a world that not only *is*, but from the beginning also aids or hinders the activity that constitutes it. Its rationality is one of values and reasons, not merely of quantifiable causal relations. So loving and hating are no longer irrational but can be understood in terms of the web of value relations that render my world meaningful. Not putative causes but reasons make them intelligible.[30]

The lifeworld on which phenomenology focuses is not some forgotten "natural" world to be discovered in our antelapsarian past.[31] Nor is it some putative "deep" reality uncovered by plumbing the depth of our unconscious. Such metaphysical constructs become necessary when we ignore the world of our life and treat our theoretical construct as reality. Then we understandably have to invent hidden forces and alternative realities to account for their conduct. When, however, we set aside our theoretical world and see the world of our experience, value laden and meaning structured, we can shave them off with Ockham's razor.[32]

That is the point. Husserl is not inventing alternative realities but rather pointing to alternative ways of organizing or constituting the one reality amid which we live, breathe, and have our being. Yes, we can consider that reality from the perspective of a natural scientist, as abstracted from subject activities. It will be a highly useful model but in principle incomplete. We can conjure up a supernatural reality to make up the lack—or we can consider that very same reality from the perspective of a purposive subject, including the relations of value and meaning that structure a subject's world. The rationality or intelligibility of the world so considered or constituted will not be mathematical and causal but rather the rationality of value and meaning—for that is in fact how we constitute our life-world.

Who, though, is the *we* of whom we speak? And can we speak of a *we* at all or are we dealing at best with a plurality of I's, fused into a community solely by an empirical consensus? Do our subject-related value and meaning structures have an intrinsic intersubjective validity? Can we claim, for instance, that benevolence is a positive value per se, a priori, or is that no more than an empirical consensus of a community of speakers?[33]

This is where Husserl's conception of eidetic structure, described in later writings even more misleadingly as *transcendental subjectivity*, proves its worth, though not without some unpacking. First of all, *subjectivity* is not *a subject*, just as *objectivity* is not *an object*. Objectivity is the characteristic of a reality defined by relations among objects. Similarly subjectivity is a characteristic of a reality defined by relations involving subjects. Subject*ivity* means a network of subject relations.

Secondly, transcendental does not mean transcendent. Transcendent means simply going beyond, contrasted with immanent, wholly enclosed.

So the chair that I see not only in my imagination but presume to exist even when I close my eyes can be said to have a *transcendent* existence, that is, reaching beyond my imagination into space-time. By contrast, the term transcendental, here on loan from Kant,[34] means *of a higher level*, on which the intelligibility of the lower level is contingent. Its opposite would be empirical, not immanent. Stretching the point rather recklessly, we could speak of the triangular structure of experience, *doer—doing—done*, as a *transcendental* structure instantiated by the empirical content I—see—a goat (or, less colorfully, ego—cogito—cogitatum).[35]

Husserl's basic recognition is that subject experience is rendered intelligible by such a *transcendental* structure. It is experience constituted as an intelligible whole by purposive activity and, already as such, it has a structure independent of and prior to the preferences of a particular agent. The *we* that constitutes the lifeworld is not a set of individual I's. It is *we in principle, we* as a pure possibility of any possible I, on which the intelligibility of any set of individual I's depends.

This is an absolutely crucial point that Husserl obfuscates hopelessly with his arcane terminology. Perhaps it is best made indirectly, by example:[36]

- So for any oxygen-inhaling being, fresh airy places are desirable, dank dark dungeons detestable. This basic value structure holds for all of *us*, oxygen-inhaling beings. The *we* is not a collection of empirical I's or their preferences but a pure possibility, independent of our preferences. Though an individual smoker may prefer a smoke-filled cellar, it remains intersubjectively valid that a forest clearing is in principle (or *eidetically*) more desirable for *our type* of being. Smoke-filled cellars are not bad "objectively." They are bad for subjects, but for subjects *as such*, for a subject in principle. The point, in a different idiom, is that the intersubjective project is not constituted by whim or preference of reflection, but already by the prereflective activity of living. This holds for plants and animals as well as for humans. The project their life represents is more basic than their reflective preference. Though all humans, addicted to motorcars, were to opt for an atmosphere laced with carbon monoxide, this would not change the hard fact that such atmosphere is bad for them by the very nature of the life project of oxygen-inhaling beings. *Eide* are not "essences"; they are niches in the web of interwoven lives. Or, in yet other words, *intersubjectivity is constituted primordially by subject activity, only secondarily and partially by subject reflection;*

- Regardless of my individual preference, because I am a vulnerable subject conscious of my vulnerability, trustworthiness
  is a virtue and treachery a vice. As this individual subject, I
  might invert that valuation and claim to prefer interesting vil-
  lains to boring saints, but that does not change the transcendental rule valid for such subjects in principle;
- Or again, because I am a being who becomes actual only by
  becoming incarnate, my relation to my embodiments—to my
  body, to the tools of my trade, to my homeland, to my companions—is crucial to my identity. A theft is a crime against
  me not because I am greedy but because it violates a relation
  fundamental to my mode of being.[37]

Out of those examples emerges the basic contribution of transcendental phenomenology—the discovery of the autonomously functioning
structure of relations that structures our lifeworld, derived in principle
from purposive activity, making it intelligible and providing the basis for
intersubjectively valid judgments of value and meaning.[38] We need neither mystical intuition nor alternative realities. Clear perception and faithful articulation of our world as constituted by life will do quite nicely,
thank you.

Finally, a twenty-first-century afterthought: Is Husserl's phenomenology—with its conception of the world constituted as a meaningful
whole by the presence of life, of its type structure of functions,[39] and its
critique of dualism—an anticipation of evolutionism in sociobiology?

Once we strip phenomenology of its obscurantist terminology, it does
rather seem so. The great transformation in the philosophy of science over
the last quarter century is precisely the shift from physics to biology as the
science of norm. That shift entails most emphatically a shift from a
mechanical to a teleological ordering. However much the reductionists
may strive to reduce biology to a biophysics, life remains intrinsically a
purposive activity. For the purposes of unified science, the opposite direction may ultimately prove more promising. Rather than treating biology
as a flawed imitation of physics we might more profitably treat physics as
a privative version of biology, "lifeless" matter as a privative version of
life.

Is not that what Husserl proposed in commending a shift from the
theoretical world of physics to the lifeworld as the initial given? In one
sense, definitely. The conceptual root of the *crisis of European sciences* of
which he speaks does lie in the decision to take the value- and meaning-
neutral world of physics as the norm of reality. The lifeworld with its firm
type structure or *Typik* constituted by life, by purposive activity, is the

world of biology. It is its purposiveness that grounds Husserl's response to the crisis. Instead of the meaning-free rationality of the physical world supplemented by a Ouija board, Husserl proposes the meaning-structured rationality of life's world. Sociobiologists do the same.

And yet not altogether. It is *Ideen II* that points to the difference. Here, in addition to the world constituted by physical theory and the world constituted by life, Husserl speaks of the *personalistische Welt* constituted by *spirit* [sic]. Terminologically, it is deucedly awkward even in German, doubly so in English and triply in Czech. At least in German and English there is the saving grace of the term "personalistic" which Husserl borrows from Max Scheler as a synonym for *geistig*. That makes the point: the world as constituted by responsible freedom, the world that includes moral categories of right and wrong in addition to the natural categories of good and bad, represents a distinct reality. Humans live not only in life's world, but also in freedom's world. The sociobiological shift from physics to biology as the science of norm, now itself under heavy attack, is not enough. We would need another shift to history as the normative science, with biology and physics as its reduced versions.

That, though, is the topic for another time.[40] For now, let us be content with this much. We set out from the dilemma of value-free rationality supplemented by irrational value, looking for a more adequate conception of rationality. We have found it in the phenomenological conception of the value-laden, meaning-structured rationality of the lifeworld. No, we do not need to supplement instrumental reason with irrationality, the computer with a Ouija board, in order to prefer healthy forests to profitable clear-cutting. We only need to bracket our world construct, open our eyes to the world of our life with its structure of meaning and value, and base our conception of rationality on its intelligible structure or *transcendental subjectivity*.

Yes, I would plead with Husserl for a life in reason. Irrationality of goals empowered by rationality of means, a Ouija board empowered by a computer, is deadly dangerous. However, let it be the reason of *the understanding heart*.

Notes

An earlier version of this chapter was presented at the KIRA Conference, Amherst, MA/USA, 4 August 2000.

1. For the purposes of this chapter, I shall draw on three of Husserl's works: *Ideen zu einer reinen Phänomenologie und phänomenologischen*

Philosophie, Erstes Buch, *Allgemeine Einführung in die reine Phänomenologie*, 2d ed., Husserliana, vol. 3–1, ed. Karl Schuhmann (The Hague: Martinus Nijhoff, 1976) [cited hereafter as *Ideen I*]; *Ideas Pertaining to a Pure Phenomenology and to a Phenomenological Philosophy. First Book. General Introduction to a Pure Phenomenology*, trans. Fred Kersten (The Hague: Martinus Nijhoff, 1982) [cited hereafter as *Ideas I*]; *Ideen zu einer reinen Phänomenologie und phänomenologischen Philosophie*, Zweites Buch, *Phänomenologische Untersuchungen zur Konstitution*, Husserliana, vol. 4, ed. Marly Biemel (The Hague: Martinus Nijhoff, 1952) [cited hereafter as *Ideen II*]; *Ideas Pertaining to a Pure Phenomenology and to a Phenomenological Philosophy*, Second Book. *Studies in the Phenomenology of Constitution*, trans. Richard Rojcewicz and André Schuwer (Dordrecht: Kluwer Academic Publishers, 1989); and *Die Krisis der europäischen Wissenschaften und die transzendentale Phänomenologie*, Husserliana, vol. 6, ed. Walter Biemel (The Hague: Martinus Nijhoff, 1962) [cited hereafter as *Krisis*]; *The Crisis of European Sciences and Transcendental Phenomenology*, trans. David Carr (Evanston: Northwestern University Press, 1970) [cited hereafter as *Crisis*]; and *Die Krisis der europäischen Wissenschaften und die transzendentale Phänomenologie. Ergänzungsband: Texte aus dem Nachlass 1934–1937*, Husserliana, vol. 29, ed. Reinhold N. Smid (Dordrecht: Kluwer Academic Publishers, 1993). However, this is not a historical paper: though I believe I present a legitimate reading of the texts in question, my purpose is to draw on them in dealing with a contemporary problem, not to establish yet once more "what Husserl really meant."

2. Lest I be accused of confabulating, I would refer the reader to the United Nations report, *Global Economic Outlook 2000*, the annual Human Development Reports of the United Nations, and the annual *State of the World* reports issued by the WorldWatch Institute in Washington, D.C., USA, one of which is available in Czech as *Stav světa 1998*, trans. Ivana Binková et al. (Prague: Hynek, 1998).

3. Here I have in mind philosophers like Martin Heidegger ("Die Frage nach der Technik" in *Vorträge und Aufsätze* [Pfullingen: Neske, 1954]), biologists such as W. D. Hamilton ("The Genetical Evolution of Social Behaviour" in *Journal of Theoretical Biology* 7 [1964]:1–52) or philosophizing sociobiologists such as Edward O. Wilson (*Consilience* [New York: Knopf, 1998]) or James Lovelock (*The Ages of Gaia* [New York: Norton, 1988], esp. 229–40) and my comments thereto in Erazim Kohák, *The Green Halo* (Chicago: Open Court, 1999], 129–54), though I am speaking primarily of a type of thought rather than of a specific thinker.

4. For detailed analysis, see *Krisis*, Pt. II, §§10–27.

5. This is the theme of Husserl's last two public lectures presented in 1935 beyond the reach of the Nazis, in Vienna and in Prague; see *Krisis*, §§1–15; *Ergänzungsband*, 103–39; and *Krisis*, 314–48/*Crisis*, 269–99.

6. This is most emphatically *not* intended as a characterization of all philosophers of that persuasion. Many of them are thinkers of intense moral commitment but who, for good and sufficient reason, refuse to seek a metaphysical underpinning for their conviction. See, for instance, Richard Rorty's noble and passionate commitment to liberal values in *Contingency, Irony and Solidarity* (Cambridge: Cambridge University Press, 1989), esp. 73–95. For reasons that will become evident below, I am again describing a type of thought, not an instance thereof. Cf. the conception of *Typik* in *Krisis*, §51.

7. Quoth Husserl, "We are now certain that eighteenth-century rationalism and the way it sought to assure European humanity of a new grounding was a *naiveté*. Should one, though discard the *true* meaning of rationalism together with this naive—and ultimately even nonsensical—rationalism? . . . Is not the irrationality of irrationalism in the end just a narrowminded and mistaken rationality, even worse than that of the old rationalism?" *Krisis*, §6, my translation [*Crisis*, 16].

8. Husserl lays the groundwork for such dynamic reading of reason already in *Ideen II* (note esp. §60) though the terminology of *Geist*, doubly unfortunate in English translation, obscures it. Compare, however, the "self-realization of reason" in *Krisis*, §73.

9. See the appendix "Realitätswissenschaft und Idealisierung" in *Krisis*, 279–93 ["Idealization and the Science of Reality," *Crisis*, 301–14], as well as ibid., §9.

10. I have not been able to determine when the empiricists first took to describing immediate givens as *brute*, meaning presumably *as appearing to brutes*, i.e., to presumably nonreflecting beings. However, the sublime data of romantic intuition as described by depth ecologists are presumed to have the same quality of unreflected immediacy. Irrationalism, it appears, need not be bestial, though it is no less irrational for it. See Kohák, *The Green Halo*, 118–28

11. It is also Husserl's great credo in face of the Nazi tide in his Prague and Vienna lectures (*Krisis*, §§1–6 and pp. 314–48/*Crisis*, 269–99), unfortunately often misread as an ode to the Enlightenment. More careful reading—and some attention to the historical background— cf. Schuhmann, *Husserl Chronik* (The Hague: Martinus Nijhoff, 1977), 459 ff., note esp. entry on 21 September and for 12–18 November 1935—shows this to be a superficial misunderstanding. Especially

the statement about philosophers as *officials of humanity* in *Krisis*, §7, needs be read as defiance of the notorious Nazi *Beamtengesetz*, which stripped Jewish scholars, administratively state employees, of their academic office.

12. In justice to Descartes, see Jan Patočka's analysis, "Cartesianism and Phenomenology" in *Jan Patočka: Philosophy and Selected Writings*, ed. E. Kohák (Chicago, University of Chicago Press, 1989), 284–325, and of course Husserl's treatment in *Krisis*, §§16–20. Husserl's treatment of Descartes is far more sensitive than that of subsequent critics of putative Cartesianism.

13. For the benefit of those born out of season, one shilling (or *bob*) was twelve pence, so that two shillings, three pence, two pence, half-penny and two quarter pennies added up to two shillings six pence. A crown, by my day struck as a commemorative denomination only, had a nominal value of five shillings, so that a half-crown, in common circulation, was indeed worth 2/6. The sole point of the example here is to stress the independence of the sum on the all-too-human mathematical notation.

14. Actually, most writers appealing to feeling and custom tend to use them as an argument for *not* dropping it—or, more generally, for tempering human intervention in the world, as in the case of ecological writers like Arne Naess (*Ecology, Community, and Lifestyle* [Cambridge: Cambridge University Press, 1989]) or authors represented in John Seed's manual, *Thinking like a Mountain* (Philadelphia: New Society, 1988). Their shared assumption is that reason means instrumentality—and that value (therefore) requires irrationality. It is an assumption shared, ironically, by people like Hans Reichenbach in his classic *The Rise of Scientific Philosophy* (Berkeley: University of California Press, 1951)—and Carnap and Hume long before them. Both, Husserl might say, are heirs of the unfortunate dualism whose rise he traces in *Krisis*, §§10 ff. and 64 ff.

15. This is a point stressed most usefully by sociobiologically oriented writers like E. O. Wilson, whose work is available to me only in its Czech translation. I would recommend specifically the concluding chapter 15, "Natural Ethics," in *The Diversity of Life* (*Rozmanitost ivota* [Prague: Nakladatelství Lidové noviny, 1995]) and, in this specific context, chapter 7, "From Genes to Culture," in *Consilience* (*Konsilience* [Prague: Nakladatelství Lidové noviny, 1999]).

16. Jan Patočka, "Two Senses of Reason and Nature in the German Enlightenment" speaks of Nazism as combining *an irrationality of goals with a rigid rationality of means*. See *Jan Patočka*, 157.

17. See James Lovelock, *The Ages of Gaia* (New York: Norton, 1988), 229–40; also Kohák, *The Green Halo*, 133–35.

18. As we shall see below, it is the rationality (=intelligibility or simply *the way the world makes sense*) when we consider it as constituted by the presence of life (so in its subjectivity), which means *ab initio* in terms of value and meaning, not simply of mathematization, though not in individual empirical preference but *in principle* (hence transcendentally.) Would *living rationality* be less misleading? Late in *Krisis*, §72, Husserl speaks of *absolut fungierende Subjektivität*, autonomously functioning subjectivity, confirming the importance of the concept of *niche*. Thereof more below.

19. Here I refer to *Ideen I*, §§1–4, usually described as *eidetic bracketing*, often omitted as a wholly unremarkable shift to abstract thinking— which it would be, were we to take *Wesen* to mean traditional essence rather than an *ideally possible mode of functioning* or a *niche* in a systems-theoretical sense used in ecology, as we shall propose.

20. See specifically *Ideen I*, §§66–70. However, in his introduction Husserl warns of the *ärgerlichen Äquivokationen* ("vexatious equivocation") of *Wesen* (*Ideen I*, 8 / *Ideas I*, xxii)—one of whose meanings I take to be the etymologically justified *characteristic way of being*, cited in the 1903 edition of Eisler's *Handwörterbuch d. Philosophie*, current while Husserl was writing his *Ideen I*. That may actually best fit Husserl's intent.

21. As Husserl uses the term in his Vienna lecture, it has no pejorative connotations. Rather, it means simply what we have called *life in fact*, in unquestioning acceptance of brute or sublime given, which he calls *Objektivismus*. See especially the conclusion of the first part and then the analysis in *Krisis*, 339 ff. / *Crisis*, 292 ff., and the conclusion, *Krisis*, 347–48 / *Crisis*, 299.

22. *Experience* is my term. Husserl opts for *Bewusstsein*, literally *bewusstsein*, what is and is known. However, since the English equivalent, consciousness, tends to suggest mind-contents rather than reality as known, I opt for the term experience in spite of its own problems. In any case, if in doubt, consult *Ideen I*, §§33–55.

23. The metaphor of the world as a playing field, *Spielraum*, is one of Martin Heidegger's valuable contributions to phenomenology; cf. *Sein und Zeit* (Halle: Niemeyer, 1929); *Being and Time*, trans. Joan Stambaugh (Albany: State University of New York Press, 1996), esp. §§22–24, valid no matter how regrettable we consider the romantic dead alley into which he led it—or the political slant of esp. §§74–76.

24. Meaning, as we are using it, is essentially a relational reality: an X is meaningful iff it can be integrated in a network of relations. Husserl's contribution is the recognition of the meaning-bestowing function of activity—and the recognition that this is a transcendental, not an empirical, function. See *Ideen I*, §55 and *Krisis*, §35.

25. Husserl's own examples are invariably taken from geometry or formal logic. It was Heidegger who recognized the experiential applicability of Husserl's analysis, though not, it seems, the problem it entails: the more formal our analysis, the more universal—and empty; the more full, the weaker the claim to universality and the thornier the problem of universality in cultural diversity, cf. *Krisis*, §36. A suggestion of a solution seems to be present in Husserl's emphasis on *stufenweise Aufbau* and levels of universality.

26. Husserl never quotes Goethe's translation of John 1:1, "Im Anfang war die That," and his traditional terminology obscures the dynamics of his analysis, but note his treatment of the *Ich kann* as basis of personal identity in *Ideen II*, §66 a) and b).

27. Here note his emphasis on *Getreuer Ausdruck klarer Gegebenheiten*—faithful expression of clear givens—in *Ideen I*, §66 and utter exclusion of *mystischen Gedanken*—mystic thoughts—in §3.

28. To the best of my memory, the statement that "to be is to be a function of a variable" comes from W. V. O. Quine or perchance A. J. Ayer; in any case it is too succinct a gem to omit simply because I no longer recall the source.

29. Cf. Husserl's analysis in *Ideen II*, §§1–4. Whether this analysis can subsume the much later reductionist theories of W. D. Hamilton, J. Maynard-Smith, or E. O. Wilson is another question on which we can only touch later.

30. Here note Husserl's analysis of reason and cause in *Ideen II*, §56, assumed though seldom acknowledged by all his followers.

31. Heidegger recognizes the possibility of this misunderstanding and addresses it in *Sein und Zeit*, §11, though with limited success as even his own writings testify. Cf. *Vorträge und Aufsätze*, 181 ff. and passim.

32. Husserl does mention Helmholtz's metaphor of two dimensional beings and distinguishes living on the surface and living in depth in *Krisis*, §32. Closer reading, however, shows he is thinking of his familiar distinction, which we described as one between *living in fact* and *living in reason*, not one between an overt and a hidden content.

33. There is a clue worth noting in *Krisis*, §54.b where Husserl speaks of the *Ur-Ich*, proto-I, which is simply personal identity as our *ideale Möglichkeit*, which is neither singular nor plural but rather pure type.

34. Husserl explains his somewhat idiosyncratic use of the term in *Krisis*, §26, though the full sense of the term can best be followed in his own tracing of the transcendental motif in §§56–72.

35. E. O. Wilson seeks to cast doubt on what Husserl would call transcendental subjectivity by composing an exhortation an ant queen might make, praising the moral law of ants (*Consilience*, ch. 7, p. 167

in the Czech edition). Yet that is just the point: Wilson can conjecture what that law would be because the life world of ants has its transcendental subject structure! Husserl's recognition in *Krisis*, §72 makes precisely the point that such structure is not simply human.

36. Here the examples are again mine, *not* Husserl's, and, in the light of his emphasis on apodictic rigor, it seems doubtful whether he would accept such an extension. Yet this is the direction in which his late work points and the way in which I believe it needs go if it is not to end up in intuitive fantasy or learned obscurantism. While Husserl would rather err on the side of caution, I think it useful to risk on the side of daring.

37. Long ago, I attempted to sketch such a transcendental derivation of moral law in Kohák, *The Embers and the Stars* (Chicago: University of Chicago Press, 1989), 74–76, albeit with indifferent success.

38. This is nearly a paraphrase of Husserl's summary of the achievement of transcendental phenomenology: . . . *die absolut fungierende Subjektivität zu entdecken, nicht als die menschliche sondern als die in der menschlichen, oder zunächst in der menschlichen, sich selbst objektivierende*—"to uncover the autonomously functioning subjectivity which objectifies itself not as but in, or initially in, human subjectivity," *Krisis*, §72, my translation [*Crisis*, 262].

39. Husserl speaks of *die Typik*, the characteristic structure or type structure in *Krisis*, §51 in ways strikingly similar to those of some sociobiologists, as for instance Edward O. Wilson in *Consilience*, esp. ch. 7 and 8.

40. I have touched on it briefly in *The Embers and the Stars*, 129–30, and in papers dealing with personalism, as "Selves, People, Persons: An Essay in American Personalism" in *Selves, People, Persons*, ed. Leroy Rouner (Notre Dame: Notre Dame University Press, 1992), 17–36, or "Personalism: Towards a Philosophical Delineation," *The Personalist Forum*, 13, no. 1 (Spring 1997): 3–11, though none of those are more than brief hints of a topic badly needing exploration.

CHAPTER 3

The Possibility of a Constitutive Phenomenology of the Environment

LESTER EMBREE

Introduction

"Constitutive phenomenology" names the position of the mature philosophy of Edmund Husserl (1859–1938). It publicly began with his *Ideen I* of 1913, and it is also the central tendency of the phenomenological tradition.[1] Unfortunately, however, little has been done thus far within this tendency with respect to the environment. Rather than seeking why this has been the case, it is more important on this occasion to show the possibility of carrying out such work in the future.

As a first approximation, it can be said that constitutive phenomenologists chiefly engage in what are technically called "noetico-noematic reflections." Somewhat less technically, they can be said reflectively to observe "encounterings of objects" and "objects-as-encountered." In this way, phenomenologists of this tendency attempt to account for objects through reference to the consciousness or, better, through reference to the encountering of them. On the basis of reflective observation of encounterings and objects-as-encountered, one can develop descriptions in both particular and general terms, and the resulting analyses can serve not only to clarify environmental encounters but also to show how environmental action can be justified.

The expression "encountering" is preferable to that of "consciousness" because it can be more easily specified as cognitive, valuational, and especially volitional—the locution "volitional consciousness," for example, could be comprehended as "consciousness of willing" rather than as referring to willing itself. "Encountering" is also preferable to "experienc-ing" for the same reason. Nevertheless, as used here, "encountering" has an extremely broad signification whereby one can not only valuationally and volitionally encounter various objects but also encounter oneself and one's groups as well as others and theirs, encounter the previously encountered past, encounter fictive objects, or encounter ideal objects.

Most constitutive phenomenology has thus far emphasized cognitive encountering—that is, modes of experiencing, including sensuous and inner perceiving, on the one hand, and, on the other hand, remembering, expecting, and symbolic, pictorial, and indicational experiencing, along with the justified believing for which such modes of experiencing can serve as evidence. Here the emphasis will be on positionality rather than experiencing, and more specifically, on valuing and willing (and objects as valuationally and volitionally encountered). Moreover, and also unlike much previous work in the tendency, the personalistic or, better, cultural attitude will be emphasized over the naturalistic attitude.[2]

The following exposition addresses how the environment can be approached not only naturalistically but also culturally, and how envi-ronmentalism can be political as well as, in a rather broad signification, aesthetic. Further environmental phenomenology of the constitutive kind should then be seen not only to be possible, but plausible.

Naturalistic Science, Naturalism, and Culture

Although the expression "ecology" is often extended to encompass much more, particularly in Europe, in the United States it chiefly designates a biological discipline concerned with organisms and their environments. This discipline also includes work in chemistry, geology, meteorology, and other naturalistic sciences. What it centrally addresses can be called vital or organic nature—that is, living things—and the theoretical attitude in which it addresses them is, in the terminology of Husserl's *Ideen II*, "naturalistic," the naturalistic attitude being a specification of the natural attitude coordinate with the specifically personalistic (=cultural) attitude in that work. On the basis of theories about aspects of this sort of nature, there can be scientific technologies, including what is sometimes called environmental engineering, which is not a science but is nevertheless sci-entific, that is, science based.

Both the naturalistic science and the naturalistic-scientific technology that relate to the environment have been exploited in the *naturalism* in human thought that has been spreading since the Renaissance. While good science, and technology based on it, are self-critical and modest enough to avoid construing their cognitive approach as paradigmatic for epistemology and their findings as metaphysical claims, naturalism—whether in philosophy or common sense—willfully does so in both respects. Phenomenologists ought to oppose scientism, but not science.

The first contribution of a constitutive phenomenology of the environment is therefore to provide the analysis in terms of which the "nature" correlative to the naturalistic attitude is an abstract part of the cultural world.[3] This is not a matter of the subtle and sophisticated construction produced and constantly refined in the astonishing history of naturalistic-scientific thinking over recent centuries, which is one of humankind's greatest achievements. Instead it is the nature that phenomenologists increasingly call "lifeworldly nature" and that is encountered in sensuous perception and hence prior to all construction in thinking. Once abstracted from the remainder of the concrete cultural world, this perceived nature is premathematically spatial, temporal, and causal and includes physical things, vital or organic things, and among the latter, things that also have mental lives—that is, humans as well as nonhuman animals.[4]

In the grip of naturalism, one might well wonder how such a sensuously perceivable nature, which includes the nature of ecological science, could be considered an abstraction. But if one is willing to suspend what is habitually taken for granted and to reflect carefully, one can recognize that the world in which one finds oneself living is always already fraught with *values* and *uses* for us. Since the students in a professor's classes play roles in the educational situation as much as the professor does, they are more than specimens of *homo sapien sapiens*. Similarly, desks and lawns are more than geometrically shaped wooden (or plastic) objects and curious monocultures of exotic flora. Phenomenologically, they are "cultural objects" and make up "cultural situations" within "cultural worlds."

"Cultural objects," in the broad signification that *includes* cultural situations and worlds as well as cultural objects in the narrow signification, are not merely objects of sensuous perception with the appresentations whereby some are also constituted as alive and some even as conscious; they are not merely objects of such types of experiencing and of the believing they give rise to and sometimes justify, but are objects of valuing and willing as well. The grass, trees, and buildings of a campus may be beautiful or ugly for the professor, and she may also strive to make her students stay awake, study, and learn. Pretheoretically, this world is where humans fundamentally live their lives. It is called the "lifeworld" by Husserl and subsequent constitutive phenomenologists. Even though the emphasis in his work is on lifeworldly nature, which could be further specified as the lifeworldly environment, the lifeworld is concretely cultural for Husserl. The adoption of the naturalistic attitude requires abstraction from the values and uses of cultural objects and yields naturalistic objects.

When one does begin to take cultural objects seriously, however, a huge problem quickly looms that can be called "subjectivism." Values and uses vary not only with the individual, but also with the group, for example, a campus differs sometimes subtly and sometimes grossly in value and use for students, for professors, for gardeners, and for administrators; whereas, it seems easy to believe that there is one and the same "nature" there for all. Naturalism thus opposes subjectivism by focusing on nature as allegedly "objective." Values and uses might then be considered not to matter at all or not even to exist. But more often they are considered artificial determinations added to naturalistic objects. They might even be considered products of interpretation—that is, concepts. But by reflecting on cultural objects, one can recognize that such objects not only do not necessarily include concepts, but also that they do indeed have different values and uses for different individuals and groups of humans (and even for nonhuman animals). And one can indeed recognize, in addition, that values and uses can change, while the naturalistic components, such as color and shape, of the objects-as-encountered stay the same.

What the phenomenologist can ask at this point is, first, whether an object in everyday life—which is a life in which we originally value and will as well as experience and believe—can be *concretely* devoid of value and use for us. Second, she can ask whether the assertion that all cultural objects include not only naturalistic components, like color and shape and growth and metabolism but also values and uses, is not itself an objective claim, a claim about what holds for the objects encountered by all relevant individual and collective subjects—even though it is a claim different in kind from the one about "objective nature" in naturalism. Beyond this, one can wonder whether there are values and uses that actually do hold for all subjects; for example, whether health is preferred to illness by all and whether at least all healthy animals strive to remain alive. It is not necessary that all values and uses be objective or, better, nonrelative in one or the other of these ways for the charge of subjectivism to be refuted, only that some of them be objective.[5]

Many people tend to confuse the cultural with the artifactual. The latter is made up of objects deliberately modified by human action. Certainly more and more objects are being modified by deliberate action and very little on earth remains unaffected by at least inadvertent human action. But what are here called "cultural objects" may or may not be artifacts. For example, the position of the sun in the sky is used to judge if it is morning, noon, afternoon, or even night, and it has yet to be modified by human action. Nor are the stars modified; yet they are beautiful. To have a use or a value does not depend on the naturalistic properties of an object being humanly affected. On earth, we may have a favorite stone outcropping to sit upon halfway along our regular walk in the woods; it has thereby become a seat for somebody, but it does not have to be modified physically—nor even moved from one place to another—in order to serve that purpose.

The case of the outcropping-seat can also illustrate how cultural objects can have their potential uses actualized or their previous uses changed. In the latter respect, before it became a seat, the outcropping might have marked the point on the path where one would turn around to go home, and it can thereafter have both uses. After one first wills something to be or to serve a purpose, that willing begins to be habitual or, for groups, to be traditional. When well instituted, a use (or a value) is something that objects present themselves with or are encountered as having prior to any other operations subsequently performed on them. Operations are engaged in by an I or by a group of I's, while habitual encountering is not engaged in and instead simply goes on by itself within mental life when evoked by the situation. Being traditional also implies that objects, situations, and worlds can have the same values and uses for members of a group; "sociocultural world" is then a useful alternative expression.[6]

Without a doubt, matters are more complicated in philosophy as well as in science if the cultural is not excluded, but avoiding complexity is hardly a virtue. One way to avoid or, better, evade such complexity consists in taking over unquestioningly not only the naturalistic attitude but also the unreflectiveness of most naturalistic science and technology—in other words, refusing to reflect. That is not vicious in the naturalistic science of ecology, but it is indeed vicious if carried beyond naturalistic science—especially since there are clearly other approaches to the environment in science and philosophy when one remains in a concrete and cultural attitude. Several such attitudes can now be analyzed to show further what constitutive phenomenology, going beyond Husserl's letter but in his spirit, can accomplish regarding the environment.

Cultural Science of the Environment

Cultural attitudes toward the environment display various degrees of sophistication. If one remains in the cultural attitude and has professional training, one may engage in one or another cultural disciplines.[7] To begin with, among these disciplines there are the cultural *sciences*—for example, ethnology, history, and sociology, and also primate ethology. When not overwhelmed by naturalism, these sciences consciously relate to cultural objects. Recent decades have seen recourse in these sciences to ecological orientations that treat humans and other primates as belonging to ecosystems and use ecological models to explain aspects of human life. Others resist this because they want to emphasize human mental life, but it could be that both these approaches are incomplete and that a combination of the two is more adequate.

Then again, various attitudes toward humans, nonhuman animals, plants, and so forth, can be described according to the groups of humans that share them, and how such attitudes change over time can also be studied. The rise of environmentalism itself could then be a theme for history, as, of course, it has been. Primate ethology can also be considered a cultural science and approached ecologically, which is one reason why "cultural science" is preferable to "human science." Reflection on how ethologists investigate primate life seems as possible as reflection on research into the lives of children and of members of dramatically different societies. And if adult, "civilized," and educated humans do share the earth with human and nonhuman others, they might seek to understand how these others encounter the environment in the same and different ways.[8]

There is much interest in wild animals, plants, wetlands, and the like among at least American environmentalists, and thus interest in the relatively untamed as well as utterly wild areas. At the same time, however, humans are overwhelmingly concentrated in cities, and hence, that is where practically all overpopulation is produced; that is where most resources are squandered; that is where pollution is chiefly produced as well as suffered; and that is where decisions are made affecting tame as well as wild areas. Humans are not only the animals most harmful to the planet but also the ones most able to modify their own behavior. Hence, human environmental encountering within cities deserves cultural-scientific research for environmental reasons, and the same goes for technologies based on the cultural sciences. Environmentally considered, the ecosystems of humans today are mostly urban. Other than fellow humans and their pets (including fish), house plants, and parks, and also cockroaches, rats, and weeds, and some birds, what is organic about a city? Or does this question require recognition that city life is in many ways parasitic on country life?

The cultural sciences can best begin with the environmental thinking that occurs on the commonsense level prior to science. Reflection on such commonsense thinking can rely on Alfred Schutz's constitutive phenomenology, even though the closest he comes to appreciating nature in his writings is in the use of an Irish Setter as an example of the nesting of everyday typifications, and this even though Schutz was an avid hiker in the Alps and Rockies. Beginning from commonsense thinking, which is based on everyday encountering and basic culture, is pertinent to investigating the mutual understanding (and misunderstanding) between individuals and groups with pro- and antienvironmental attitudes. But that any nonhuman animals have accessible insider interpretations of their own actions, objects, situations, or relationships is doubtful.

This is not the occasion to survey environmental thinking in the cultural sciences. Present purposes are served if it is merely recognized that such thinking exists and that its subject matter includes various types of encountering and the environment-as-encountered, the environment being an abstract part of the cultural world that is not only an object of valuing and willing, but is also fundamentally vital or organic and sometimes even psychophysical or, better, somatopsychic. Access to such a thematics is indeed possible in the cultural sciences, and clarification of how that access is possible—beginning with refraining from abstracting from the concrete cultural world—can be accomplished in constitutive phenomenology. Similarly, and at least as importantly, the use of cultural-scientific knowledge in the shaping of social policy and action can in addition become a theme for reflection from the standpoint of constitutive phenomenology.

Philosophically, the differences between humans and nonhuman animals—and, in addition, the difference between animals and plants as well as other biological orders—all deserve mention as problems for future phenomenological reflection, even if such reflection is not necessary for the purpose of the present part of this chapter, which is simply to clarify the possibility of a constitutive phenomenology of the environment.

Aesthetic-Recreational or Valuational Environmentalism

Cognitive disciplines or sciences are not the only sort of cultural discipline. There are also *valuational disciplines*, which are disciplines in which one aims not at producing knowledge or at affecting events in the world, but at producing the enjoyment of this or that. Landscape architecture is a discipline of this sort. Then again, landscape painting and its study can also emphasize the environment in the sophisticated ways characteristic of disciplines, and there is even such a thing as "eco-criticism" within the study of literature. But these are not the most widespread ways in which the environment is appreciated.

For one thing, there is a great deal of simply visiting nature; that is, hiking, mountain climbing, sleeping under the stars, living minimally by carrying in one's food (and carrying out one's garbage), watching birds and bears and whales, and so on. Such practices are no doubt enhanced when one has more knowledge about what one is enjoying, but sophisticated knowledge is not necessary for enjoyment to occur. Environment appreciatings like these do encourage support for the protection and restoration of ecosystems, but these are consequences of encounterings rather than the encounterings themselves, which are encounterings in which valuing rather than believing or willing predominates and values correlatively predominate in the objects-as-encountered—something that can be reflectively observed merely through looking at the magazines distributed by such organizations as the Sierra Club or the Audubon Society.

Environmental magazines are regularly filled with beautiful photographs of ecosystems and wild animals. Valuational encounterings are then based on what seems best called representational awareness and this can be analyzed phenomenologically.[9] What one is straightforwardly experiencing is the river and the fish or the bear in the meadow, but one can easily recognize that this experiencing is founded on an experiencing of colored shapes on the magazine page. Moreover, one easily learns that millions of people look at perfectly similar magazine pages and thereby experience and appreciate the self-same part of the environment.[10]

Another form of environmental valuing occurs in hunting. Certainly there are environmentalists deeply concerned with animal rights and opposed to hunting, but there are also hunters and fishers who love to be out of doors, and there are certainly many more hunters than animal-rights activists. Both of these types of people value environmental matters, and both engage in activities beyond hiking and looking at magazines. For example, duck hunters, in addition to actually hunting ducks, might actively preserve duck environments and build breeding ponds where ducks are protected from nonhuman predators. Nevertheless, at least when the hunters and fishers in the rich countries eat or release their prey and are thus not commercial hunters and fishers, what chiefly happens is enjoyment, and the practical activities of recreational hunters and fishers are directed toward this end. Those who support animal rights no doubt appreciate nonhuman animals, but typically go beyond appreciation into political action to stop or otherwise affect the course of events, so that such activities are best discussed under our next heading.

If these types of environmental encountering are predominantly valuational, then they can be considered aesthetic in a broadened signification. It is this axiotic type of positional characteristic predominant in the object of such encountering as well as the valuational positional component predominant in the encountering itself that makes this type of environmental encountering different from the cognitive types of encountering discussed in our previous sections. However, valuing is not always positive, for those concerned with animal rights often disvalue hunting, and many hunters probably disvalue same animal-rights advocates in return.

Some may consider eco-spiritual and eco-feminist approaches to the environment valuational. However, these are better considered attitudes that raise questions and present alternatives to many previous attitudes of cognitive and volitional as well as valuational sorts. How far is the domination and exploitation of women analogous to the mistreatment of the ecosphere? Are both behaviors essential to masculinity? Can women be the source of new and better attitudes toward not only humans but also the environment? Then again, can walking in the woods be an encountering not merely of the beautiful wilderness or wild-seeming environment, but also an encountering of community with the trees and mountains, who have moral status for the humans walking among them, so that in relation to them one is in contact with higher powers? Would one then not only disvalue but actively oppose the ravaging of something holy in order to make toilet paper just as easily made by recycling junk mail? Is the dominating, controlling ("managing"), and exploiting of other species deeply disrespectful? Such questions can also be pursued in constitutive phenomenology.

Yet another sort of attitude emphasizes believing, valuing, and willing, and deserves mention. This can be characterized as *antienvironmental attitudes*. Examples of this type abound and cannot be ignored if there is to be any hope of changing or replacing them. Some forms are quite overt, but others are more subtle—and perhaps the more to be feared— such as the attitudes of many city dwellers for whom the rest of the earth is nothing but resources for their pursuits and priorities. A thorough examination of Western culture and its impacts on other continents in this perspective requires extensive historical foundation and is hence far beyond the limits of this chapter.[11]

Practical-Political Types of Environmental Encountering

Believing or valuing often do not predominate in some types of encounterings of the environment, and this is so on levels ranging from sophisticated disciplines down to everyday life. Rather, what predominates is *volitional*. This can take the form of positive willing ("willing for") or negative willing ("willing against" or diswilling) something for its own sake or for the sake of something else and, correlatively, the objects-as-encountered volitionally can have the characteristics of being positive and negative ends or means. (Here "uses" can cover means characteristics as well as ends characteristics, just as "value" can cover both intrinsic and extrinsic values, with means having extrinsic uses and ends having intrinsic uses.) This parallelism of types of values and uses might lead to confusion unless one is clear about the difference between valuing and willing and, as mentioned, constitutive phenomenology involves reflecting on the encountering in which the encountered is constituted. The explanation of the origins of habit and tradition referred to above for willing also holds for believing and objects-as-believed-in and for valuing and objects-as-valued. Moreover, "skill" seems chiefly to connote volitional or practical habits, but extending this word to desirable habits of valuing and believing seems worth considering.

Another expression from the practical sphere that might be broadened is "technology." Environmental engineering, which was briefly mentioned above, is a form of technology, and technology would seem to involve use of equipment in order to affect the course of events.[12] Not all technology is, on this definition, science based, because to use a broom is to use equipment invented long before science to affect the cleanliness of the floor. Interestingly, people can also be used as means; for example, professors are used by students to get an education. And of course nonhuman animals have often been used as means. Possibly the expression "technology" is today more frequently used to refer to the use of inanimate devices than to the use of horses or colleagues. But the important thing in this connection is to recognize the uses that nonhumans and humans have within the the sphere of volitional encountering and objects-as-volitionally-encountered.

There are many types of routine volitional encounterings or, better, practices that relate to the environment. Farming, for example, is unlike much of city life in clearly and directly relating to nonhuman objects that are in their foundations organic or vital. But such objects are also cultural. For the farmer the soil has its use, as do crops in the ground as well as harvested, the weather, the change of the seasons, the barn, farm workers, and so on. Farming is thus a sort of environmental encountering of the volitional or practical kind, and one can easily see how it too can be analyzed noetico-noematically.

The animal rights movement has been mentioned. It is readily conceived as a matter of volitional encountering, which is to say willing for the humane treatment of nonhuman animals and willing against humans who treat such animals badly. This is volitional or practical but it also *political*. What makes it so? For one thing, there seems to be more in the way of expressed rationale or justification in this connection than typically occurs in, for example, commercial farming (although many organic farmers are indeed deeply concerned with justifying their practices in environmental terms and engage in collective action for this very reason). And while farming might be done by an individual without a sense of participating in any collective effort, the opposite would seem the case for political action. For a third thing, the role of valuing in the background of willing is usually clear in politics, since it is often referred to in justifying the willing.

By no means is all politics concerned with the environment. Most of it is still highly *anthropocentric,* which is to say that it relates to the environment as something to be exploited for exclusively human purposes. Yet one can now conceive of a politics in which the highest goal is the preservation and even reconstruction of the biosphere called Earth, within which humans may still be considered a species with intrinsic value and preserved for its own sake, but they would not by any means be the sole species to be valuationally encountered in this way. Humans can learn to be *biocentric.*

Environmental politics can be practiced on international, national, and regional levels and can also be practiced in schools and homes. It is increasingly institutionalized in green parties and institutions for special advocacy, but there has long been a growing environmental movement on the popular level much like the women's movement and the civil rights movement. Furthermore, environmental politics is increasingly informed by environmental science, which is desirable. But the basic principles— that one ought not foul one's own nest; that clean rather than polluted air, water, and food are healthier for humans and other species; that waste ought to be disposed of safely; that the human population needs to be reduced by several billion; that exotic organisms cause trouble; that biodiversity is preferable to monocropping, and the like—can easily become matters of common sense. Indeed, school children easily understand "Reduce, reuse, recycle!"

Conclusion

In order to make a *prima facie* case that constitutive phenomenology can be employed with respect to the environment, it has been contended above that the environment is first of all part of the cultural world—that is, made up of objects that not only have a naturalistic foundation that is vital or organic, but are also valued and willed in pretheoretical human life. When current politics is considered in the United States, it has to be admitted that environmental issues are not yet central, but the fact that they have become prominently peripheral in various sophisticated disciplines and also in everyday life after merely forty years of the environmental movement can reduce one's pessimism.

The emphasis here has been on valuing and willing, rather than on believing and the forms of experiencing that can serve as evidencing that most constitutive phenomenology has been heretofore focused on. Phenomenologists in non-constitutive tendencies may not have been clear about the axiotic and praxical dimensions recognized in constitutive phenomenology. The terminological pair of "encountering" and "objects-as-encountered" has been employed as the generic heading under which experiencing, believing, valuing, and willing fall, with one of the latter three predominating.

Mental or encountering life can either be a matter of operations in which an I is actively or passively engaged or it can be habitual or traditional, and there are belief characteristics along with intrinsic and extrinsic values and uses that are correlative with positive and negative believing, valuing, and willing. This general scheme has been specified for the environment in similarly broad terms. All of this can be refined. Preferential valuing, for example, has not been hitherto mentioned, but can be found in many easy as well as difficult cases. Then again, single values and uses, emphasized for convenience in the above exposition, are actually rare, while structured systems of values and of uses are not. Beyond its capacity to clarify—that is, reflectively to observe, analyze, and describe valuing and willing, which can be specified for the environment—constitutive phenomenology includes a theory of how reason or justification can be turned to in order to contend that one or another course of believing, valuing, or willing is right. This issue has not been addressed in the present chapter.[13] The above taxonomy of environmental encounterings is not normative, but can be made so.[14]

And, finally, while most constitutive phenomenologists recognize what Husserl called the "constitutive phenomenology of the natural attitude," which can suffice for many philosophical purposes, most phenomenologists of this type also accept the transcendental phenomenological *epochē* and reduction, and that procedure too can be used for purposes of *ultimate* justification.[15] But these dimensions of the constitutive phenomenology of the environment are beyond the scope of this chapter.

Notes

The author thanks Betsy Behnke and Ted Toadvine for reactions to an earlier draft of this essay, but they are not responsible for any mistaken opinions still expressed here.

1. Lester Embree et al., *Encyclopedia of Phenomenology* (Dordrecht: Kluwer Academic Publishers, 1997).

2. Concerning how there have been theories of value and action in constitutive phenomenology from the outset, see Lester Embree, "Some Noetico-Noematic Analyses of Action and Practical Life," in *The Phenomenology of the Noema*, ed. John Drummond and Lester Embree (Dordrecht: Kluwer Academic Publishers, 1992), and "Advances regarding Evaluation and Action in Husserl's *Ideas II*," in *Issues in Husserl's "Ideas II*," ed. Thomas Nenon and Lester Embree (Dordrecht: Kluwer Academic Publishers, 1996).

3. Cf. Lester Embree, "There is no Naturalistic *epochē*, Reduction, and Purification," in *Interculturelle Philosophie und Phänomenologie in Japan*, ed. Tadeshi Ogawa, Michael Lazarin, and Guido Rappe (Munich: Indicum, 1998), 75–84.

4. Cf. Lester Embree, "The Problem of Representational Adequacy or How to Evidence an Ecosystem," in *The Prism of the Self: Philosophical Essays in Honor of Maurice Natanson*, ed. Steven Galt Crowell (Dordrecht: Kluwer Academic Publishers, 1995).

5. Cf. Lester Embree, "The Constitutional Problematics of Non-Relativity or How to Dump Garbage in Nobody's Backyard" in *Phenomenology and Skepticism: Festschrift for James M. Edie*, ed. Brice R. Wachterman (Evanston: Northwestern University Press, 1996).

6. For a convergent account of explanation, see Lester Embree, "A Gurwitschean Model of Culture or How to Use a Spearthrower," in *To Work at the Foundations: Essays in Memory of Aron Gurwitsch*, ed. J. Claude Evans (Dordrecht: Kluwer Academic Publishers, 1996).

7. Lester Embree, "Introduction: Reflection on the Cultural Disciplines" in *Phenomenology of the Cultural Disciplines*, ed. Mano Daniel and Lester Embree (Dordrecht: Kluwer Academic Publishers, 1994).

8. Concerning infants, so-called primitive humans, and apes in phenomenological perspective, see Aron Gurwitsch, "Critical Study of Edmund Husserl, 'Nachwort zu meinen Ideen zu einer reinen Phänomenologie und phänomenologischen Philosophie,'" *Deutsche Literaturzeitung* (1932). Translated in Aron Gurwitsch, *Studies in Phenomenology and Psychology* (Evanston: Northwestern University Press, 1966).

9. Lester Embree, "The Phenomenology of Representational Awareness," *Human Studies* 15 (1992).

10. Cf. Lester Embree, "Problems of the Value of Nature in Phenomenological Perspective or What to do about Snakes in the Grass," in *Phenomenology of Values and Valuing*, ed. James G. Hart and Lester Embree (Dordrecht: Kluwer Academic Publishers, 1997).

11. But a good place to begin is Alfred W. Crosby, *Ecological Imperialism: The Biological Expansion of Europe, 900–1900* (Cambridge: Cambridge University Press, 1986).

12. Lester Embree, "A Perspective on the Rationality of Scientific Technology or How to Buy a Car" in *Lifeworld and Technology*, ed. Timothy Casey and Lester Embree (Washington, D.C.: Center for Advanced Research in Phenomenology and University Press of America, 1989) and "An Environmental Phenomenological Examination of Electric Vehicle Technology," in *Technology and Environmental Philosophy*, ed. Marina Banchetti, Lester Embree, and Don Marietta, *Research in Philosophy and Technology* 18 (1999): 115–30.
13. Cf. Lester Embree, "Phenomenology of Action for Ecosystemic Health or How to Tend One's Own Garden" in *Environmental Philosophy and Environmental Activism*, ed. Don Marietta and Lester Embree (Lanham: Rowman and Littlefield, 1995).
14. The most radical reform within constitutive phenomenology has been proposed by Dorion Cairns, for whom philosophy is not merely knowledge of even volitional-practical life but culminates in a life of justified action itself, and this is something that can be specified for the environment. Cf. Dorion Cairns, "Philosophy as a Striving toward Universal *sophia* in the Integral Sense" in *Essays in Memory of Aron Gurwitsch*, ed. Lester Embree (Washington, D.C.: Center for Advanced Research in Phenomenology and University Press of America, 1984).
15. Lester Embree, "The Non-Worldly Grounding of Environmentalism," *Pondicherry University Journal of Social Science and Humanities* 1 (2000).

CHAPTER 4

Prolegomena to Any Future Phenomenological Ecology

JOHN LLEWELYN

What Is Phenomenology?

Is phenomenology a help or a hindrance to a philosophical ecology or a philosophy of the environment? It might seem to go without saying that before this question can be answered definitively, the terms in which it is posed would have to be definitively defined. But not even provisional definitions are easy to give at the outset for some of the terms. Recall, to begin with, Merleau-Ponty's acknowledgment in the preface to *Phenomenology of Perception* that no definitive answer has been given to the question, What is Phenomenology? It may well be that phenomenology is essentially resistant to being defined, if to define is to deliver an account of an essence understood as a statement of necessary and sufficient conditions. So that if phenomenology is, as is sometimes said, the science of the essence of what appears, there would apparently be no essence of phenomenology and no phenomenology of phenomenology. But if, as is commonly said, phenomenology is a descriptive science, then its findings need not be essences understood as necessary and sufficient conditions for something. If we still want to say that what it seeks to describe are essences, essences will have to be more flexible, for example clusters of features of which a more or less wide number will belong to what instantiates the concept in question, no particular one of the cluster being bound to belong to each instance. It is not surprising that the concept of phenomenology has to be understood as a family resemblance if it includes phenomenology of conception, phenomenology of perception, and phenomenology that comes to exceed both conception and perception in the

51

course of the history of the word's use by, to go no further back in the history of philosophy, Hegel, Husserl, Heidegger, Merleau-Ponty, Levinas, and so on. As the bearer of the first of these proper names would insist, given that there is a historical dimension to the logic of the Concept as such, there is a historical dimension to the logic of the concept of phenomenology.

According to the construal of essence as family resemblance, historical circumstances play a part in determining which features belong to the cluster of those from which different selections are made in different exemplifications of a concept. This historical dimension of conceptuality is acknowledged in the appeals to etymology that are made in the style of phenomenology practiced sparingly by Heidegger in *Being and Time* and more sparingly in the style of thinking, no longer called by him phenomenology, to which he later turned. Making an appeal both to the etymology of a concept and to the concept of etymology, it is illuminating to note that the Welsh word usually translated as "essence" or "quintessence" is *hanfod*. The second syllable of this verbal noun is a mutation of *bod*, which is equivalent to the verbal noun "being." The first syllable, deriving perhaps from an obsolete preposition, has the sense of descent, as in *hanes*, history or story, and the further sense that what the story would tell is clandestine, something concealed. This last notion is conveyed in Latin and Greek by the prepositional components of *substantia* and *hypostasis*. It is the notion of property, propriety, or properness conveyed by *ousia*. This ontological notion corresponds to the phenomenological notion that to get to the truth of something is to unconceal, as suggested by the Greek *a-lêtheia*. According to Heidegger there is more than correspondence here. "Ontology is possible only as phenomenology."[1] "Phenomenological ontology" is a pleonasm. That this is so is spelled out in the words *Sein* and *Dasein*. "Sein braucht Dasein." Being needs and uses Dasein. The *Da* is the where and opening of the appearing and concealing of being.

Of course, one immediately wishes to interpolate, what is hidden may be a ground or it may be a causal or historical antecedent; of course, it goes without saying that we must distinguish chronological or temporal genesis from logical origin or ground. But the two words "of course" themselves sometimes hide what is not a matter of course and does not go without saying. If the principle of all principles of phenomenology according to Husserl is self-evidence,[2] the self-evident must be scrupulously distinguished from what only appears to be self-evident. Here we strike again upon one of the features that belong to that selection of features highlighted in Heidegger's conception of phenomenology. Linguistic appearances to the contrary, phenomenology is not only the study of what appears (*phainomai*), but also of what disappears. Were we not already aware that Heidegger takes seriously the thought he sees expressed in the word *a-lêtheia*, the thought that there must be an original darkness for something to come to light, we might wonder whether Heideggerian phenomenology is in contradiction with phenomenology more naively understood. We might wonder whether his phenomenology of the concept of phenomenology exemplifies the paradoxical capacity of a concept to include mutually incompatible features in the cluster of those on which users of the term denoting it draw in different contexts. Writers who have speculated on the genetic analysis of concepts include Dugald Stewart, Payne Knight, Karl Abel, Freud, Wittgenstein, and Robert Musil. The last three of these have noted that a semantic cluster may embrace opposite elements. Of a concept like premeditated murder, justice, or scorn, Musil writes, "a multiply branching and variously supported chain of comparisons is possible among various examples of it, the more distant of which can be quite dissimilar to each other, indeed distinct from each other to the point of being opposite (*Gegensatz*), and yet be connected through an association that echoes from one link to the next."[3] This does not render the term that denotes such a concept unusable, since the concept is not defined in the Aristotelian manner by necessary and sufficient conditions or genus and differentiating property (the way President Clinton defined "sexual relation"?), but is one based on family resemblance (the way "sexual relation" was defined by the president's critics?). Does the admission of this degree of openness of texture put an end to logic, reducing logical or conceptual necessity to anthropological, psychological, historiological, or sociological contingency? Not if the concept of logical necessity is itself based on family resemblance so that logical necessity is not simply opposed, as the necessity of systems of formal logic and mathematics is traditionally opposed, to the empirical contingency usually associated with the sciences of anthropology, psychology, and the like. It is precisely this opposition between formally rational necessity and empirical contingency (hence the opposition referred to earlier between logical origin or ground and chronological or temporal genesis) that Husserl and those inspired by him portray as derived by abstraction from and dependent for its meaning on motivation by involvement in a concretely inhabited world. Meaning is not originally either meaning defined by the principle of noncontradiction or meaning defined by empirical ostension. This dualism of meaning, one of the "dogmas of empiricism," presupposes what Husserl calls a lifeworld and Wittgenstein a form of life. It is this that gives point both to the formally analytic a priori and to the synthetic a posteriori.

Kant had already argued that this dualism presupposes the synthetic a priori. But he had argued this by transcendental deduction from what he claimed to be the fact, one agreed on by rationalists and empiricists alike, that human experience is chronologically successive. Husserl and Heidegger (and Bergson), in their different ways, set out to show that this alleged fact is one that holds at best only for the temporality of the world of Newtonian science. They maintain that this chronology of clocks and the synthetic a priori concepts and principles deduced as the condition of its possibility presuppose a temporality of preconceptual experience. This preconceptual experience is not that of an inner psychological continuum of impressions or ideas or contents, an internal projection or reflection of the external world of physical objects. As Heidegger in particular tries to show, this preconceptual experience is not initially a perceptual one in which a subject represents an object either in the space of an external world or in the space of what is taken as that world's internal duplicate. Rather is it in the first place one in which the opposition of a subject and an objective external world is shown to be an outgrowth from a complex bedrock of one's behabitive being-in-the-world.

Ecologies and Environments

The hyphens in this complex *in-der-Welt-sein* are Heidegger's reinterpretation of the hyphens in the complex of *noesis-noema* and *cogito-cogitatum* that are fundamental in Husserl's essentialist phenomenology. It is on the sense given to these hyphens that hinges the answer to the question whether Husserlian or Heideggerian phenomenology is a help or a hindrance in articulating a philosophical ecology or philosophy of the environment. If the Husserlian *noema* and *cogitatum* are intentional accusatives, we shall have reached a field of research more fundamental than that of the empirical or theoretical objects of the natural sciences. But will we not have stayed with the same structure of objects or objectives over against subjects? And if transcendental subjectivity constitutes objectivity, is not objectivity a way of being subjected to the subject? If so, will not the objects (*Gegenstände*) of the natural world of which the phenomenological objects (*Objekte*) present the form also be subjected to the subject, perhaps subjugated by it? It may be said that the inference that it will be is invalid, because for something to be subjected to or subjugated by something else it must first be there, already constituted, as Husserl would say, and it is in the manifold intentional acts of *noêsis* or *cogitare* that this constitution consists. When a chef puts together the ingredients of a Christmas pudding, he is neither exercising mastery over the pudding nor releasing it from bondage. Until the pudding is made, it is only to the ingredients that he can be doing either of these things.

Does not this clarification leave standing the fact that all *noesis* is understood by Husserl as an act of meaning or intending? Here another clarification is called for. Does one perform two acts of will whenever one does something and means to do it? If one does, must one not perform an infinite series of acts, therefore none? However, without supposing special acts of will, and without supposing either that intentionality as a phenomenological feature of all mental acts or of all consciousness implies that something is performed willingly (for also what is done unwillingly may display intentionality in the sense described by Husserl and Brentano), is not this mental intending still haunted by a ghost of will even when this is no longer conceived dualistically as a ghost in a machine or on analogy with a pilot in a ship? Otherwise, how are we to explain the translation in some contexts of Husserl's word *meinen*, "to mean," by *vouloir dire*, a French expression which, anyway, echoes the expression *sagen wollen* that is already used in German as one alternative to *meinen*, as illustrated in Hegel's discussion of sensible certainty in *The Phenomenology of Spirit*?[4] Both are ways of marking that someone wants, wishes, or desires what she or he does or says to be taken as such and such, for instance, considering here only acts of speech, as predicating a property of a thing or as a denial, as a question or, indeed, as the expression of a want, wish, or desire. So they are expressions of the subject's subjectivity, whether or not, through their noematic objectivity, they necessarily subject the things of the subject's environment to that subjectivity. Even if those things, human or nonhuman beings, are not enslaved to the human ego, the human ego seems to be accorded a certain priority. The ego is at least their master in a metaphorical sense. And that bodes ill at least for a deeper philosophical ecology.

A sense of what a deeper philosophical ecology might be can be conveyed by contrasting it with a philosophical ecology that is compatible with the at least figurative dominion of the ego that appears to be implied by the account of the noetic-noematic structure given so far. The advocate of this shallower version could begin to dispel the impression of egological dominance by saying that other egos have the same access to power over me as I have to power over them. As Hegel in his phenomenology of recognition and Sartre in his phenomenology of the look maintain—the first optimistically, the latter pessimistically in *Being and Nothingness*, though less pessimistically in *The Critique of Dialectical Reason*—arrangements can be instituted by which conflicts between the interests of human beings can be at least temporarily resolved, and through them one ego will be making concessions to another. These arrangements will have to include ones that safeguard the sustainability of the natural resources necessary for the survival of human society. They may go as far as to include

ones that foster concern for the welfare of nonhuman beings. Nevertheless, at the shallowest end of philosophical ecology, that concern for the
welfare of nonhuman beings will be dictated ultimately by concern for the
welfare of human beings. Shallow ecologism thus described would be an
environmentalism that sees the non-human as the environment of the
human.

It is to a shallow ecologism of this sort that the hyphen of the noetic-
noematic structure of Husserlian phenomenology seems to point—at least
as we have analyzed it so far. Very much the same has to be said of the
first stage of the analysis of Dasein's being-in-the-world carried out in
Being and Time. That first and, Heidegger insists, provisional stage
describes how everyday Dasein inhabits its world for the most part. That
Welt is an *Umwelt*, where the *Um* marks not only Dasein's being *surrounded by* its world, but marks also the world's being *for* Dasein, *um-zu*.[5]
First and foremost, the world occupied by everyday Dasein is not a totality of objects or things present to consciousness. Nor is it a totality of
facts—which in any case are liable to being regarded as abstract and complex objects or things. It is rather a totality of utilities and disutilities,
goods or means to the discovery or production of goods that are expected
to answer human needs or desires.

A theological turn will be given to the discussion at this point by
some. They will maintain that the world's answering to human needs and
desires has to be subsumed under the human being's answering to God,
and that the adjustment of the world to humanity is not a humanocen-
trism, but a ground for seeing human life in relation to a nonhuman
center. Taking this turn would entail discussing whether the theological
philosophy of ecology that might emerge from doing so would still be a
shallow ecology. One recalls Heidegger's warning, considered disingenu-
ous by many of his readers, that when he writes of Dasein's propensity to
fall prey to the world (*verfallen*), this term is not to be taken to express any
negative value judgement.[6] If, as Heidegger implies, "inauthentic"
(*uneigentlich*) in his use of the term does not express a value judgment
either, it follows that a conception of ecology that sees the world as subservient to man and an ecology which sees the world and man as subservient to God are both inauthentic. Any conception of Dasein and
Dasein's *oikos* is inauthentic if Dasein's being-in-the-world is not ultimately for the sake of being. For both the humanocentric and the theocentric ecologies, whether we call them shallow or deep, see the human
being as "fallen among objects in the world," rather as an apple might
find itself fallen among other apples on the ground in Eden or elsewhere.
This is how these ecologies see not just human or nonhuman beings of the
world. If the humanocentric ecology makes room at all for an other-
worldy being called God, both it and the theocentric ecology see all beings

as "fallen among objects in the world." For God's or a god's being a being in a world other than ours is in Heidegger's sense a mode of worldliness, a mode of his or her or its being "with us," albeit, so to speak, in a room for whose door we may not possess the key: present in the mode of absence. Heidegger is not the first to observe that even to place God beyond our world in a superworld of his own is to bring him down to the level of apples, sticks and stones, cabbages and kings. God is thereby dedivinized. Being is more holy than a God so conceived—and Heidegger says this too of such a reifying conception of the Good and of value quite generally.

This is why no negative value judgment is being made when he writes that Dasein has a propensity to fall prey to the world and to occupy its world in an inauthentic way. This statement is a phenomeno-ontological one. Such statements are value neutral. My value judgments, whether expressing a positive or a negative evaluation or indifference, evince my having fallen prey to the world. But what this means is simply that they are ontic judgments I make of beings in the world, including human beings, regarded inauthentically as simply entities alongside me. In authentic regard beings are regarded in their being. What does this statement mean? Can it be understood in a way that does not subordinate beings to being? If being is more divine than God understood as a being, is it not *a fortiori* more divine than any other beings too, especially if these are understood as having been created by God? Is this to say that being is higher or deeper than beings? If so, would a deep ecology whose depth is the depth of being be an ecology that sacrifices beings at the altar of being? The thought that it would might arise from the tendency manifested throughout the history of metaphysics to construe being as a being of one sort or another. And this thought is encouraged by the assertion that being is higher or deeper than beings. However, what is higher or lower than a being is another being. Being as such, being as expressed by a verbal noun, is not a being, any more than a verbal noun is a noun, however difficult it may be to avoid construing it as one. That is why the history of the many different metaphysical constructions of being as a being has to be deconstrued, and why it is so difficult to do this even with hindsight—perhaps precisely because of hindsight, because deconstrual seems to require us to jump over our own shadow.

A section of a chapter of the book in which this difficult deconstrual is written up would deal with the history of the topic with which this present chapter began, phenomenology. That chapter would show in detail how Heidegger's phenomenology of time as the meaning of being relates to Husserl's preoccupation with the temporality of consciousness. That chapter would stress, as it must be stressed here and now, that although intentionality may, as noted earlier, retain a trace of will (the "faculty" given prominence in the German Idealism, Kantianism, and Neo-Kantianism from which Husserl and Heidegger strive to become distentangled), the will of any individual Dasein is minimal in what Husserl calls passive intentionality, passive genesis, and passive synthesis. It would be all too easy to reify passive intentionality and to see it as an impersonal force in conflict with the intentionality of individual Dasein. But we can think that Husserl admits this reification only if we forget his insistence that the point-source of temporality cannot be named. For an analogous reason no such "dialectical" conflict between Dasein and *Sein* can have a place in the interpretation of *Being and Time* if what Heidegger does in that book is extend and bend Husserl's teaching of the unnamability of the genesis of time into a teaching of the meaning of being. As already noted, Dasein and *Sein* use and need each other, but in the way that in the *Sein* of Dasein the genitive is double, both objective and subjective, as grammarians say, if misleadingly in this context of all contexts; for Dasein is not a subject and *Sein* is not an object, since neither *Sein* nor Dasein is primarily an entity, although they may be inauthentically thus ontically conceived. This does not mean that there cannot be a Dasein. Heidegger regularly uses "Dasein" as a place holder for what other philosophers call and sometimes he himself calls a human being, *Mensch*. What he aims to convey in using this word is that Dasein is indeed a place holder. Ontologically and existentially, Dasein is the "where," the *Da*, that makes being possible, makes being its possibility, its *Seinkönnen*. As Heidegger says of language, traditionally proposed as that which differentiates man from nonhuman animals, Dasein is the house of being, being's *oikos*, the ecologicality of being.

A philosophical ecology deeper than one concerned only with the human being's environment would be one that follows up the consequences of the thought that as well as having an environment the human being is part of the environment of nonhuman beings. Would it follow that the kind of theological ecology referred to above is deeper than one-sided humanocentric environmentalism? Not necessarily, if to say that one account is deeper than another is to say that it is more comprehensive, wider. For it is not clear that an account according to which whatever is nonhuman is for the sake of the human is any less comprehensive than one according to which whatever is nondivine is for the sake of the divine. "Deep ecology" is not a notion for which we can realistically expect to find generally agreed necessary and sufficient conditions. At the present moment in the history of reflection on it there is no agreement on the list of features on which applications of the expression would draw. Definition is bound to be somewhat stipulative. This does not mean that it is bound to be arbitrary. Reasons are required and a case has to be made out. Paradoxical though it may seem, cases may have to be cited without our being able to define the concept under which it is claimed that they fall. Here there is as much learning to be done as there is teaching. Here the distinction between definition and description breaks down. Merleau-Ponty says of Husserlian phenomenology that "It is a matter of describing, not of explaining or analyzing."[7] Nor of defining, one might want to add, since what Husserlian phenomenology purportedly describes is essences. And Heidegger says that the expression "descriptive phenomenology" is tautological.[8] But what is it to describe an essence? What is it to describe? Wittgenstein bids us consider how many different kinds of thing are called "description."[9] Might not one of these things be definition according to necessary and sufficient conditions or by genus and differentia as in classificatory botany? If so, such definition could not be simply opposed to the description of essence. On the other hand, the essences that phenomenology is said to describe could still be more open-textured. Whether they are or not will depend on what we learn when we patiently allow our descriptions and definitions to be guided by "the things themselves," by the *Sachheit* of the things under investigation, where, let it be noted in anticipation, the German word *Sache* corresponds with the English word "sake."

So Heidegger writes of phenomenological description that it "has the sense of a prohibition, insisting that we avoid all nondemonstrative determinations." Here demonstration is showing in the sense of the Greek word *phainesthai*, which, let it too be noted in anticipation again, is middle voiced. Hence applying Heidegger's phenomenology to phenomenology itself and to ecology, how tightly or loosely these are to be defined or described remains to be seen. And if, with regard to the *logos* of phenomenology or ecology, a modern Socrates objects, as the ancient Socrates so often does to his interlocutors, that he is asking not for stories but for an *eidos*, a sharply delimited specification of essence, he must be told that stories and histories may be what the situation asks for here. He must be reminded of Aristotle's advice not to expect in fields of discourse like ethics what might be sought in mathematics.[10] Giving reasons for defining deep ecology in this way or that, and giving reasons for advocating deep ecology rather than shallower varieties, will be in large part the telling or retelling of stories, describing concrete experiences, perhaps performing them in one way or another.

Performance

One way of moving beyond phenomenological description or of rethinking description as performance is illustrated by the history of Heidegger's move "through phenomenology to thought."[11] If phenomenology is a move from philosophy that sets up the definition of essences or concepts as its ideal to philosophy that describes best by giving examples or exemplars, Heidegger's later thinking is a move that supplements such description with performance, the singing of song, in both a wide and a narrower sense of the word. Indeed, with the help of, although not always in unison with, Hölderlin, Goethe, George, Mörike, Rilke, and the thinker-scientist-poets by whom Plato and Socrates were moved, not always successfully, to try to write sober prose, Heidegger sings the word "word" and thereby each thing that calls to be called by a name or a proname or some other part of speech. Perhaps the philosopher and the poet and the scientist working together may alter by complicating what one may risk calling a *Weltanschauung*, notwithstanding Heidegger's qualms about what goes by that name. This word may be risked because it can mean both how human beings regard the world and how the world regards human beings, how it concerns us. To think regard in this latter ethical or "ethical" sense, which may be "deeper," because presupposed and therefore prone to be hidden by the former sense, is to rethink the sense and directionality (*Sinn*) of the hyphens of noesis-noema and of being-in-the-world. This is what Heidegger's thinking of the ecology of what he calls the Fourfold (*Geviert*) or Fouring (*Vieren*) would do, with its emphasis on the interdependence of the components, which he calls earth, sky, mortals, and gods, and his emphasis on their being each of them according to its own way of being or essencing, *fügsam seinem Wesen*.[12]

Is Heidegger's emphasis equal? Or does it reflect the priority given to the human being in the chorus from *Antigone* that Heidegger quotes?

> Wonders are many on earth, and the greatest of these
> Is man.

As earlier with "deeper," so now with "greatest," priority must be heard in Heidegger's terms as priority of the ontological over the ontic. He is invoking Sophocles in the service of giving the philosophical reminder that Dasein, "man," is the *locus* and *logos* of being. No slur is being cast upon beings that are un-*Da*. Heidegger is simply spelling out preconditions both of casting slurs and praising to high heaven. These include the notions of fairness and unfairness, justice and injustice, truth and untruth presupposed in judgments we make about things natural, nonnatural, or supernatural. But the truths of such judgments presuppose in turn primordial truth as the dis-closure, *a-lêtheia*, and opening that is Dasein's *Da*. Similarly for the justice or injustice of such judgments. They too presuppose primordial justice, the order that the particle *fug* echoed in Heidegger's *fügsam* is intended to denote, itself an echo of the Greek *dikê*, meaning an original justice or organization of the world, on which Heidegger bases his fourfold ecology.

No particular order of evaluative priority can be inferred from this basis as to the worth of, say, the organic in comparison with the inorganic or the earth in comparison with the sky. The constituents of Heidegger's fourfold are incomparable, for they are not separable from one another. Each is implicated in and implicates the others.[13] So if any of these regions is for the sake of another, it is also for the sake of itself. This does not mean that a thing belonging to one region cannot be for the sake of another thing of that region or for the sake of a thing of another region. It does, however, suggest that when such supposed intraregional or crossregional subservience is placed in the wider coregional perspective, invidious comparisons cease to be attractive. In the words of the poet, scientist, and phenomenological ecologist John Muir, who is remembered by an inscription on a granite slab in Wisconsin as "the most rugged, fervent naturalist America has produced, and the Father of the National Parks of our country":

> Poison oak or poison ivy (*Rhus diversiloba*), both as a bush and a scrambler up trees and rocks, is common throughout the foothill region up to a height of at least three thousand feet above the sea. It is somewhat troublesome to most travelers, inflaming the skin and eyes, but blends harmoniously with its companion plants, and many a charming flower leans confidingly upon it for protection and shade. I have oftentimes found the curious twining lily (*Stropholirion Californicum*) climbing its branches, showing no fear but rather congenial companionship. Sheep eat it without apparent ill effects; so do horses to some extent, though not fond of it, and to many persons it is harmless. Like most other things not apparently useful to man, it has few friends, and the blind question, "Why was it made?" goes on and on with never a guess that first of all it might have been made for itself.[14]

If it might have been made by God, it is made to His Greater Glory only if God makes it for itself and us for ourselves. So a sustainable human economy would be sustained justly, *fügsam*, only if it cooperates with a sustainable economy for nonhuman beings, with an environmentalism that is not unidirectional, but a synergic ecology. An opening is made for this thought when Heidegger reminds us and himself that being needs beings, and when in saying this it is not only human or Dasein-ish beings that he means.

No more can be claimed here than that an opening is made for this thought. Heidegger's phenomenology and the "other thinking" he declined to call phenomenology does not entail this other thinking of the nonhuman other. It only enables it. It enables it precisely by softening the hardness of the logical must, by passing from phenomenological methodology to hodology, to a being underway—*tao*, he is ready to say[15]—on a path that this other thinking suggests we could follow if we could learn again to think deponently, depositionally, to speak in something like the middle voice, poised between the putting of a question and being put into question, in the pause of the open question, on the way to language, in the moment of the *question savoir* for which *savoir* is no longer an *avoir* and least of all a *s'avoir*, a self-possession.[16]

At the end of the *Cartesian Meditations* Husserl writes:

> The Delphic motto, "Know thyself!" has gained a new signification. Positive science is a science lost in the world. I must lose the world by *epoché*, in order to regain it by universal self-examination. *Noli foras ire*, says Augustine, *in te redi, in interiore homine habitat veritas*.[17]

Heidegger's phenomenology of inauthentic everyday being-in-the-world and of falling into entanglement in it echoes Husserl's words. Following a way toward which Husserl's words point, therefore, in the pause of phenomenological suspension, which is a losing of the world of objects and of the self as having fallen among them, he finds the world given back. It is given back not just to oneself, but to itself. Acceptance of the invitation to enter into yourself, *in te redi*, leads to an *in te redditus*, a gift of the world that is a *foras ire*, an exiting from interiority through the world's being accepted as a gift, and therefore as a ground for gratitude.

Gratitude to whom or Whom, to what or What? What Heidegger calls *seinlassen*, letting-be, lets us leave this question open, at least for a moment, now and then. It allows us to not close off the thought that gratitude may be due simply to the things themselves, and that this dueness may be the ligament, alliance, reliance, and truth of the *religio* treated in the work *De vera religione* from which Husserl's citation from Augustine comes. If, following Augustine, Descartes found God already at home in the *cogito*, following Heidegger following Husserl one may find that the interiority of that home is an exteriority in which one is not altogether at home, but *un-heimlich*. This is in part because one cannot be grateful to oneself. It cannot be to oneself that the debt of gratitude is due. But gratitude and its owing are not enough. It is not enough because its owing is still owed to a self-owning. It is a return for services rendered to me. Even if I think I am not worthy of the benefit I have received, even if what is conferred is a sheerly gratuitous grace, I am still at the center of my world—or at one of its centers if the geometry of that world is the geometry of an ellipse. To be elliptical is to fall short, to be incomplete. But the ellipsis described by gratitude does not fall short enough. Its incompleteness is insufficient, so to speak, because it is described in terms of sufficiency and its lack. Here we have to speak so-to-speakingly not because we have to speak metaphorically in the semantically semiological sense of metaphor. Nor is the having-to of our having to speak so-to-speakingly the having-to of the hard logical must. Both harder and softer than the must of logical entailment is the must of a necessity that is not based on my need or on a logico-conceptual requirement of my language, but on the absolute need in which other things stand. Another thing's absolute need is not and is not based on a particular lack. In that sense it has no basis. My response to it is both the most and the least gratuitous response in the world. In the phenomenology of Husserl the motivation of the intentionality of consciousness, even when it is complicated by his references to passive genesis, is (on the assumption that one's own self is the center) centrifugal. The response that is due to another's absolute need, absolute responsibility, is motivated otherwise. The intentionality of its motivation is (still on the assumption that one's own self is the center) centripetal, an affection from outside that bypasses my consciousness—and my subconsciousness and unconsciousness too, if these are conceived as subliminal analogues of consciousness.

Justice Adjusted

In my transhumanistic response to the humanism of the other human being toward which Levinas works in response to the essentialist phenomenology of Husserl and the eksistentialist phenomenology of Heidegger, the moment when, now and then and always and always already, I am addressed by the other human being is also the moment, the momentum, the movement, and the motivation when any existent whatsoever addresses me, whether or not it, he, or she speaks the same language as I do—or any language at all where language is taken in the traditional Aristotelian way as a property that distinguishes the human from other living beings. My response to the address of another human being is not a response to the other's being an instance of the concept humankind. It is, as Levinas puts it, a response to the other's face. The other's face is the other's nonphenomenal singularity. Singularity is not particularity. The singularity beyond the sign, the uniqueness that in *Otherwise than Being or*

Beyond Essence Levinas calls a face and a trace, is beyond essence in this Aristotelian sense and beyond essence or *essance* in the verbal sense of *Wesen*. But is it beyond being? How can it be beyond being (and non-being), beyond *Sein* and Dasein (and *Nicht-sein*) if, when we try to extend the application of Levinas's word "face" to all things, we extend it to every thing's to-be?

The being beyond which Levinas's title says his doctrine goes is not just the *existentia* of Scholasticism. It is also being as taken beyond *existentia* by Heidegger: being as thought not through the Latin third person *est* or the German *ist*, "is," but through the first person *bin*, with its sense of to dwell and to shelter, as in German *bei*, the *bu* of Sanskrit, the Scandinavian *by* and the Scots *burgh*.[18] When this sense is read back into the Latin *existentia*, being regains the sense in which to-be-there, Dasein, is to inhabit a world, not just to be in the space of a world in the manner of un-Dasein-ish objects.

As Heidegger's later thinking of things in the ecology of the fourfold can help us understand, once we come to think of things as other than only objects, their being too is seen as more than Aristotelian *hoti estin* or Scholastic *existentia*. This does not mean that all things are now seen to exist in the manner of Dasein. It means rather that they exist in ways of their own which may be Dasein-ish or not, but are never the way only of objects over against subjects or indeed as objects over against Dasein. A thing is no longer a mere what. But its existence does have a way, a mode, perhaps a mood. There is an adverbial how to it, which makes it possible for us, if not for it, to ask what it would be like to exist in that way. This makes a lot of sense at least for animals, even if to ask this question of plants and the nonliving will be judged by many to be an indulgence in pathetic fallacy. If pathetic fallacy is the projection of human or Dasein-ish capacities upon the nonhuman and non-Dasein-ish, then pathetic fallacy does not respect the differences among the many ways of being. Ecological *Fügsamkeit* is flouted. The challenge is to maintain respect for an ecological justice that allows for difference without dominance. The challenge is to rethink justice in the way it is thought in Plato's *Republic*, but in a way in which the republic extends beyond the human and beyond the vertical hierarchy of the great chain of being, in a way that would mean refiguring justice in the soul so that the purely rational and the purely sensory would be abstractions from and aspects of an irreducibly ambiguous imagination. One platform from which to launch this idea would be the imagining of an original position like that imagined by John Rawls,[19] except that we are to imagine a state in which it is not only undecided what role in society we are to fill, but undecided also whether we are to be human or nonhuman and in what way nonhuman. The idea of metempsychosis could have a similar effect. If you are to come back into the world as a chicken or a fox, you may be strongly inclined in your lifetime now to take out membership of the Society for Compassion in World Farming and the League Against Cruel Sports. Ecological ethics built on such a foundation would, however, be an ethics based ultimately on self-interest. This ethics would still be a transhumanly ramified prudence.

If we look to Kant or Levinas for the basis of a transhuman ethics that transcends prudence we come up against the fact that both of them restrict underivative ethical responsibility to beings that speak. Levinas argues persuasively that ethics grounded solely in respect for a universal moral law is a violent masquerade of ethics because it fails to respect the other human being in its singularity. An ethics in which respect is limited to my being face to face with another would also be violent, because it is blind to the injustice it is bound to do to the third party. So respect of both kinds, for the case and for the face, have somehow to be hybridized if an ethics that is not glorified prudence is to be possible. In other words, a certain sort of systematicity is retained by Levinas, but it is not one in which terms are defined by their internal relations, as in the structuralism that was all the rage when he was writing his major works. Levinas has more than one way of maintaining the difference between terms. My difference from another human being is established first by my restrictedly egological enjoyment within the walls of my home. This corresponds but is not equivalent to Heidegger's saying that, for Dasein, to exist is to dwell. One reason why this is not equivalent is that according to Levinas the eksistentiality of Dasein as described by Heidegger is so preoccupied with what it is *for* that it cannot admit Dasein's enjoyment of what it lives *from*. My egological separateness and independence get "accomplished" and "produced," according to Levinas's genealogy of ethics, when the other human being picks me out, makes me stand out as a uniquely singular one from the impersonal one of *das Man*, by charging me with a responsibility unshared by anyone else. It is only through this asymmetrical relation of relations that human sociality can be ethical.

Whatever one may think of the bearing Levinas's phenomenology or postphenomenology has on the phenomenological ontology of *Being and Time* (the work of Heidegger to which he says he is attending above all), is it unthinkable, horrified though Levinas would be at the thought, that his doctrine and Heidegger's doctrine of the fourfold might be adapted to each other to produce at least a prolegomenon for a future ethical ecology? Recall that the regions of things that make up the Heideggerian fourfold (though we are not committed to a fold of only four) and the things of those different regions belong to each other. This does not mean that we possess them or that they possess us, any more than that we possess ourselves (*s'avoir*). Possession and the belonging, *zugehören*, of which Heidegger writes in "Das Ding" is for him more like a *zuhören*, one thing's so-to-speak hearing the voice of another. The openhanded nonpossessiveness of this so-to-speak hearing and speaking is not altogether unlike that of the caress of erotic love with its accompanying sweet nothings expressed in not yet fully formed sentences, which according to Levinas anticipate the fully articulated ethical saying in which I am possessed by the other. For Levinas too, possession is the hearing of voices, a kind of persecution mania, ethical psychosis, madness that is the "accomplishment" of rational responsibility because never accomplished, always beyond limit, infinite, unfinished: never enough, because absolutely beyond sufficiency.

But while what obsesses in what Levinas calls possession and psychosis is the other human being, it has to be asked why the other that obsesses me cannot also be the nonhuman. Levinas's reluctance to take this question seriously is connected with his fear of "hasidic" (Buberian), inebriated participation and confusion of every being with every or any other. As noted earlier, he sees a provisional salutary solution in the hypostasis of an ego enjoying itself, enjoying itself by enjoying the fruits of the earth from which it lives, a state which, whether or not it is prior to or presupposed by the being-thrown-ahead of itself of everyday Dasein, still, like this latter, lives its life without questioning that the world is for the human ego. Another salutary solution is intimated in the following words of John Muir:

> The one deer that he started took a different direction from any which this particular old buck had ever been known to take in times past, and in so doing was cordially cursed as being the "d—dest deer that ever ran unshot." To me it appeared as "d—dest" work to slaughter God's cattle for sport. "They were made for us," say these self-approving preachers, "for our food, our recreation, or other uses not yet discovered." As truthfully we might say on behalf of a bear, when he deals successfully with an unfortunate hunter, "Men and other bipeds were made for bears, and thanks be to God for claws and teeth so long."[20]

It has to be conceded that any ethics or "ethics" based on this reminder might be only a glorified prudence and utilitarianism for nonhumans, or for humans and nonhumans, which latter, as Muir here implies, may include God. How much less exclusive can one get? Levinas is more exclusive than Muir. He does not think that a nonhuman and nondivine being might have a sake whose center of gravity is itself. This is a difficulty for him because a sake or, as he would say, a face is that which speaks. To face is to say, *dire*. But he himself underlines that this saying is not the speech act that is distinguished from and opposed to what is said, the *dit*. It is the saying, the *Dire*, that allows this opposition to be made. So, rather as Levinas equates the face's saying with the looking at me of its eyes, can we not say of nonhuman beings that we regard them not simply as objects, but, as Levinas himself occasionally says of human beings, that they *me regardent*; that is, they are my concern?

Heidegger writes in "Das Ding": "Remembering them in this way, we let ourselves be concerned by the thing's worlding being (Dergestalt andenkend lassen wir uns von weltenden Wesen des Dinges angehen)."[21] He goes on: "Thinking in this way, we are called by the thing as the thing. In the strict sense of the German word *bedingt*, we are be-thinged, the conditioned ones. We have left behind us the presumption of all unconditionedness." On the one hand, the conditionedness here is not just one of alimentary and other suchlike causal dependence. Nor, on the other hand, does it mean only that the worlding of other things is dependent on the thinking and speaking that mortal things do. Nor, thirdly, is the different way of thinking envisaged simply a different *Weltanschauung* understood as a different attitude (*Einstellung*) taken up toward things; not if that means seeing things in a new framework (*Gestell*). That would still be representation, seeing things as objects, even if in a more complicatedly objectivating way. If the new thinking called for is ecological, it must be so in a nonobjectivating way, and it must also be in some sense phenomenological, notwithstanding Heidegger's avoidance of the word because he and we have used it so much that it has become a concept we believe we have grasped. For Husserl phenomenology is motivated by the imagination.[22] So it can survive as a living science only if the imagination continues to be open to risks, including the risk to which Levinas fears it is exposed, the risk of defacing the human being. One of the risks to which phenomenology is exposed is that of seeing the nonhuman being as only for the sake of the human being or Dasein. From poets and scientists, phenomenological ecology may learn to be concerned not only with arriving by variation in imagination at invariants; it may learn also a capacity for the incapacity that leaves room at the edge of the *oikos* for the wild, the undomesticated.

Ancillae Phaenomenologiae

Himself a man of science, but of science otherwise imagined, John Muir writes of men of science:

> The men of science and natural history often lose sight of the
> essential oneness of all living beings in their seeking to classify
> them in kingdoms, orders, families, genera, species, etc. . . . while
> the Poet and Seer never closes on the kinship of God's creatures
> and his heart ever beats in sympathy with the great and small as
> earth-born companions and fellow mortals dependent on
> Heaven's eternal laws.[23]

The same must be said of the science of ecology. The aesthetic, the ethical,
and the scientific belong to each other. Together they make up an ecology,
like the so-called faculties of the mind, which in Kant's three Critiques
read together are mapped on to the imagination writ large, larger than
Plato's republic.[24]

Philosophy has traditionally been ready to listen to the sciences. It
has sometimes been ready to think of itself as either the highest of them
or as the handmaiden of the highest of them, the science of God. Whether
or not phenomenology considers itself to be a science, any future phenomenological ecology will continue to listen to the natural and human
sciences if its imagination is to be stretched not only toward the planet
("planetary thinking"), but toward the universe and the universal via the
generic, the specific, and the particular. But if phenomenological ecology
is to be fully attentive, its imagination will keep the particular in touch
with the singular. That is to say, it will remain ready to listen also to the
poet; and if its phenomenology is a science, it will also be an art. Heidegger writes that thinking, instead of taking up a different point of view, is
called to make a step back, a *Schritt zurück*. Among other things, Heidegger invites his reader to reread the so-called Pre-Socratics, who were scientists and poets and theologians and thinkers before the faculties of the
mind and of the universities were separated, and before the faculty of philosophy was sectioned off into logic, philosophy of science, epistemology,
metaphysics, ethics, aesthetics, political theory, philosophy of history, and
so on. But this step back is to be made in order that we may make a step
forward. It calls to be made in the pause (*Aufenthalt*) of *Ent-sprechen*. *Ent-
sprechung* is co-respondence. But spelled as Heidegger spells it, with a
hyphen, it can be heard simultaneously as dis-speaking, sygetics, the ring-
ing of silence, *das Geläut der Stille*. An antecedent of this has already been
heard, Levinas says, in the Saying that is, not the correlative of a said, but
the ethical and anarchic passivity without which language is no more
than a *flatus vocis*.[25] Notwithstanding all the burdens and aporias it brings
already when confined to relations among beings that "have the word," is
not responsibility shirked unless it is directed, and as directly, to beings
that do not have the word? Do not "dumb creatures,"—those passed over

in silence who cannot speak for themselves—call to be spoken for in the most serious sense of the word "call," a sense that crosses Heidegger's *Heissen* with Levinas's *Dire*? A limiting case of such advocacy would be saying that we should respect, and acknowledge the meaningfulness of, the silence of the beings on behalf of whom we speak. But, if only in order for there to survive beings toward whom this respect and acknowledgment is to be shown, our speaking on their behalf may have to take the form, despite the risk of appearing paternalistic, of protesting against certain practices, for example, the poaching of tigers in Thailand to turn their bones, claws, and penises into allegedly tonic tablets or aphrodisiac soaps for men rich enough to afford them.

The risk of sinking into the neutrality of the impersonal being of the "there-is" remains. So too, however, does the opposite risk of a parochiality in the scope of our conception of justice. Both risks can be met if the Good, the *epikeina tês ousias*, is the beyond *of* being, being's beyond, commanding beings not hierarchically from above, but at the heart of a chiasmus. Levinas's fear of suffocation in being is a figment of a lack of imagination, a lack of that without which reason is empty and sensibility is blind. If phenomenological ecology is ontological it will also be ethical, the ontological and the ethical exceeding each other chiasmically. The ethical will in turn be chiasmically crossed with the aesthetic, and poietic representation as the production of something standing for something or somebody will be crossed with practical and political representation as somebody standing up for something or somebody. Only in this way will philosophy, not least the philosophy of Heidegger or the philosophy of Levinas, make belated acknowledgment that it has let preoccupation with one's own death or lethal indifference to other human beings turn its regard from the perishing or destruction of nonhuman beings.

So far these prolegomena for a nonexclusive phenomenological ecology have included God or gods among the nonhuman beings that compose that ecology, while allowing that this inclusion might be of a nonhuman being or of nonhuman beings entering in to the *oikos* from an absolute exteriority. However, in responding to the questions just touched on of the death of the personal subject or of the personal as such, and of the death or destruction of the other, a thoroughly nonexclusive phenomenological ecology cannot exclude a priori what is proclaimed as the death or destruction of God. On one interpretation of this, what is proclaimed is that God is killed by being represented as a being. Bearing in mind that two of the three passages cited above from John Muir have invoked God as Creator, and taking as points of departure our citation of Heidegger's statement that being is more divine than any being and our more recent remarks about creative *poiêsis*, phenomenological ecology might find a future in going back to Husserl's thought that the engine of phenomenology is imagination. Your imagination and mine, but also imagination as it speaks to us through language, which Heidegger calls the house of being, being's *oikos*. One word that is spoken through this *ecologos* is the word "divine." The—or a—so-called root meaning of this word is to shine. It communicates therefore with *mico*, to flash, as of the imagination.

It is no surprise then that, as observed in our opening section, the concept of phenomenology is always liable to surprise us, that it is always on the move, always beginning again, always ahead of itself, if its motor is imagination, *Phantasie*, understood not as a power to conjure images but as something like middle-voiced *phantazesthai*, where creative power is inseparable from patient *attente*, responsive attention, feel, touch, tact, attempt, temptation. Understood in this way, imagination exceeds itself only because it lets itself be exceeded, allows itself to be overcome by surprise. As *ecologos*, the language of imagination has the "divine tendency," *die göttliche Neigung*,[26] to open itself to what is not yet at home in the *oikos*. It is therefore open to the surprises thrown up in its own verbal play, for example the surprise that the so-called root meaning of shining attributed to "divinity" branches out also into "divining," prophesying, guessing. So that if it is no longer thinkable that God is a being, it may still be thinkable that God is the human being's being kept guessing: shining, but also being kept in the dark, the provocation of imagination understood not as the power to produce images, but as patience before the unimageable. Therefore if imagination is the handmaiden of phenomenology, so also would be theology.

Notes

1. Martin Heidegger, *Being and Time*, trans. John Macquarrie and Edward Robinson (Oxford: Blackwell, 1962); trans. Joan Stambaugh (Albany: State University of New York Press, 1997), 35.
2. Edmund Husserl, *Ideas Pertaining to a Pure Phenomenology and to a Phenomenological Philosophy, First Book: General Introduction to a Pure Phenomenology*, trans. Fred Kersten (The Hague: Martinus Nijhoff, 1982), §§24, 141.
3. Robert Musil, *The Man without Qualities*, trans. Sophie Wilkins and Burton Pike (New York: Knopf, 1995). I thank Percy Jack for drawing my attention to this passage. For comments on what is said by the other writers named in the text at this point, see John Llewelyn, *Derrida on the Threshold of Sense* (London: Macmillan, 1986), chapters 5 and 6.

4. For a discussion of some of the complications to which this connection has given rise see John Llewelyn, "Meanings Reserved, Reserved, and Reduced," *The Southern Journal of Philosophy* 23, Supplement (1993), 27–54.

5. Heidegger, *Being and Time*, 15 and §15.

6. Heidegger, *Being and Time*, 175.

7. Merleau-Ponty, *Phenomenology of Perception*, trans. Colin Smith (London: Routledge & Kegan Paul, 1962), viii.

8. Heidegger, *Being and Time*, 35.

9. Ludwig Wittgenstein, *Philosophical Investigations*, trans. G. E. M. Anscombe (Oxford: Blackwell, 1953), 24.

10. Aristotle, *Nichomachean Ethics*, 1094b, 11–12.

11. William J. Richardson, *Heidegger: Through Phenomenology to Thought* (The Hague: Nijhoff, 1967).

12. Martin Heidegger, *Poetry, Language, Thought*, trans. Albert Hofstadter (New York: Harper & Row, 1975), 182; *Vorträge und Aufsätze*, vol. 2 (Pfullingen: Neske, 1954), 55.

13. Heidegger, *Poetry, Language, Thought*, 178–80; *Vorträge und Aufsätze*, 50–52.

14. John Muir, *My First Summer in the Sierra* (Edinburgh: Canongate, 1988), 14.

15. Martin Heidegger, *On the Way to Language*, trans. Peter D. Hertz (New York: Harper & Row, 1971), 92; *Unterwegs zur Sprache* (Pfullingen: Neske, 1959), 198.

16. The expression *"question-savoir"* is Merleau-Ponty's. See *The Visible and the Invisible*, trans. Alphonso Lingis (Evanston: Northwestern University Press, 1968), 129; *Le visible et l'invisible* (Paris: Gallimard, 1964), 171.

17. Edmund Husserl, *Cartesian Meditations*, trans. Dorian Cairns (The Hague: Nijhoff, 1960), 157; *Cartesianische Meditationen* (The Hague: Nijhoff, 1950), 183.

18. Heidegger, *Being and Time*, 54.

19. John Rawls, *A Theory of Justice* (Oxford: Oxford University Press, 1972), 223. See John Llewelyn, *The Middle Voice of Ecological Conscience: A Chiasmic Reading of Responsibility in the Neighbourhood of Levinas, Heidegger and Others* (London: Macmillan, 1991), 35 and 192. I can underline how important for my argument is the coherence of the notion that human beings may be advocates for nonhuman beings if I reproduce here the following comment by an anonymous editorial reviewer of this chapter, which is itself a case of such advocacy: "Rawls claims that his ethic is not one based essentially on self-interest, but rather is a Kantian ethic based on rational choice. It just so happens that the most rational universalization in this instance is one

that maximizes self-interest. Yes, this is hogwash, but it is his position. This is why, for instance, a tree can't enter the Original Position.
It supposedly has no rationality that would be left behind the Veil of
Ignorance." On my argument the most rational universalization for
the human advocate in the Original Position would be more universal than the universalization contemplated by Rawls and Kant.

21. John Muir, *A Thousand Mile Walk to the Gulf* (Boston: Houghton Mif-
    flin, 1916), 58.
21. Heidegger, *Poetry, Language, Thought*, 181; *Vorträge und Aufsätze*, vol.
    2, 53.
22. Husserl, *Ideas I*, §§4, 70, 140.
23. John Muir, "Thoughts on the Birthday of Robert Burns," cited by
    Graham White in his introduction to John Muir, *The Wilderness Jour-
    neys* (Edinburgh: Canongate, 1996), xviii.
24. See John Llewelyn, *The Hypocritical Imagination: Between Kant and Lev-
    inas* (London: Routledge, 2000).
25. Emmanuel Levinas, *Otherwise than Being or Beyond Essence*, trans.
    Alphonso Lingis (The Hague: Martinus Nijhoff, 1981), 135; *Autrement
    qu'être ou au-delà de l'essence* (The Hague: Martinus Nijhoff, 1978), 172.
26. G. W. F. Hegel, *Phenomenologie des Geistes* (Frankfurt am Main:
    Suhrkamp, 1970), 92.

CHAPTER 5

Heidegger's Phenomenology and Contemporary Environmentalism

MICHAEL E. ZIMMERMAN

The phenomenology developed by Husserl and transformed by Heidegger provided the basic conceptual distinctions for much of twentieth-century continental philosophy. In addition to challenging customary conceptions of selfhood, language, and metaphysics, continental philosophy has also contributed significantly to postmodern ethics and multicultural theory by criticizing humanism and theo-logo-phallo-centrism. In the domain of environmental philosophy, however, continental philosophy initially played a less influential role than did Anglo-American philosophy, which sought to justify the extension of moral standing to nonhuman beings. A number of continentally oriented philosophers, however, began questioning the metaphysical presuppositions of modern moral philosophy, especially as "extended" to nonhuman beings, and began exploring whether thinkers such as Heidegger, Nietzsche, and Merleau-Ponty could help clarify issues pertinent to humanity's attitude toward nature.[1]

In what follows, I continue that exploration by examining the extent to which Heidegger's phenomenology can contribute to environmental philosophy. His theoretical approach to preserving nature differs from the Anglo-American one in two major and intertwined ways. First, his approach cannot be adequately conceived in terms of the debate between anthropocentrists, who say that inherent value belongs only to humans and that nature has only instrumental value, and biocentrists, who say that nature itself has inherent value with which human values are continuous. Although Heidegger's thought is sometimes described as anthropocentric, he himself sharply criticized anthropocentrism. Yet he was no biocentrist, because he believed that humankind is discontinuous with

73

nature as understood by physics, chemistry, biology, and psychology. Second, Heidegger's approach to preserving nature is not axiological, but ontological. That is, he does not propose to discover some property in natural beings that is "inherently valuable." Indeed, he maintains that the very concept of "value" arose along with the power-hungry modern subject. Hence, extending value to nonhuman beings encompasses them within the same subjectivity that is central to technological modernity.[2] Instead, Heidegger's approach to limiting humanity's destructive treatment of nature was ontological. In his view, for something "to be" means for it to manifest itself, in the sense of being interpreted, understood, or appropriated by human Dasein. Dasein's encounter with beings occurs in the temporal-historical clearing opened up through Dasein. Because Dasein neither produces nor owns this clearing, but rather exists only insofar as it has been appropriated *as* this clearing, Dasein is summoned to "let beings be," by allowing them to manifest themselves in their various kinds of intelligibility.

In his early work, which sought access to being as such by analyzing the being of human Dasein, Heidegger indicated that nature primarily manifests itself as a resource for human ends, and secondarily as an object for the natural sciences. He hinted at other modes of nature's being, but did not adequately develop them. By the 1930s, concerned about the perceived subjectivism and anthropocentrism of his early work, he approached being without engaging in extensive analysis of Dasein's Being, although he always emphasized the close relation between being and human Dasein. His later phenomenology, ever more hermeneutical in orientation, amounted to a radical uncovering of insights gained by the phenomenological ontology of previous great thinkers, above all Aristotle.[3] Heidegger interpreted crucial Aristotelian concepts, such as *physis, energeia, dynamis, kinesis,* and *metabole,* in ways that offer fruitful alternatives to traditional readings of Aristotle. Recently, in an essay attempting to demonstrate Heidegger's pertinence for environmental philosophy, Nancy J. Holland maintains that Heidegger's version of Aristotle's view of nature differs dramatically from the modern scientific view, which objectifies nature. Holland does not point out, however, that much of contemporary environmentalism endorses the scientific view of nature, including the idea that humans are simply one species among others. Hence, there is no easy way to reconcile Heidegger's view of nature and humankind with the environmentalists' view. Even more troubling for those attempting such a reconciliation is Thomas J. Sheehan's contention that Heidegger himself concludes that his talk of a "new beginning," a postmetaphysical, nondomineering, and eco-friendly encounter with beings, is internally inconsistent with his own thought. If Sheehan is right, the nihilism of modern technology is the inevitable outcome of Western history as understood by Heidegger.

Early Heidegger's Phenomenological Analysis of Nature as Human Resource

Despite his debt to Husserl, whose account of "categorial intuition" in *Logical Investigations* foreshadowed his own understanding of being, Heidegger redefined phenomenology in his own way.[4] Agreeing with Husserl that phenomenology's methodological aim was to get back to "the matters [*die Sachen*] themselves," Heidegger maintained that the matters most in need of disclosure and simultaneously most difficult to disclose were *ontological*. In *Being and Time*, he defined phenomenology by first analyzing the term into its roots, phenomenon and logos.

Phenomenon, he writes, "means *that which shows itself in itself*, the manifest" (BT 51/SZ 28).[5] Ordinarily, what show themselves are beings of various kinds, accessible to what Kant called "empirical intuition." But beings are not what Heidegger has in mind by the phenomenological concept of "phenomenon," which concerns "that which already shows itself in the appearance prior to the 'phenomenon' as ordinarily understood and as accompanying it in every case" (BT 54-5/SZ 31). Kant maintained that space and time—the pure forms of intuition—are phenomena that appear *prior to* the appearance of objects of experience. Typically, space and time are not noticed as such; instead, attention is given to things appearing within the horizons opened up by space and time. A true phenomenon, then, does not show itself directly, but instead makes it possible for beings as such to appear.

Heidegger defines *logos*, the other element of phenomenology, as "discourse" (*Rede*), which Aristotle explained as *apophainesthai*. "The logos lets something be seen (*phainesthai*), namely, what the discourse is about. . . . Discourse 'lets [something] be seen' *apo* . . . that itself of which the discourse is [about]" (BT 56/SZ 32). This letting be seen makes possible truth, *aletheia*, which Heidegger defines not as "correctness" in judgment, but instead as taking something out of its hiddenness or dis-covering it. Synthesizing his analysis of phenomenon and logos, Heidegger defines phenomenology as "To let be seen from itself that which shows itself, just as it shows itself from itself" (BT 58/SZ 34). But what needs to show itself through phenomenology is *not* what primarily shows itself—that is, various kinds of beings—but instead that which lies hidden: being. Although concealed from ordinary view, being "belongs essentially to what thus first and for the most part shows itself [beings], so much so as to constitute its meaning and ground" (BT 59/SZ 35). According to Heidegger, "This being can be covered up so extensively that it becomes forgotten and no question arises about it or about its meaning" (BT 59/SZ 35). Seeking to uncover what has been hidden in the Western tradition—being, phenomenology amounts to ontology, correctly understood. Indeed, philosophy itself is "universal phenomenological ontology" (BT 62/SZ 38).

Early Heidegger maintained that human Dasein's temporality constitutes the "world" in which beings can manifest or present themselves insofar as they are interpreted "as" something. To speak of the "being of beings" [*das Sein des Seiendes*], then, means to speak of how beings reveal themselves in the clearing within which human Dasein's interpretative activity occurs. Synonyms for "clearing" (*Lichtung*) include: the "world," "absencing" (*Abwesen*), and "nothingness." This clearing—and not the being of beings—constitutes *the* central topic of his thinking. Indeed, he maintained that metaphysics has long asked: "What is the being of beings?", but phenomenological ontology asks: "What is being *as such*?" By "as such," Heidegger meant the conditions needed for beings "to be," in the sense of manifesting themselves *in their intelligibility* or *in their availability* to Dasein.

Beings do manifest themselves in limited ways to animals, Heidegger maintained, but only the interpretative comportment of human Dasein is capable of disclosing the complex intelligibility and meaningfulness of beings.[6] Early Heidegger, influenced by Kant, emphasized the intrinsic relation between manifesting or presencing (*Anwesen*) and the transcendental temporality or absencing (*Abwesen*) necessary for such manifesting. By presencing, Heidegger meant the ways in which beings make themselves available for understanding, interpretation, and use by human Dasein. Presencing tends to conceal itself; indeed, beings can appear as beings only insofar as attention is turned *away* from presencing and *toward* the beings that appear. The work of metaphysicians, which involves uncovering and describing the being of beings, has been so difficult precisely because of this self-concealing aspect of presencing. Even more hidden, however, is the condition for such presencing, namely, the clearing, understood first as Dasein's temporality, transcendence, and later as *Ereignis*. To emphasize the fact that traditional metaphysics had overlooked the temporal dimension required for the presencing or self-manifesting of beings, Heidegger sometimes distinguished between his own concept of being (*Sein*) and the metaphysical conception of being or "beingness"(*Seiendheit*).

Ereignis, which Sheehan translates as "opening up the open [the clearing]," constitutes the "third term" that makes possible the reciprocal relation between the self-manifesting of beings, on the one hand, and the interpretative and appropriative behavior that allows manifesting to occur.[7] For Heidegger, "openness" or "*Ereignis*" name what he regarded as being as such. So hidden is the clearing or *Ereignis* that thinkers of the stature of Plato and Aristotle overlooked it. Heidegger used phenomenology to point out the primal "phenomena"—presencing, understanding, and the clearing in which the former two stand in relation to one another—by virtue of which our encounter with secondary "phenomena"—beings—can take place. A particularly powerful phenomenological method is needed to disclose Being and the clearing, because of their own tendency to conceal themselves. Early Heidegger used "formal indication" to describe the demanding phenomenological practice that Dasein employs as an inquirer to address its own self-concealing mode of being as transcendental temporality.[8]

If early Heidegger said that beings could not "be" apart from the temporal-historical clearing constituted by human Dasein, later Heidegger added that beings cannot "be" apart from language (*logos*), which he virtually equated with *Ereignis*, the opening within which beings become accessible to human Dasein's interpretative activity. It is from this concept of language that Jacques Derrida derives his claim that there is nothing "outside the text." Such notions disturb those environmentalists who insist that nature is robustly real, independent of being known, perceived, encountered, or spoken of by humans.[9] Heidegger himself expended a great deal of effort attempting to clarify the relation between the seeming "independence" of beings, on the one hand, and the fact that they can "be" only within the temporal-historical world, on the other. As I have explained elsewhere, Heidegger developed a "realism" regarding beings, and an "idealism" regarding Being.[10] That is, Dasein does not invent or create nature, as in some kind of subjective idealism, but instead is dependent on nature. Nevertheless, insofar as a being may be said "to be," it must be revealed *as* something, that is, as intelligible, as meaningful, as useful. In 1929, Heidegger wrote: "Although being [*seiend*] in the midst of beings and surrounded by them, Dasein—as existing—has always already surpassed nature.[11] The apparent "alreadiness" of natural beings and their resistance to human intervention are basic features of beings that Dasein discloses in encountering them.

Criticizing the naïve realism of natural science, early Heidegger argued that the interpretation of beings as "present-at-hand" objects independent of human experience derives from the more primordial everyday experience of beings as ready-to-hand tools or instruments for human purposes. In disclosing not just artifacts, but natural beings as ready-to-hand (for example, the forest as timber and the wind as power for windmills) everyday human Dasein discloses beings as they are "in them-selves" (BT100–101/SZ 70–71). The priority assigned by Heidegger to productivity and to the instrumental understanding of Being led Hubert Dreyfus to depict *Being and Time* as one of the final stages in production-ist metaphysics, of which later Heidegger was to become so critical.[12]

At first glance, the claim that "in themselves" (*an sich*) beings are instruments for human use seems to be a throwback to primitive anthro-pocentrism. In contrast, scientists say that a tool is "in itself" an object formed of materials shaped according to certain specifications. The use to which a tool is put is secondary to its primary ontological status as a material artifact. Conceding this point, Heidegger writes: "That the world does not 'consist' [*besteht*] of the ready-to-hand shows itself in the fact (among others) that whenever the world is lit up . . . [e.g., when tools break down, get in the way, or get lost] the ready-to-hand becomes deprived of its worldhood so that being-just-present-at-hand comes to the fore" (BT 106/SZ 75). For tools to function *as* tools, neither their being nor the world in which they are involved may become explicitly manifest. The "inconspicuousness" and "unobtrusiveness" of tools are positive onto-logical traits that characterize the "being-in-itself" of beings ready-to-hand. In saying that "the world lights up," Heidegger means in part that we become more aware of the being of tools as things intertwined in com-plex sets of reference relationships ("the worldhood of the world"). As such awareness arises, the tool shows itself more as (and thus "becomes") an object present-at-hand; our capacity for working with it as a tool diminishes; we understood what it "is" differently. In other words, for tools to show up as tools, their being as ready-to-hand must conceal itself or "hold itself in." This self-concealing or "holding-in" is what Heidegger means by saying that readiness-to-hand constitutes how things are "in themselves."

For Dasein to encounter beings *as* beings, Dasein must have an a priori understanding of the being of the beings in question. Drawing on Aristotle, Heidegger maintained that Dasein's temporal mode of being (existence or openness or transcendence), involves a two-fold movement (*kinesis*) of excess and regress.[13] Always already, prior to any empirical encounter with beings, Dasein exceeds, steps beyond, or transcends itself and moves toward the intelligibility or meaningfulness (being) of beings. This movement constitutes the clearing in terms of which being can be understood. Simultaneously, however, being withdraws, conceals, or effaces itself, such that Dasein regresses or moves back toward the beings whose being has been thus understood. Ordinarily, Dasein is unaware that such ontological motion and understanding make possible our every-day dealings with beings. Wrongly assuming that all understanding is at the level of beings, Dasein typically conceals not only the ontological difference between being and beings, but also the clearing in which Dasein can encounter beings as beings. Dasein's everyday "preontological" understanding leads us to encounter beings—including natural beings—primarily either as tools or as raw material. Bruce V. Foltz maintains, however, that strategic and methodological factors help to explain why Heidegger emphasizes this instrumental understanding of being. In his insightful book on Heidegger and environmental ethics, Foltz writes:

> The primacy of the practical in this case (and elsewhere) is intended strategically to emphasize our involvement with nature and how involvement alone discloses it as meaningful—thereby dislodging the detached stance of theoria and "beholding" from their long dominance in the Western understanding of nature.[14]

As Foltz and others have noted, *Being and Time* does not reduce nature to the either/or of instruments or scientific objects, but instead alludes to (but does not explore) alternative modes of nature's being, including the romantic. In 1929, Heidegger referred to nature in "a primordial sense" that cannot be understood either as readiness-to-hand or in terms of virtually any human relationship.[15] Later Heidegger's idea of the self-concealing "earth," and his analysis of central concepts in Aristotle's thought seem to have been efforts to reveal this primordial nature. In a moment, we will see the extent to which Heidegger's Aristotle analysis can be read as consistent with environmental philosophy's concern to justify protecting nature from needless exploitation.

First, however, let us discuss briefly another aspect of Heidegger's early thought that is important for environmental philosophy, namely, his claim that Dasein's being is care. In part, this claim emphasizes that Dasein is not a disembodied intellect, but instead radically finite, embodied, being-in-the-world for whom beings *matter*. Dasein cares for itself when it frees itself *from* inauthenticity (self-deceptive and self-disowning flight into beings), and when it frees itself *for* authenticity (affirmation that one is the mortal, temporal, historical openness in which beings can manifest themselves). Dasein cares for other beings when it lets them be, in the sense of allowing them to manifest themselves in terms of their own inherent possibilities. Dasein exists not for itself alone, but instead in the service of the self-manifesting of beings. By defining human Dasein in this way, Heidegger sought to go beyond the "humanism" that defines humanity as existing solely for itself.

In 1941, he quoted an old Greek saying, *meleta to pan*, "Take into care beings in the whole."[16] Taking beings into care means not only intervening ontically to preserve them, but more importantly holding open the clearing in which they can show up *as* beings. The former kind of caring may be misguided unless the latter kind takes place appropriately. In 1946, describing Dasein as the "shepherd of Being," Heidegger urged people not to disclose beings exclusively as raw material for modern technology.[17] Hence, he agreed with many others who, during the past two centuries, have asserted that there are aspects of natural phenomena that cannot be revealed by modern science and technology. Recognition of this fact, so it has been argued, may provide the basis for a respect for natural beings, a respect lacking in the modern technological disclosure of nature.

Heidegger's talk of "letting things be," "caring for beings," and being the "shepherd of Being" may strike some as both paternalistic and as possibly consistent with the human effort to take over the planet. In view of human population growth and the enormous scale of technical-industrial power, however, there may be little alternative to human efforts to manage the planet, however daunting and dangerous that task may be. But, even the idea of "caring" for beings disturbs those environmentalists who seek to protect wild and pristine nature from any human interference. Today, however, critics insist that human intervention in the natural world has occurred to such an extent that there is no "pristine" nature, if by that is meant nature untouched by human hands.[18] What Bill McKibben calls "the end of nature," then, has been taking place for many centuries.[19] Many contemporary thinkers argue that nature is in important respects a human construct, both in the sense that "nature" can show up only within a cognitive-linguistic framework and in the sense that terrestrial "nature" has been so shaped by human activity. Even if environmentalists concede the constructed character of nature, however, they point out that it is worth our effort to preserve remaining relatively wild nature and to restore damaged lands to a more healthy (if not "original" or "pristine") condition.[20]

Raised within an area long worked by human hands, Heidegger almost certainly preferred that landscape to "wild" nature, of which there was little if any in central Europe even in the 1930s. Moreover, as he makes clear in *Introduction to Metaphysics*, human Dasein is the most uncanny of all beings, because "Everywhere humanity makes routes for itself; in all the domains of beings, of the overwhelming sway, it ventures forth, and in this very way is flung from every route."[21] Virtually destined to intervene in and to do violence to "nature" (*physis*), humankind so distinguishes itself from other beings that humankind becomes homeless, not a member of the natural community. Heidegger's student, Hans Jonas, read his teacher as an a-cosmic thinker with strong resemblances to the Gnostics of the early Christian era.[22] Karl Löwith, another student, argued that Heidegger's sharp distinction between humankind and the rest of reality was analogous in some ways to Cartesian dualism.[23] Given human Dasein's role in the self-manifesting of beings, other critics ask, how far removed is Heidegger from the anthropocentrism of which he claims to be so critical?

Heidegger criticized the anthropocentrism that arose, over many centuries, from Aristotle's definition of the human as *zoon echon logikon*, "rational animal."[24] By the nineteenth century, increasingly governed by materialistic naturalism, Western thinkers were describing humankind as nothing more than clever animals. In contrast, Heidegger insisted that human being is essentially different—separated by an abyss—from animal being.[25] Sometimes, he insisted that this difference ought not to be read as downplaying the importance of animals, each of which is complete in its own way.[26] At other times, however, Heidegger asserted that even more important than the very survival of the planet was maintaining human Dasein's link with the clearing at work through Dasein.[27] Of course, all of this clashes with the sensibility of most contemporary environmentalists, who regard humans precisely as intelligent animals and who maintain that humankind is not more valuable than the whole living planet.

Aristotle's Pretechnological Disclosure of Beings

By the 1930s, Heidegger developed in more detail his contention that the Western understanding of being had declined since its great beginning in ancient Greek thought. Asserting that modernity was the nihilistic culmination of the ever-increasing self-concealment of being as such—that is, the clearing that makes possible human Dasein's knowledge and appropriation of beings—Heidegger claimed that the powerful, but constricted technological understanding of being was turning the earth into a gigantic factory and humanity into the most important raw material. To prepare the way for a "new beginning" that would disclose beings in alternative ways, he contrasted the early Greek understanding of being with the nihilistic modern understanding. Ostensibly, Western history began when ancient Greek Dasein was appropriated or opened up (*vereignet*) as the site through which beings can "be" in the sense of being disclosed. This appropriation involved the violent ripping apart within Dasein of the opening needed for the self-manifesting of beings. In 1935, Heidegger wrote:

> But the human being is urged into such Being-here, thrown into the urgency of such Being, because the overwhelming as such, in

order to appear in its sway, *requires* the site of openness for itself. The essence of Being-human opens itself up to us only when it is understood on the basis of this urgency that is necessitated by Being itself. [. . .]

[T]he almighty sway of Being violates Dasein (in the literal sense), makes Dasein into the site of its appearing, envelops and pervades Dasein in its sway, and thereby holds it within Being.[28]

According to Heidegger, early Greek thinkers experienced the violence and strangeness involved in humankind's effort to know and to shape *physis*, usually translated as "nature." At times, however, Heidegger virtually equated *physis* with *ousia*: being, presencing, manifesting. Central to *physis* is *kinesis*, the movement by which a living being brings itself into presence by continually going back into itself in order to unfold itself. Despite his genius, Aristotle did not fully understand the relation between presencing and human Dasein; nor did he recognize the necessity for the temporal clearing (*Ereignis, Lichtung*) in which that reciprocal relation could hold. Nevertheless, Heidegger drew on Aristotle's concept of *kinesis* to explain how the "movement" of human temporality opens the clearing in which beings can be encountered *as* beings. Heidegger believed that the decline of the West began when Plato interpreted being as constant presence (*Anwesenheit*), *eidos*, the eternally unchanging form. Entirely concealed in this ontology is the clearing, the no-thingness, or the *nihil* within which such *eidos* can first make itself available or intelligible to human Dasein. According to Heidegger, millennia of obliviousness to the *nihil* makes possible the most fundamental kind of nihilism.

Not surprisingly, in view of Plato and Aristotle's own use of metaphors drawing on handcraft production, the Romans interpreted Greek philosophy as productionist metaphysics: "to be" means "to be produced," for example, to cause something merely potential to be actualized. Metaphysics became the quest for Being, now defined as the ultimate cause, ground, or foundation for beings. Never fully revealed to the ancient Greeks, and now more hidden than ever, is the clearing that makes possible Dasein's interpretative encounter with beings. With the wedding of Christian philosophy to baleful Latin translations of crucial Greek philosophical terms, the ultimate ground became the self-producing God. Later, Descartes turned human reason itself into that ground, by asserting that for something "to be" means for it to be representable as a clear and distinct idea of the human subject. Because only quantifiable phenomena are thus representable, being became identified with the objects of the mathematical sciences. Nature was thus deprived of any status apart from that of an object for scientific analysis or raw material for modern technology. Certainly, nature is left with no "inherent worth" or "intrinsic value," in the parlance of contemporary environmental ethics.

Heidegger, Aristotle, and Environmental Philosophy

Recently, Nancy J. Holland has argued that in his lecture-course, *Aristotle's Metaphysics Θ 1–3*, Heidegger not only sketches the origins of the technological understanding of being, but also provides "an alternative account of the relation between Dasein and the natural world, based on a different understanding of being, an alternative with arguably important implications for contemporary ecological questions."[29] This alternative reconciles the relative independence and integrity of beings with the fact that they "are" only insofar as they manifest themselves within the clearing constituted through Dasein. Holland would presumably agree that because Dasein does not itself create the clearing, but instead is appropriated *as* it, Dasein is obligated to "care" for beings in part by letting them present themselves in ways that accord with their own inherent possibilities.

In his course on Aristotle, Heidegger focused not on *physis*, but rather on the meaning of two terms profoundly related to it, namely, *energeia* and *dynamis*, usually translated as actuality and potentiality. He emphasized that *dynamis* means force and capability, as well as possibility. Aristotle himself defined *dynamis* as "the origin of change, an origin which as such is in being other than the one which is itself changing, or, if the originary being and the changing are the same, then they are so each in a different respect."[30] Heidegger, however, disagreed with the prevailing view that producing (*Herstellen*) is the key for understanding *dynamis* as the origin of change.[31] Moreover, he emphasized another, little-noticed aspect of *dynamis*, namely, *Ertragsamkeit*, or "bearance," meaning both bearing-fruit and bearing-with or enduring and resisting. "Bearance refers to *dynamis* as the foundation for what withstands any attempt to change for the worse or to destroy."[32] This sense of bearance, as Holland points out, may be discerned in Heidegger's later concept of "earth," which "shatters every attempt to penetrate into it." Even the scientific-technological will to mastery is impotent in the face of the self-concealing, enduring earth.[33]

The other aspect of bearance involves the *dynamis* in its "for doing, for producing: in the orientation toward what is to be produced, there is the reference to what can be produced."[34] That which is produced is the *ergon*, or product. Aristotle's opponents, the Megarians, maintain that the

actuality (*energeia*) of the work is nothing other than what has been produced, what "is" really there. For the Megarians, power resides only in
the act of power; that is, they equate Being with what is "present" in the
sense of a being (*ergon*) whose production is complete. Although there is
some truth in saying that the actuality of artifacts lies in their being the
final product of productivity, this is not an adequate way to characterize
all modes of being, including the natural and the divine. Moreover, the
Megarians' exclusive focus on what is present or actual concealed not
only the complex movement (*kinesis*) of living beings that go back into
themselves in order to bring forth other aspects of themselves, but also
the human *kinesis* by virtue of which Dasein holds open the temporal-
linguistic clearing in which *physis*—presencing, self-manifesting,
self-unfolding—can be revealed as such. As Holland comments, the
Megarians' error of equating being with the *ergon*

> is later compounded by the evolution of our understanding of
> nature itself, first, as the object or result of an act of (divine) cre-
> ation, and then as the merely "present-at-hand," the object of sci-
> entific investigation or technological manipulation.[35]

Heidegger noted that bearance as endurance plays not only a negative role, but a constructive one as well. For Greek thinking, the limits
imposed by material are crucial in the formation of a being. The grain of
the wood figures into the production of a cabinet. For the technological
understanding of Being, in contrast, natural beings—the earth—are
treated as if they involved no inherent limits whatsoever.

> The birch tree never oversteps its possibility. The colony of bees
> dwells in its possibility. It is first the will which arranges itself
> everywhere in technology that devours the earth in the exhaus-
> tion and consumption and change of the artificial. Technology
> drives the earth beyond the developed sphere of its possibility
> into such things which are no longer a possibility and are thus
> the impossible.[36]

Elsewhere, Heidegger wrote: "The earth can show itself only as an
object of assault. . . . Nature appears everywhere . . . as the object of technology."[37] Today, all things are "challenged forth" to be interchangeable
raw material. The technological understanding of being involves a disastrous combination of subjective idealism and naïve realism. On the one
hand, modern humankind reduces everything to the status of an object
for the cognizing subject. Swallowing everything up, the modern subject

interprets all things in accordance with their value for promoting the subject's drive for power and security. Eventually, in the fulfillment of the technological age, even the subject-object distinction is overcome insofar as everything is transformed into interchangeable raw material.[38] On the other hand, having forgotten its essential openness for the being of beings, modern humankind adheres to a naïve realism, according to which humans are merely one species among others.[39] Heidegger's antinaturalistic conception of humankind had the virtue of allowing him to distinguish his thought from the racism of National Socialism, even though he supported this movement in hopes that it would save the West from nihilism. For some environmentalists, however, Heidegger's refusal to conceive of humankind as simply another species imbedded in the organic "web of life" puts him in the camp of anthropocentric humanism, which conceives of nature primarily instrumentally.[40]

Still, Holland maintains, Heidegger's defense of the integrity of natural beings provides the basis for defending them from exploitation by modern technology. She maintains that "we must respect the natural world in its own terms, acknowledging the limits as well as potential of its 'bearance.'"[41] A little later, she writes: "The actuality [of a being] is independent of perception, but the perceptibility is not. This is what underlies Heidegger's doctrine of what one might call 'metaphysical respect.'"[42] Such respect arises from acknowledging the relative independence and integrity of beings, which may be what Heidegger had in mind when he once spoke of their "dignity" (*Würde*) in distinction from their "value."[43] Although such respect might form the basis for an environmental ethic, critics would expect Heidegger to define both the meaning of and the basis for the "dignity" of beings. Philosophers have not yet agreed whether one can successfully identify and defend any property—ontical or ontological—which would require us to accord "inherent worth" even to humans, much less to animals and plants, not to mention the ecosystems, mountains, and rivers regarded as so worthy by many environmentalists. Heidegger's brief accounts of the "dignity" of living beings usually focus on their being as *physis*. But for him, *physis* somehow means both the self-manifesting of beings within the clearing and the process whereby an organism unfolds its own structure in the life-process. Heidegger never adequately reconciles these two aspects of *physis*.[44] Critics charge that, by overemphasizing the former sense of *physis*, Heidegger ends up in a kind of "ontological aestheticism," which celebrates the beauty of the self-manifesting of beings at the expense of their merely "ontical" characteristics.[45] Whether or not such a critique is justified, greater clarity is needed regarding Heidegger's conception of *physis*.

Obstacles to a "Green" Interpretation
of Heidegger's Phenomenology

Elsewhere, I have argued that Heidegger's lack of interest in cosmology, his antinaturalistic stance (including his insistence that humans are not animals), and his relation to National Socialism create obstacles to reading his thought as consistent with contemporary environmentalism and/or Green politics.[46] Here, however, I focus attention on a possibility that would pose an even more fundamental problem. The possibility is that Heidegger's own thought—despite his own personal or political preferences—is consistent with modernity's project of the technological domination of nature.

At times, Heidegger indicated that humankind may undergo a transformation that will initiate a nondomineering way of disclosing beings. Some commentators, however, including Thomas J. Sheehan, contend that such a transformation would be inconsistent with the basic thrust of Heidegger's thought. According to Sheehan, Heidegger saw no escape from the nihilism of technological modernity.[47] For Heidegger, nihilism has two senses: nihilism I and nihilism II. Nihilism I refers to technological modernity's attempt to disclose all beings as raw material. Nihilism II refers to a culture's obliviousness about the *nihil*, the clearing, *Ereignis*, which makes possible Dasein's interpretative and practical encounter with beings. *Ereignis* cannot be grasped by the human intellect, which is capable only of comprehending beings *as* beings. Allegedly, nihilism II makes possible nihilism I; that is, the obscuration of *Ereignis* makes Dasein blind to its ontologically unique endowment. Consequently, Dasein interprets itself merely as the clever animal seeking control of everything through modern science and technology. Sheehan argues, however, that in Heidegger's own view, Aristotle's thought—which is central to the entire Western tradition—ultimately leads to nihilism I. Moreover, even if a few philosophers point toward *Ereignis*, thereby minimally easing nihilism II, this fact cannot in and of itself influence nihilism I. Whether or not Dasein catches a sideways glance of *Ereignis*, Western Dasein will inevitably increase its capacity for disclosing and manipulating beings. Given the reciprocal relation between the beings that tend toward manifesting themselves and the human Dasein that discloses them, total technological disclosure of beings cannot be avoided. Sheehan adds that the ethical, political, and social challenges posed by the looming possibility of the total disclosure of beings must be met with means other than those used by Heideggerians meditating on *Ereignis*.

At one time, Heidegger did seem to think that disclosing nihilism II could transform nihilism I. In fact, he defended his involvement with National Socialism as part of his own philosophical effort to overcome (*überwinden*) nihilism. Later on, however, having abandoned this disastrous political engagement, he spoke not of *Überwindung*, but rather of *Verwindung*. As Sheehan comments, *Verwinding* involves not the overcoming of nihilism I, but instead of "a 'freeing' of oneself from social and cultural nihilism by seeing its rootedness in a deeper and unsurpassable 'nihilism' that is in fact the human condition."[48] If Sheehan is right, Heidegger's well-known utterance that "only a god can save us now" is best read ironically, given his views about the inevitability of Dasein interpreting beings ever more completely. Further, his talk of a dispensation (*Geschick*) that may enable Dasein to interpret beings in a nondomineering way is best read as an instance of mythologizing that has been described as Heidegger's "private religion."[49]

Sheehan observes that understanding everything as raw material is possible only insofar as Dasein exists within the clearing that allows Dasein to encounter and to interpret beings as beings. Heidegger remarked: "Even if the contemporary and closest humankind, technologized and equipped to the utmost, is in a planetary condition for which the general distinction between 'war and peace' belongs to things gone by, even then humanity still lives 'poetically' on this earth. . . ." Immediately, however, he adds the following: ". . . but he lives in essential opposition (*Gegenwesen*) to poetry and hence without need and therefore [is] inaccessible for its essence."[50] Here, Heidegger gives with one hand what he takes away with another. True, modernity *does* disclose the being of beings, but *not* the poetizing mode of being heralded by Hölderlin, nor the self-blossoming mode of being—*physis*—revealed by Aristotle. To experience an alternative way of disclosing beings, Heidegger maintained, humankind must become attuned to its own profound lack, its ontological need. Self-assertive humankind discloses all beings as flexible raw material without any internal limits. Such disclosure is a nihilism that correlates with humanism, "the ideology which asserts that human being is fulfilled in abetting the limitless availability and intelligibility of everything that is."[51]

At times, Heidegger suggested that humankind reject modernity and become open for a new mode of ontological understanding that enables Dasein to become rooted again in the earth. Elsewhere, however, he indicated—for example, in his essay "On the Question of Being," dedicated to Ernst Jünger—that there is no alternative to the technological disclosure of being, which involves the correlation between nature as raw material and Dasein as the *Gestalt* of the worker-soldier who uses such raw material for gaining ever greater power.[52] Many commentators on Heidegger conclude that the technological disclosure of beings decreases Dasein's overall capacity for ontological disclosure. Sheehan maintains, however, that far from offering a constricted disclosure of beings, modern science reveals them more thoroughly than ever before. Hence, he asks: "Why are they [technological disclosure and *Ereignis*] correlative in an apparently zero-sum way, such that the increase in the power and domination of the *Gestalt* of the worker would necessarily entail the decrease in the power of appropriation [*Ereignis*]?"[53] The scientific-technological disclosure of beings has made possible extraordinary improvements in human well-being, but that same disclosure also poses enormous social, ethical, and political problems associated with nihilism I. Nevertheless, according to Sheehan, the technological disclosure of beings does *not* arise from the historical constriction in or human obliviousness to the clearing/*Ereignis*. Humankind has always been and remains oblivious to the clearing. The technological disclosure of beings is the perhaps inevitable result of humankind exploiting its capacity for uncovering, understanding, and manipulating beings.

Heidegger assigned to human Dasein an extraordinary position, outside the great chain of being and cosmos, but inside *Ereignis*. Heidegger rendered Parmenides' famous saying, "Being and thinking are the same" (*to gar auto noein estin te kai einai*), as "There is a reciprocal bond between apprehension [Dasein's ontological understanding] and being."[54] This "guiding principle of Western philosophy" names *Ereignis*, that is, the groundless opening that makes possible Dasein's interpretative encounter with beings. Heidegger stated: "We always say *too little* about 'being itself' when, in saying 'being,' we leave out presence *to* the human *essence* and thereby fail to recognize that this [human] essence itself goes to make up 'being'."[55] If Dasein is essentially openness for the self-manifesting of beings, beings themselves are inherently inclined to make themselves completely accessible to human Dasein. As Sheehan says, "entities are ontologically '*ad hominem*'."[56] Hence, nihilism I (technological modernity) arises not because *Ereignis* conceals itself (nihilism II), but instead because *Ereignis* occurs at all:

> Insofar as the essence of entities entails their presence to human cognition and will, it also entails that they are disposed to be picked up and used, to be reshaped as *poioumena*—and endlessly so. The endless accessibility of the real is at the core of the Greek-Western vision of being, which from the pre-Socratics up to Heidegger, has affirmed the infinity of the intelligibility (and thus the transformatibility) of *to on*, an infinity that is correlative to the infinite reach of *nous*.[57]

If Sheehan is right, there is no basis in Heidegger's own ontology for his critical portrayal of modern technology as nihilism I, the highly attenuated disclosure of beings resulting from nihilism II, the allegedly increasing concealment of *Ereignis*. Contrary to Heidegger's yearning for the post- or nontechnological era of the fourfold (earth and sky, gods and mortals), and contrary to some environmentalist's longing for a less domineering treatment of nature, Sheehan argues that

> we would be doing being-itself no favors if we just let entities 'be' in the sense of leaving them pristine and untouched, perhaps even unknown. To let entities *be* means to let them *be present*, that is, to take them as endlessly engagable. And we do that by endlessly engaging them . . . , and yes, by letting them be submitted to the domination of the worker in the inevitable humanization of nature and the naturalization of man.[58]

In effect, Heidegger maintained that from their own side beings "want" to be disclosed and utilized by humankind. *Ereignis* itself entails this. Moreover, according to Aristotle, insofar as humans pursue their desire to know, they are seeking to become godlike. Humans can become godlike because they share to some extent in God's own nature. Sheehan writes:

> But this means that, whether or not the project is ever actually fulfilled, Aristotle has opened up to human beings the possibility of the total knowledge (and along with that knowledge, the control) of everything that is insofar as it is. Aristotle's theology is the first technology, and modern technology is only the last theology. The "death of God" begins with the first sentence of the Metaphysics, and after it nihilism will be only a mopping up exercise. . . . [H]enceforth in Western thought *theos*, the highest instance of *physis*, will be a symbol for the goal and scope of technology: the humanization of nature and the naturalization of man.[59]

In this exegetical *tour de force*, Sheehan concludes that the ontological kernel of Heidegger's thought is consistent with the progressive ideologies according to which humankind is both capable of and entitled to transform nature in infinite ways. Clearly, this conclusion would be palatable neither to most Heideggerians nor to most environmentalists, for whom progress amounts to an ideological justification for the exploitation of nature. In Sheehan's view, however, Heidegger's dislike for modernity reflected personal and political considerations that cannot be reconciled with the gist of his thought. Sheehan seeks to rescue Heidegger from neo-Christian eschatology, according to which Being will one day reveal itself again, thereby saving humankind from technological nihilism.[60] According to Sheehan, the real *eschaton* concerns "the ultimate, unsurpassable *factum*," that humankind lives "into and out of appropriation [*Ereignis*]."[61] Humankind must come to terms with both the insecurity and power imposed by this destiny; that is, nihilism II, obliviousness to the clearing/*Ereignis*. Philosophers may learn something profound from Heidegger's discussion of the clearing, but, writes Sheehan, "the future of the humanization of nature and naturalization of man, is decided not in classrooms or philosophy conferences, nor in libraries or texts. It is being decided in the hills and in the streets, in the boardrooms and the *maquilas*."[62]

By making the preceding remark, Sheehan indicates that his own views differ in certain respects from those of Heidegger. Although apparently agreeing with Heidegger that humankind is endowed with an apparently limitless capacity for disclosing and utilizing beings, Sheehan believes that there is no basis in Heidegger's own thought for a "new beginning" that would alter this capacity. Moreover, he disagrees with Heidegger's yearning and evident preference for preindustrial ways of life, perhaps in part because the positive contributions of modernity are so valuable. What Sheehan does not spell out, however, is the basis for the decisions that need to be made in the hills, streets, boardrooms, and factories with regard to how humans will live in a world ever more characterized by humanity's technological prowess. One suggestion: If humankind is the disclosing being (as opposed to Marx's productive animal), the issues of justice and ethics have to do with enhancing conditions that enable everyone to engage in disclosive activities to the best of their abilities, and eliminating those conditions that deprive people of such opportunities.

Concluding Remarks

Because Sheehan is the leading exegete of Heidegger's Aristotle-interpretation, readers must take seriously his striking conclusions that nihilism II cannot be overcome, that Heidegger's thought is ultimately irreconcilable with social nostalgia and antianthropocentric environmentalism, and that Western history involves not a decline from a great beginning but instead the gradual (aka progressive!) unfolding of humankind's extraordinary capacity for knowing and utilizing beings. Many Heideggerians, however, particularly those who affirm Heidegger's pertinence for environmental philosophy, would complain that Sheehan either ignores or minimizes aspects of Heidegger's thought that suggest the possibility of a nondomineering disclosure of nature.[63] Moreover, even if such Heideggerians concede that later Heidegger mythologizes being (which supposedly reveals itself, hides itself, initiates new beginnings, etc.), they could argue that his analysis of early Greek thinking reveals that there are conceptions of being alternative to the technological one. The fact that the technological understanding of being happens to prevail in the current historical epoch does not mean either that it is inevitable or enduring.

Presumably, the excesses of the technological disclosure of beings could be tempered by acknowledging two things: first, following Aristotle, that living beings tend both to preserve and to unfold themselves according to their own internal possibilities; and second, that humans have a responsibility to respect the integrity and relative independence of natural beings, even though often using those beings in order to serve human ends. If the Kantian doctrine of respect for persons is based on insight into human existence, as Heidegger himself suggested, then respect for animals, plants, and even ecosystems may be based on insight into their *own* modes of being, as Holland suggests in the essay we discussed earlier. The fact that plants, animals, and ecosystems "show up" *as* beings only through Dasein's interpretative activity does not give Dasein a license to treat such beings arbitrarily, any more than the fact that other persons show up through such activity gives Dasein license to treat persons without due respect. Endowed with great disclosive capacities, Dasein is also burdened with unparalleled responsibilities to "care" for beings.

Although agreeing that modern technology culminates Aristotle's metaphysics, Heidegger also maintained at times that the technological disclosure of beings is as narrow as it is powerful. In regard to how living beings are disclosed by modern science and technology, Heidegger stated that

> *an original reference to things is missing.* . . . We feel that what zoology and botany investigate concerning animals and plants and how they investigate it may be correct. But are they still animals and plants? Are they not machines duly prepared beforehand of which one afterwards even admits that they are "cleverer than we are"?[64]

Environmentalists may also refer to Heidegger's famous contrast between earth and world to support Holland's contention that for Heidegger, beings have an intrinsic resistance to complete disclosure in any particular world, Greek, Roman, medieval, or technological. Discovery of such internal resistance occurs in ordinary temporality, not in the ecstatic temporality of *Ereignis*. Questions to be posed here include these: Does the fact that living beings happen to display such resistance place us under a moral obligation to avoid altering or harming such beings? In other words, does "is" entail "ought"? Environmental ethicists know, of course, that there are no easy answers to such questions, nor should such answers be expected from Heidegger, who explicitly declined to develop an ethics.

In times, Heidegger did contest the conclusion that the technological disclosure of beings exhausts their possibilities, even if such disclosure does enable "infinite" discovery about and shaping of such beings. Beings can be encountered, interpreted, and used in ways other than as scientific objects or technologically pliable stuff. In his Plato lectures from 1931, for instance, he wrote the following concerning the limitations of the scientific understanding of beings:

> It is a question for itself whether, through that science, the being [*das Seiende*] has become more being [*seiender*] or whether something totally different has inserted itself between the being and cognitive man, as a result of which his relationship with the being has been eroded, his instinct for the essence of nature driven out of him—and his instinct for the essence of man choked.[65]

According to Sheehan's reading, however, Heidegger misspeaks himself here. There is no "thing" that can be placed "between" human cognition and beings, since the open, clearing, or no-thingness constitutes the "between" of knowing and beings known "open" or "clearing." The kinds of "things" that lead to a distorted disclosure of beings are bias, prejudice, ignorance, or malice. If humankind has an "instinct" for the essence of nature, that instinct involves the capacity for ever more effective ways of disclosing aspects of that essence, including the ecological sciences. Alternatives to scientific modes of disclosure do persist, including art and ritual. Arguably, however, as Heidegger himself conceded, the most penetrating disclosures are taking place through the natural sciences. To suggest, as Heidegger did, that such disclosure are merely "correct" and not ontologically "true" begs the question of the status of the latter kind of truth, especially if it is supposed to be something other than the capacity for understanding the being of beings, as this is described in *Being and Time* and elsewhere.

Perhaps the ontological truth in question pertains to the disclosure of the "openness of the open," *Ereignis*, a rare event that constitutes an end in itself and the high point of human existence. By virtue of such truth, apparently the highest degree of self-transparency possible for human existence, Heidegger allegedly was able to draw important conclusions about the obscure relationship between knowing and being. In some (but not all!) respects, such truth corresponds to the truth position occupied in the first *Critique* by Kant, who made truth claims about the nature of human cognition, truth claims that do not conform to the kinds of truth claims that are legitimated in that *Critique*. Here, it is important to note that Galileo and Newton were able to make profound discoveries about material nature, without any knowledge whatsoever of the transcendental conditions (allegedly) necessary for such discoveries.

Analogously, whether or not "man's" instinct for its own essence is choked—that is, whether or not Dasein is more or less able to catch a glimpse of the clearing that makes possible humanity's encounters with beings—makes no difference with respect to the ongoing activity of disclosing, understanding, and utilizing beings. Sheehan puts this provocatively: "[O]ne can embrace mystical worldviews (as the dying Aquinas allegedly did) which, to the degree they are oblivious to the open, are formally no different from the materialist worldviews of Antiphon or Stalin."[66] Although initially shocking, Sheehan's claim seems consistent with Heidegger's own understanding that authenticity (*Eigentlichkeit*) is an end in itself. Surrendering to the transformational mood of anxiety allows Dasein to experience directly the groundless opening-up (*Ereignis*) of the temporality that makes possible every encounter with beings.

In his excellent biography of Heidegger, Rüdiger Sanfranski argues in a way that seems consistent with Sheehan's view. For Heidegger, authenticity is an extraordinary intensification of human existence, a very rare, even blissful disclosure of the temporalizing no-thingness at work through Dasein.[67] Despite generating inexpressible wonder and terror, such a disclosure offers no insights about the structure of beings, nor any necessary revelations about political and ethical matters.[68] Science and other disciplines seek to disclose those structures, just as moral direction must be worked out by individuals and/or communities on their own and as best they can, without the assistance of either *Ereignis* or eternal grounds. Hence, Heidegger's ideas of *Gelassenheit* and "letting things be" may be read not as recommending a less domineering attitude toward nature, despite Heidegger's remarks to the contrary. Instead, *Gelassenheit* may involve taking up a detached attitude toward modern technology, whose all-controlling impetus not only cannot be halted, but *ought* not to be halted.

Seen from this perspective, modern technology is simply Dasein doing its thing with increasing effectiveness. Guidance for decision making must come from a source other than *Eigentlichkeit* or *Ereignis*.

Even the maxim that I cited earlier—namely, that great ability (e.g., the capacity to disclose beings as beings) confers equally great responsibility—cannot be derived from the experience of *Ereignis*. Apparently, then, we must conclude that the source of Heidegger's frequent criticisms of modern technology (nihilism I), including the destruction of nature, must be other than nihilism II, that is, constriction of Dasein's experience of *Ereignis*, the opening of the open. That true source for Heidegger's critique of nihilism I may itself be manifold, including conservative ideology, anticommunism, romantic love for nature, contempt for commercialism and mass society, and so on. Even if Heidegger did insist that the technological disclosure of being is merely partial, then, Sheehan is right that Dasein cannot expect the future dawn of a posttechnological, nondomineering clearing. Instead, there are far better grounds for thinking that "this is it." If so, the progressive reading of Western history, according to which humankind will eventually achieve a godlike power over beings, would make more sense than Heidegger's reading of history as a decline into the nihilism II (concealment of *Ereignis*) that makes nihilism I (modern technology) possible.

Some of the difficulty involved in reading Heidegger as an eco-friendly thinker may be traced to his abandonment of the moral dimensions of esoteric Christian theology and Greek philosophy, particularly Platonism. Among other things, esoteric Christians and Platonists share the view—*mutatis mutandi*—that beyond the realm of creatures or beings, and even beyond the plane of being itself, one may discern an ultimate that cannot be designated as a creature, being, or phenomenon. Mystical Christians describe the Godhead beyond the historical divinity as an abyss, an *Ab-grund*, a nothingness. Plato speaks of the *agathon* as lying beyond the being of beings. For both mystical Christianity and Platonism, the Ultimate lies beyond good and evil, at least in respect to how these are understood by mortals. Both mystical Christians and Platonists, however, acknowledge that both before and after those rare moments of insight into the Ultimate, humans exist within societies governed by moral codes that are not merely arbitrary, at least insofar as a serious degree of moral goodness is typically a prerequisite for someone seeking to move beyond beings and being to the Ultimate. In other words, Christian and Greek mysticism presupposed the validity of ethical strictures in everyday life. Furthermore, one may discern in Christian and Greek mysticism an element also presupposed by esoteric Buddhism; namely, that ever greater wisdom—including the extremely demanding and terrifying truth about ultimate no-thingness—spontaneously generates ever greater compassion. Jesus called upon his followers to care for the needy, hungry, and oppressed; Plato indicates that the prisoner who leaves the cave and discovers the Ultimate is bound to return to the cave in order to assist others to know the liberating truth; and Mahayana Buddhism indicates that the Bodhisattva vows to renounce ultimate enlightenment—even after having tasted it—until all sentient beings are saved from suffering. Typically absent from Heidegger's thought, despite occasional remarks to the contrary, is this theme of the reciprocal relation between ontological wisdom and ontical compassion. Perhaps Heidegger's encounter with Nietzsche helps to explain this lacuna. In any event, insofar as Heidegger developed no ethics, and insofar as compassion is not explicitly included in his discussion of insight into *Ereignis*, the central core of his thought provides inadequate guidance for environmental philosophy, even though—due to motives that lie outside the core of his thought—Heidegger certainly did exhibit concern about the destruction of nature by modern technology.

Missing from Sheehan's insightful critique of efforts to read Heidegger as a protoenvironmental philosopher is a moral and/or political basis for contesting and resisting—as he apparently wishes to do—at least some of the totalizing practices of modern technology. Insofar as Sheehan is evidently a progressive thinker who also admires aspects of the idea that humankind exists as the disclosing being, he might call for a social ethics that alters institutions and allocates resources in ways that maximize the capacity for each individual to disclose beings to the best of his or her abilities, instead of being compelled to disclose beings primarily in accord with requirements imposed by oppressive governments, corporations, and other social institutions. Another way for Sheehan to reconcile a progressive reading of history, from Aristotle to modern technology, with Heidegger's reading might involve introducing the concept of panentheism, which Sheehan—like most moderns—prefers to exclude. According to panentheism, Spirit manifests itself in evolutionary processes in terms of an enormously complex hierarchy, which includes material nature and consciousness, but Spirit is not exhausted by any such manifestation. Spirit is the clearing, understood as absolute nonduality. Giving rise to humankind as an agent that interprets beings, Spirit fulfills itself in the evolutionary process by which humans (and comparable beings elsewhere) discover and actualize their own incipient divine powers of disclosure and creation. To maximize these powers within humankind, humans must struggle to put into place various conditions—material, cultural, social, institutional, personal. These struggles are defined as progressive insofar as they either expand humankind's disclosive capacity or else protect such capacity from various forms of oppression. Such an evolutionary panentheism, details of which I cannot develop here, emphasizes that Spirit transcends but also accompanies the universe.

According to the perennial wisdom shared by many versions of panentheism, *compassion*—including compassion for all sentient beings—spontaneously arises with increasing *wisdom*. A wiser humankind would treat all sentient being less brutally than we do today. The capacity for technological control over beings does not constitute wisdom, but neither does wisdom involve denying that such power may or even ought to be the destiny of our species. Sharing with Nietzsche and other moderns an antipathy for the otherworldliness of the onto-theological tradition, Heidegger reduced Spirit's transcendence to the radical finitude of Western Dasein. In doing so, however, he—like other moderns—not only omitted the prospect of divine compassion, but also limited the possibility of a serious dialogue among contemporary cosmologists, environmental philosophers, and teachers from diverse spiritual traditions.[69]

Notes

My thanks to Frank Schalow and Thomas J. Sheehan for their critical suggestions, which improved this essay. Remaining shortcomings are exclusively my responsibility.

1. See for example, George S. Cave, "Animals, Heidegger, and the Right to Life," *Environmental Ethics* 4 (1982), 249–54; Michael E. Zimmerman, "Toward a Heideggerean *Ethos* for Radical Environmentalism," *Environmental Ethics* 5, no. 3 (Summer 1983), 99–131; Bruce V. Foltz, "On Heidegger and the Interpretation of Environmental Crisis," *Environmental Ethics* 6, no. 4 (Winter 1984), 323–42; Laura Westra, "Let It Be: Heidegger and Future Generations," *Environmental Ethics* 7, no. 4 (Winter 1985), 341–50; Michael E. Zimmerman, "Implications of Heidegger's Thought for Deep Ecology," *The Modern Schoolman* 64 (November 1986), 19–43; Leslie Paul Thiele, "Nature and Freedom: A Heideggerian Critique of Biocentric and Sociocentric Environmentalism," *Environmental Ethics* 17, no. 2 (Summer 1995), 171–90; David Abram, "Merleau-Ponty and the Voice of the Earth," *Environmental Ethics* 10, no. 2 (Summer 1988), 101–20; and Max Hallman, "Nietzsche's Environmental Ethics," *Environmental Ethics* 13, no. 2 (Winter 1991), 99–125.
2. See Martin Heidegger, "Letter on Humanism," trans. David Farrell Krell, in *Basic Writings* (New York: Harper & Row, 1977), 28; "Brief über den 'Humanismus' ," *Wegmarken* (Frankfurt am Main: Vittorio Klostermann, 1967), 179.

3. See Jacques Taminiaux, "Poiesis and Praxis in Fundamental Ontology," *Research in Phenomenology* 17 (1987), 137–69.

4. See John Van Buren, "The Young Heidegger and Phenomenology," *Man and World* 23 (1990), 239–72.

5. BT refers to Martin Heidegger, *Being and Time*, trans. John Macquarrie and Edward Robinson (New York: Harper & Row, 1962); SZ refers to *Sein und Zeit* (Tübingen: Max Niemeyer, 1967). I have sometimes altered the Maquarrie/Robinson translation.

6. Frank Schalow, "Who Speaks for the Animals? Heidegger and the Question of Animal Welfare," *Environmental Ethics* 22, no. 3 (Fall 2000), 259–72.

7. My analysis of *Ereignis* is indebted in part to Thomas J. Sheehan's excellent essay "On Rightly Dividing the Word: A Paradigm Shift in Heidegger Research," *Proceedings, Thirty-Fourth North American Heidegger Conference*, Marshall University, May 19–21, 2000. See also Sheehan, "*Kehre* and *Ereignis*: A Prolegomenon to *Introduction to Metaphysics*," in *A Companion to Heidegger's* Introduction to Metaphysics, ed. Richard Polt and Gregory Fried (New Haven: Yale University Press, 2001), 3–16.

8. On "formal indication," see Theodore Kisiel, *The Genesis of Being and Time* (Berkeley and Los Angeles: University of California Press, 1993); Daniel Dahlstrom, "Heidegger's Method: Philosophical Concepts as Formal Indications," *Review of Metaphysics* 47, no. 4 (June 1994), 775–95; John Van Buren, "The Ethics of *Formale Anzeige* in Heidegger," *American Catholic Philosophical Quarterly* 69, no. 2 (Spring 1995), 157–70; and Ryan Streeter, "Heidegger's Formal Indication: A Question of Method in *Being and Time*," *Man and World* 30 (1997), 413–30.

9. See Michael E. Soulé and Gary Lease, *Reinventing Nature? Responses to Postmodern Deconstruction* (Washington, D.C.: Island Press, 1995).

10. Michael E. Zimmerman, "On Vallicella's Critique of Heidegger," *International Philosophical Quarterly* 30, no. 1 (March 1990), 75–100.

11. Martin Heidegger, *On the Essence of Reasons*, trans. Terrence Malick (Evanston: Northwestern University Press, 1969), 38–39. German original ("Vom Wesen des Grundes") is on facing pages of translation.

12. Hubert Dreyfus, "Heidegger's History of the Being of Equipment," in *Heidegger: A Critical Reader*, ed. Hubert Dreyfus and Harrison Hall (Cambridge: Blackwell, 1992), 173–85.

13. My interpretation here is indebted to a number of Thomas J. Sheehan's essays, including "Heidegger's Philosophy of Mind," in *Contemporary Philosophy: A New Survey*, ed. Guttorm Floistad (The Hague: Martinus Nijhoff, 1983), 287–318.

14. Bruce V. Foltz, *Inhabiting the Earth: Heidegger, Environmental Ethics, and the Metaphysics of Nature* (Atlantic Highlands, N.J.: Humanities International Press, 1995), 34, note 3.
15. Heidegger, *On the Essence of Reasons*, 81–83.
16. Martin Heidegger, *Grundbegriffe*, Gesamtausgabe 51 (Frankfurt am Main: Vittorio Klostermann, 1981), 42.
17. Heidegger, "Letter on Humanism," 193; "Brief über den 'Humanismus'," 145.
18. See Steven Vogel, *Against Nature: The Concept of Nature in Critical Theory* (Albany: State University of New York Press, 1996); Vogel, "Nature as Origin and Difference: On Environmental Philosophy and Continental Thought," in *Conflicts and Convergences*, ed. Linda Martin Alcoff and Merold Westphal, Supplement to *Philosophy Today*, 42 (1998), 168–81; William Cronon, ed., *Uncommon Ground: Rethinking the Human Place in Nature* (New York: Norton, 1996).

    Of course, there are many critics of "strong" forms of the social construction of nature hypothesis. A sample includes: Charlene Spretnak, *The Resurgence of the Real: Body, Nature, and Place in a Hypermodern World* (Reading, Mass.: Addison-Wesley, 1997); Anna Peterson, "Environmental Ethics and the Social Construction of Nature," *Environmental Ethics* 21, no. 4 (Winter 1999), 339–58; Mick Smith, "To Speak of Trees: Social Constructivism, Environmental Values, and the Future of Deep Ecology," *Environmental Ethics* 21, no. 4 (Winter 1999), 359–76; David W. Kidner, "Fabricating Nature: A Critique of the Social Construction of Nature," *Environmental Ethics* 22, no. 4 (Winter 2000), 339–58.
19. Bill McKibben, *The End of Nature* (New York: Random House, 1989).
20. See Michael E. Soulé, "The Social Siege of Nature," in *Reinventing Nature: Responses to Postmodern Deconstruction*, ed. Michael E. Soulé and Gary Lease (Washington, D.C.: Island Press, 1995).
21. Martin Heidegger, *Introduction to Metaphysics*, trans. Gregory Fried and Richard Polt (New Haven: Yale University Press, 2000), 162; Heidegger, *Einführung in die Metaphysik*, 2d ed. (Tübingen: Max Niemeyer Verlag, 1957), 116.
22. Hans Jonas, *The Gnostic Religion: The Message of the Alien God and the Beginnings of Christianity* (Boston: Beacon, 1972). See also, Michael Pauen, *Dithyrambiker des Untergangs: Gnostizismus in Ästhetik und Philosophie der Moderne* (Berlin: Akademie Verlag, 1994).
23. Karl Löwith, *Der Weltbegriff der neuzeitlichen Philosophie* (Heidelberg: Carl Winter, Universitätsverlag, 1960), and "Zu Heideggers Seinsfrage: Die Nature des Menschen und die Welt der Natur," in *Aufsätze und Vorträge*, 1930–1970 (Stuttgart: W. Kohlhammer Verlag, 1971).
24. For a recent discussion of this issue, see Françoise Dastur, "The Critique of Anthropologism in Heidegger's Thought," in *Appropriating*

Heidegger, ed. James E. Faulconer and Mark A. Wrathall (New York: Cambridge University Press, 2000), 119–34.

25. Martin Heidegger, "Letter on Humanism," trans. Frank A. Capuzzi, in *Pathways*, ed. William McNeill (New York: Cambridge University Press, 1998); 246–49; Heidegger, *Wegmarken* (Frankfurt am Main: Vittorio Klostermann, 1967), 155–58.

26. See Heidegger's remarkable investigation of animal being in *The Fundamental Concepts of Metaphysics: World, Finitude, Solitude*, trans. William McNeill and Nicholas Walker (Bloomington: Indiana University Press, 1995); *Die Grundbegriffe der Metaphysik: Welt, Endlichkeit, Einsamkeit*, Gesamtausgabe 29–30 (Frankfurt am Main: Vittorio Klostermann, 1983).

27. See Heidegger, *Discourse on Thinking*, trans. John M. Anderson and E. Hans Freund (New York: Harper & Row, 1966), 55–56; *Gelassenheit* (Pfullingen: Günther Neske, 1959), 24–25.

28. Martin Heidegger, *Introduction to Metaphysics*, 173–74, 190; Heidegger, *Einführung in der Metaphysik*, 124, 136.

29. Nancy J. Holland, "Rethinking Ecology in the Western Philosophical Tradition: Heidegger and/on Aristotle," *Continental Philosophy Review* 32 (1999), 409–20; citation is from 413.

30. Martin Heidegger, *Aristotle's Metaphysics Θ 1–3: On the Essence and Actuality of Force*, trans. Walter Brogan and Peter Warnek (Bloomington: Indiana University Press, 1995), 57; *Aristoteles, Metaphysik Θ 1–3: Von Wesen und Wirklichkeit der Kraft*, Gesamtausgabe 33 (Frankfurt am Main: Vittorio Klostermann, 1981), 68.

31. Heidegger, *Aristotle's Metaphysics*, 75; *Aristoteles Metaphysik*, 89–90.

32. Holland, "Rethinking Ecology," 411.

33. Martin Heidegger, "The Origin of the Work of Art," trans. Albert Hofstadter in *Poetry, Language, Thought* (New York: Harper & Row, 1971), 46–47; Heidegger, "Der Ursprung des Kunstwerkes," *Holzwege* (Frankfurt am Main: Vittorio Klostermann, 1972), 36.

34. Heidegger, *Aristotle's Metaphysics*, 89; *Aristoteles Metaphysik*, 105.

35. Holland, "Rethinking Ecology," 412.

36. Martin Heidegger, "Overcoming Metaphysics," in *The End of Philosophy*, trans. Joan Stambaugh (New York: Harper & Row, 1973), 109; Heidegger, "Überwindung der Metaphysik," *Vorträge und Aufsätze* (Pfullingen: Neske, 1967), 90.

37. Martin Heidegger, "Nietzsche's Word, 'God is dead,'" in *The Question Concerning Technology*, trans. William Lovitt (New York: Harper & Row, 1977), 100; "Nietzsches Wort 'Gott ist tot,'" *Holzwege* (Frankfurt am Main: Vittorio Klostermann, 1972), 236.

38. These themes are developed in Heidegger, *The Question Concerning Technology*.

39. Martin Heidegger, *Grundbegriffe*, Gesamtausgabe 51 (Frankfurt am Main: Vittorio Klostermann, 1981), 84. See also Heidegger, "Letter on Humanism," passim.
40. See Michael E. Zimmerman, "Martin Heidegger: Anti-Naturalistic Critic of Technological Modernity," in *Ecological Thinkers*, ed. David Macauley (New York: Guilford, 1995).
41. Holland, "Rethinking Ecology," 415.
42. Ibid., 417.
43. Heidegger, "Letter on Humanism, 228; "Brief über den 'Humanismus,'" 179.
44. See my essay, "On Vallicella's Critique of Heidegger," *International Philosophical Quarterly* 30, no. 1 (March, 1990), 75–100. See also Michel Haar, *The Song of the Earth*, trans. Reginald Lilly (Bloomington: Indiana University Press, 1993).
45. See Michael E. Zimmerman, "The Limitations of Heidegger's Ontological Aestheticism," in *Heidegger and Praxis*, special issue of *The Southern Journal of Philosophy* 28 (1990), 183–89. See also John D. Caputo, *Demythologizing Heidegger* (Bloomington: Indiana University Press, 1993).
46. See Zimmerman, "Rethinking the Heidegger—Deep Ecology Relationship," *Environmental Ethics* 15, no. 3 (Fall 1993), 195–224; *Contesting Earth's Future: Radical Ecology and Postmodernity* (Berkeley and Los Angeles: University of California Press, 1994); and "Ecofascism: A Threat to American Environmentalism?" in *The Ecological Community*, ed. Roger S. Gottlieb (New York: Routledge, 1997), 229–54.
47. Thomas J. Sheehan, "Nihilism: Heidegger/Jünger/Aristotle," in *Phenomenology: Japanese and American Perspectives*, ed. Bert C. Hopkins (Dordrecht: Kluwer Academic Publishers, 1998), 273–316.
48. Ibid., 281.
49. Richard J. Kroner, "Heidegger's Private Religion," *Union Seminary Quarterly Review* 11 (1956), 23–37.
50. Martin Heidegger, *Hölderlins Hymne "Andenken,"* Gesamtausgabe 52 (Frankfurt am Main: Vittorio Klostermann, 1982), 40.
51. Sheehan, "Nihilism," 275.
52. Heidegger, "On the Question of Being," trans. William McNeil, in *Pathmarks*, ed. William McNeil (New York: Cambridge University Press, 1998), 291–322; Heidegger, "Zur Seinsfrage," *Wegmarken*, 213–54. On the Heidegger-Jünger relation, see Michael E. Zimmerman, *Heidegger's Confrontation with Modernity* (Bloomington: Indiana University Press, 1990).
53. Sheehan, "Nihilism," 284.
54. Heidegger, *Introduction to Metaphysics*, 122; *Einführung in der Metaphysik*, 154.

55. Heidegger, "On the Question of Being," 308; "Zur Seinsfrage," 235; cited by Sheehan, 293.
56. Sheehan, "Nihilism," 294.
57. Ibid., 296.
58. Ibid., 297.
59. Ibid., 308–309.
60. For a recent look at the religious dimension of Heidegger's thought, see Daniel Dalhstrom, "Heidegger's Religious Turn: From Christianity and Metaphysics to God," *Proceedings, Thirty-Fourth North American Heidegger Conference*, Marshall University, May 19–21, 2000.
61. Sheehan, "Nihilism," 314.
62. Ibid., 315.
63. See chapter 6 of Foltz, *Inhabiting the Earth*, for example.
64. Martin Heidegger, *The Question Concerning the Thing*, trans. W. B. Barton Jr. and Vera Deutsch (Chicago: Henry Regnery, 1967), 41; *Die Frage nach dem Ding* (Tübingen: Max Niemeyer, 1962), 31.
65. Martin Heidegger, *Vom Wesen der Wahrheit. Zu Platons Höhlengleichnis und Theätet*, Gesamtausgabe 35 (Frankfurt am Main: Vittorio Klostermann, 1988), 84. Cited in Rüdiger Safranski, *Martin Heidegger: Between Good and Evil*, trans. Ewald Osers (Cambridge: Harvard University Press, 1998), 220.
66. Sheehan, "Nihilism," 313.
67. Sanfranski, *Martin Heidegger: Between Good and Evil*, passim.
68. Cross cultural evidence supporting the claim that "authenticity" or "enlightenment" provide neither moral nor political compass can be found in the case of the Kyoto School of Zen Buddhism. Instigated in part by discoveries about the link between Heidegger and National Socialism, investigators have shown that during the years leading up to and during World War II, a number of Zen Buddhists—including enlightened masters such as Yasutani—used their position, authority, and Buddhism itself to justify the martial designs and racist attitudes of Japanese leaders. See James W. Heisig and John C. Maraldo, *Rude Awakenings: Zen, the Kyoto School, and the Question of Nationalism* (Honolulu: University of Hawaii Press, 1994), and Brian Victoria, *Zen at War* (New York: Weatherhill, 1997).
69. For a very useful attempt at such a dialogue, see Ken Wilber, *Sex, Ecology, Spirituality* (Boston: Shambhala, 1995).

CHAPTER 6

Nietzsche, Heidegger, and Merleau-Ponty

Some of Their Contributions and Limitations for "Environmentalism"

MONIKA LANGER

Phenomenology broadly conceived has much to offer "environmentalism." At the same time, environmentalism implicitly highlights some shortcomings of phenomenology. Without attempting to be comprehensive, this chapter will offer reflections on three classic phenomenologists: Nietzsche, Heidegger, and Merleau-Ponty. Before outlining some of their potential (or actual) contributions and shortcomings, it is necessary to indicate the main features of environmentalism.

"Environmentalism" is a popular term for an inherently very diverse and fluid series of sociopolitical movements characterized by their concern for the "environment" and their willingness to take measures to address "environmental problems." Environmentalism may be reformist or more radical. The former is anthropocentric and aims to ameliorate the environment primarily for the benefit of "anthropos" ("man"). To this end, "reform environmentalists" employ such measures as "resource management" (including "resource conservation") or technological innovations, but see no need for a fundamental change in perspective or values. A more radical environmentalism is ecocentric and seeks to improve the life of planet Earth as a whole. Its adherents believe that "nature" is sentient and intrinsically valuable. They regard environmental problems as the result of an androcentric, consumerist lifestyle, which

103

they reject. Instead, they seek to establish a way of living that is in harmony with, and enhances, all forms of life. Responsive to the needs of
nonhuman beings, they may work to restore habitats and native species,
to support community gardens and organic growers, to stop genetic engineering and animal experimentation, to halt clear-cut logging, and to
eliminate various sources of pollution. To counter consumerism, they
practice some form of voluntary simplicity. They also attempt to integrate
theory, experience, and practice.

Among these more radical environmentalists there are those who
realize that the dominant, destructive lifestyle is bound up with a profoundly flawed, dualistic ontology. Further, "eco-feminists" recognize
that the traditional subjugation of women is connected with the domination of "nature," and that both spring from the same dualistic and hierarchical ontology. Radical environmentalists emphasize the need for a
thorough, ongoing, transdisciplinary questioning of ourselves and of our
culture's dominant worldview. Rejecting the fact/value split, many of
them ("deep ecologists") stress the inextricable intertwining of all life
forms and seek "self-realization" in the widest and deepest identification
with "nature." By contrast, eco-feminists tend to caution against such
identification. They emphasize respect and care for nature understood as
a community of related but distinct beings.[1]

Various radical environmentalists have argued that the notion of
nature is itself fraught with difficulty, as are notions of environment (and
thus "environmentalism") and environmental problems. The debates concerning these notions—most particularly the notion of nature—are very
complex, extensive, and far reaching. Since they exceed the scope of this
chapter, only a few of their features can be indicated here. Debates about
nature raise a plethora of questions such as the following: Does nature
mean either "wilderness" or "wildness"? If nature is synonymous with
one of these terms, does this not reinforce a dualistic ontology (which
divides humans from nature)? Are humans identifiable with "nature"
understood holistically? If so, can any conceivable human action be considered "unnatural"? By the same token, is it possible to distinguish
between nature and culture? Is nature a human construct? Are notions of
nature connected with notions of gender in human societies? Is it possible
to find a nature unaffected by processes of social construction? Can
humans derive ethical principles from a notion of nature? Can humans
speak as, or for, nature? Can language speak "the truth" of nature? Is it
possible to develop an environmental philosophy that does not colonize
nature, if nature is conceived as fundamentally irreducible to human representations? Do notions of holism, interconnectedness, and integration
with nature invariably erase the alterity of nature?

Debates about nature occasionally make use of metaphors such as Mother Nature, Mother Earth, virgin forests, rape of the land, and rape of nature. As eco-feminist Tzeporah Berman points out, these metaphors portray the male bias in environmental discourse and perpetuate hegemonic traditions. Berman therefore calls for the creation of "a positive semantic space" and nonpatriarchal tropes for nature.[2] Similarly, Catriona Sandilands cautions that the representation of nature as female or as "home" obscures the fundamental strangeness of nature and facilitates its authoritarian colonization. Sandilands urges eco-feminists to undertake a discursive construction of nature that opens up spaces in which "the wild strangeness of nature" can be experienced. She insists that it is impossible to capture in language nature's alterity; and that human identity itself defies closure because this alterity is both in and beyond ourselves. The mysterious, wonderful wildness of nature overflows all our constructions and resists description—for "[t]he rational is always already pierced by mystery, showing the necessity of wonder."[3] Neil Evernden argues that "perhaps even wildness is an inadequate term, for that essential core of otherness is inevitably nameless, and as such cannot be subsumed within our abstractions or made part of the domain of human willing."[4]

For her part, Freya Mathews emphasizes that "Nature" itself has a "dark side"; and that decay, death, and destruction are aspects of Nature's "earthiness" that have been repressed in the traditional dualistic ontology favoring light, reason, and culture. She urges us to recognize and accept this dark side and its exemplification in human destructiveness. According to Mathews, bulldozers, chainsaws, bombs, missiles, and all our other technologies are part of "the natural order," and contribute to "the moral order" as effectively as any forest. We should honor these ecologically destructive technologies—for "we cannot honour the world if we despise our technology."[5] Mathews insists that "[t]o be prepared to accept as natural and hence to respect—perhaps to sacralize—our cities and our technologies of destruction, is to respect and re-enchant the Nature that we actually inhabit."[6] She criticizes deep ecologists' idealization of "untouched Nature" as "wilderness."

It is not surprising that environmentalists disagree so profoundly about the very meaning of nature. As Evernden points out, the concept of nature is inherently volatile and ambiguous and can be used to demand or justify virtually all lifestyles and social goals. It "is also a mode of concealment, a cloak of abstractions which obscures that discomforting wildness that defies our paranoid urge to delineate the boundaries of Being."[7] Similarly, the notions of "environment" and "problem solving" spring from, and conceal, the dualistic ontology which fuels that paranoid urge to delineate, delimit, and control Being. Thus the very terms "environmentalism" and "environmentalists" actually encourage and reinforce the rupture with, and reification of, Being, by implying that there is a world of objects surrounding us. The idea of "environmental problems" or "solutions" presupposes such an androcentric reification of Being.[8] Despite these inherent difficulties and drawbacks, environmentalism can contribute to phenomenology, as I will show in due course.

What can (or does) phenomenology contribute to environmentalism, given the tremendous diversity—and indeed, irreconcilability—of the many movements comprising it? Any contribution will necessarily be partial, since it cannot address all components (given the irreconcilability). With this proviso, phenomenology's contributions include the following: phenomenological critiques of the traditional, dualistic ontology; alternative, nondualistic phenomenological ontologies; detailed phenomenological descriptions to support environmentalists' claims concerning the primacy of lived experience; phenomenological descriptions showing the profound import of language—thus implicitly cautioning against careless use of environmental discourse; and phenomenological insights that are particularly pertinent for environmental ethics. For its part, "environmentalism" can (or does) contribute to phenomenology by making the latter's own shortcomings more evident—and thus encouraging contemporary phenomenologists to address them. Phenomenologists' resolve to limit themselves to description is one such shortcoming. Some additional shortcomings include: considerable abstractness (despite claims to the contrary), relatively little direct concern with "ecological issues," inadequate discussion of "nature," and perpetuation of phallocentrism. Environmentalism's success in prompting large numbers of people to rally to its various calls for action also implicitly raises questions about phenomenology's accessibility to the nonspecialist.[9] Further shortcomings will emerge in the course of this chapter.

Of the three phenomenologists on whom I will now reflect, Nietzsche is the most blatantly phallocentric. Yet his work is the most accessible. Nietzsche goes beyond description in repeatedly emphasizing the importance of remaining "faithful to the earth," and nonhuman animals figure quite prominently in his writings. These features, coupled with his "down to earth," colorful, witty, and engaging style, make his philosophy not only more accessible but also more concrete than is usually the case with philosophers. Nietzsche is generally classified as an existentialist rather than as a phenomenologist; and of course, he predates Edmund Husserl, who is commonly considered the founder of phenomenology. Yet Nietzsche's extensive descriptions of lived experience—and of its distortions—qualify him also as a phenomenologist in the broad sense of the term. It is worth noting too that Heidegger and Merleau-Ponty are generally considered to be both existentialists and phenomenologists. Clearly, such categorizations are mutually compatible.

Nietzsche is arguably the first to offer a sustained critique of the dominant, dualistic ontology that fuels our "environmental" crisis. As has often been noted by now, this ontology involves a host of hierarchical, binary oppositions such as: mind/body, reason/emotion, reality/appearance, culture/nature, subject/object, human/nonhuman, activity/passivity, form/matter, being/nonbeing, and man/women. In each case, the first term is exalted and the second term is devalued. Further features include the following assumptions: that absolute boundaries keep the binary oppositions intact; that time is linear; that the self is given as suprasensible mind; that clarity and distinctness are valid criteria for ascertaining Truth; and that Truth is objective, timeless, permanent, unconditional, universally valid, and absolute. This ontology claims that philosophy is the disinterested discovery of such Truth, and that philosophy proceeds from absolutely sure foundations in an absolutely clear origin. To discover Truth, the philosopher must turn away from concrete, corporeal experience and engage in solitary, abstract reflection. Such reflection aims to provide an all-encompassing system of rational ideas and ideal, absolute norms. Experience must be subsumed under these ideas and norms. This traditional ontology declares that knowledge consists in the attainment of absolute Truth and of the totalizing system based on that alleged Truth.

Nietzsche provides a radical, sustained critique of this entire traditional ontology, with the exception of the man/woman hierarchical opposition—which he unfortunately retains. *Thus Spoke Zarathustra* is arguably Nietzsche's most accessible work; and since he himself considered it his best, I will concentrate on it. The whole book is in fact a detailed critique of mainstream, dualistic ontology, and an unfolding of an alternative ontology that springs from lived experience. One aspect of that critique is the objection to abstractness. Consequently, Nietzsche couches his critique in terms which themselves emphasize concreteness. The entire work is a story (that of Zarathustra) which is rich in imagery and is told in sensuous, sonorous language. Moreover, this story itself contains multiple stories such as the ones in which Zarathustra recounts his dreams and visions. Unlike Descartes, he regards those dreams and visions as sources of wisdom. As stories within a story, *Thus Spoke Zarathustra* tacitly undermines the traditional ontological dichotomy between form and matter—a dichotomy that plays such a prominent role in mainstream philosophies from Plato through Descartes to Kant, and in their successors. Both explicitly and implicitly the book impugns traditional ontology's claim to attain absolute Truth and to articulate universal, timeless norms. In the section

"On the Spirit of Gravity" in part three, for example, Zarathustra says: "By many ways, in many ways, I reached my truth. . . . A trying and questioning was my every move. . . . 'This is my way; where is yours?'—thus I answered those who asked me 'the way'. For the way—that does not exist."[10]

The book not only shows us Zarathustra's way, but also teaches us how to go our own ways. Zarathustra therefore effaces his path behind him. He repeatedly reminds his listeners (and by extension, us) that his way is by no means desirable for everyone, and that there are multiple paths to the future. Again and again, he explicitly urges his listeners to go their own ways. In fact, he even counsels them to resist him and suggests that perhaps he deceived them.[11] The fact that Nietzsche does not speak in his own voice anywhere in the text also serves to subvert the traditional claim to absolute authority, and leaves it entirely up to the reader to evaluate the protagonist, Zarathustra. The latter's increasingly evident flaws (such as his naivety in addressing the people in the market place, his own acknowledged callousness and desire for revenge, his loss of temper, and his resort to physical violence) are designed to preclude our turning him (and by extension Nietzsche) into a new idol.[12] For the same reason, the story of Zarathustra is itself presented as being chronicled by several chroniclers whose versions differ—so that "it may have been so or otherwise."[13]

Zarathustra is himself the antithesis and subversion of the traditional philosopher. For dualistic ontology the philosopher is a disembodied, detached, dispassionately objective, and unsituated mind—a mouthpiece for pure Reason and absolute Truth. By contrast, Zarathustra is emphatically corporeal, subjective, emotional, concretely situated, and passionately involved in the world. In his teachings he demystifies traditional philosophy and unmasks the desire for pure, dispassionate rationality and absolute Truth, as a desire which is itself based on suppressed, sick passions (such as hostility to life and a craving for revenge). Far from claiming to possess absolute Truth, Zarathustra stresses the relativity and contingency of all truths—including any allegedly absolute Truth. Moreover, he shows that solitary reflection invariably becomes sterile. Hence, already in " Zarathustra's Prologue" he tires of his solitude and feels the need to rejoin other beings.

In his person and in his teachings, Zarathustra goes on to overturn the dualistic ontology's conception of the self as ego, and the ego as mind, or soul. For example, in the section "On the Despisers of the Body" in part one, he teaches that the self is the body, whereas the ego or soul (or mind) is merely an aspect of the body and is controlled by the body. As well, at various points in the story Zarathustra converses with his soul, thus indicating that the latter is no more than an aspect of his "self." Further, Zarathustra dissolves the subject/object and activity/passivity opposi- tions in teaching that both the bodily self and its ego aspect are histori- cally created, and that "the individual himself is still the most recent creation."[14] Zarathustra overturns the traditional objectification and devaluation of the body and the earth. He chastizes the despisers of the body, and advises them instead to "create a higher body for themselves." He points out that "the healthy body . . . speaks of the meaning of the earth"; and he repeatedly urges his listeners to remain true to the earth.[15] Zarathustra himself creates a dancing body from his own ashes at various junctures in the story.[16]

As a dynamically changing, corporeal self, Zarathustra teaches that there cannot be a definitive beginning or an absolutely sure foundation. Dualistic ontology attempts to secure such an origin and ground in an allegedly suprasensible realm of "reality" beyond the world of lived expe- rience—which it declares a sphere of mere "appearance." Zarathustra emphatically rejects this as a nihilistic mystification. Far from pretending to provide an absolute beginning or indubitable foundation, he stresses that the craving and quest for such certainty are symptomatic of pathol- ogy. To emphasize the impossibility of an absolute source or ground, the story of Zarathustra itself begins in midstream, "when Zarathustra was thirty years old"; and its recurrent theme is the uncertainty inherent in continual transformation. The philosopher Zarathustra himself under- goes countless transformations in the course of the story; and he teaches his listeners to celebrate the creativity that becomes possible with uncer- tainty. *Thus Spoke Zarathustra* is therefore a sustained critique of the tradi- tional stance that the philosopher should strive for a purely intellectual, abstract, dispassionate knowledge of absolute Truth.

Zarathustra teaches that there cannot be such absolute Truth or such dispassionate knowledge, and that both conceptions are illusions based on a nihilistic hostility to life. Instead, Zarathustra himself shows how to attain an ever deeper, experiential knowledge in which the unambiguous, absolute boundaries and hierarchical, binary oppositions erected by dual- istic ontology dissolve. The richness of ambiguity and multiplicity emerges, and many contingent truths replace the traditional single, (allegedly) absolute Truth. These contingent, experiential truths are cre- ated, not discovered. Zarathustra urges his listeners to create values that accord with those experiential truths. The teaching of eternal recurrence and the absence of an absolute origin also subvert the traditional notion of linear progress. *Thus Spoke Zarathustra* is itself structured as a circle con- taining multiple circles within it. The end of the story leads back to its beginning, suggesting that the truths emerging from faithful adherence to the earth become ever more profound as that adherence deepens. Ongoing becoming replaces the traditional, dichotomous opposition of being and nonbeing. In these ever deepening circles of becoming, culture and nature are dialectically related, rather than mutually opposed. This dialectical reuniting of culture and nature is symbolized by Zarathustra's journey and by his wisdom. The latter is a "wild wisdom" and is at home in the mountains—but also needs human companions to thrive. Accordingly, Zarathustra's circular journey takes him from cave and mountains, through forests, to towns; and from towns back through forests (and occasionally, over seas), to mountains and cave—and back to towns, and so on.

Unfortunately, the traditional human/nonhuman hierarchical opposition is only partially resolved in this dialectical reuniting of culture and nature. Zarathustra offers a radical critique in repeatedly describing how dualistic ontology's split between humans and "the earth" has turned humans into "cripples." Yet he does not describe its devastating effects on the earth. Moreover, for the most part, Zarathustra's perception of nonhuman animals actually reinforces their stereotypes and the traditional hierarchical ranking of humans as superior to nonhuman animals. While it is refreshing to have a host of animals in a philosophical text, it is all the more disappointing to find them portrayed so traditionally. *Thus Spoke Zarathustra* teems with animal tropes, including: snakes, lizards, crocodiles, frogs, toads, worms, leeches, glow-worms, flea-beetles, lice, spiders, ants, flies, bluebottles, mosquitoes, bees, butterflies, moths, fish, crabs, oysters, bats, mice, moles, hedgehogs, rabbits, sheep, a goat, swine, cattle, buffalo, camels, horses, asses, mules, monkeys, apes, whales, bears, lions, lionesses, tigers, panthers, wolves, dogs, cats, an elephant, eagles, falcons, vultures, owls, songbirds, doves, crows, hens, roosters, peacocks, flamingoes, a heron, a goose, and an ostrich. In addition, Zarathustra refers to "maggots," "winged worms," "bugs," "vermin," "parasites," "evil birds," "evil beasts," "savage beasts," "wild animals," "beasts of prey," "beasts of burden," "monsters," and "dragons."

Since animals thus abound in this work, it is worth considering their significance. Although they enhance the book's color, passion, wit, and accessibility, the animal tropes on the whole do little to improve the animals' status. The following examples are typical for how these tropes tend to function in the text: Zarathustra describes self-serving nationalists as foul-smelling monkeys; petty, uncreative people as "poisonous flies"; pretentious braggarts as puffed-up frogs; traditional philosophers and "preachers of equality" as impotent and envious spiders; and Zarathustra himself as a new rooster who is pecked by hens but remains unruffled by these little annoyances.[17] Bees, fish, snakes, lions, lionesses, eagles, and birds in general usually appear in a positive light in the text; whereas the rest of the animals mostly appear negatively. In both cases, the result is simply a perpetuation of their habitual stereotypes.

There is an intriguing mixture of animal and human imagery in Zarathustra's famous parable about the spirit's three metamorphoses. Through these metamorphoses, the spirit (or mind) develops a sense of embodiment and playful creativity. The spirit initially becomes a camel loaded with all the traditional values. From camel it changes into a lion who battles the dragon of traditional morality and imposes his own will instead. Since the preying lion cannot create new values, this lion turns into a life-affirming, playfully creative child for whom the traditional mind/body dichotomy does not exist. Camel and lion appear here in their usual roles as, respectively, docile beast of burden and fearless hunter. Their importance consists entirely in producing the requisite conditions for the emergence of the human being as innocent, creative child. The latter is able to do what the camel and lion cannot do. Zarathustra nowhere suggests that the child's significance consists in ushering in the camel or the lion. Despite their non-linearity, the three metamorphoses therefore maintain the hierarchical ranking of humans above animals.

There is a brief reversal of the traditional ranking when Zarathustra's animals—his eagle and snake—first appear. Zarathustra says that they are respectively the proudest and wisest animals. Adding that he himself will never be thoroughly wise like his snake, Zarathustra expresses the wish that his animals lead him. Clearly, he here acknowledges their superiority. Yet later, when they tentatively try to assume a leadership role, Zarathustra belittles and rebukes them—and eventually stops listening to them. In fact, however, his eagle and snake combined are better integrated and wiser than he. Together they symbolize the integration of male and female power and give concrete evidence of their superiority in their interpretation of eternal recurrence. They first present Zarathustra's version, which he acknowledges they have understood very well. That version is atomistically detailed and leads to nausea. His snake and eagle then offer their own interpretation, which dissolves the atomistic boundaries and poetically celebrates the intermingling of self and world in an eternal ring of becoming. If we consider *Thus Spoke Zarathustra* as a self-contained work, we can interpret Zarathustra's failure to recognize his animals' superiority consistently as another flaw on his part. The same would be true of his failure to establish genuine reciprocity with his animals. Thus we can interpret the text as actually overturning the traditional hierarchy here, so as to place two nonhuman animals above Zarathustra himself. Alternatively, we can argue that his eagle and snake are anthropomorphized and function as substitute "humans" for Zarathustra. On the latter interpretation, the traditional ranking remains intact.[18]

Nietzsche's *Thus Spoke Zarathustra* contributes to "environmental-ism" a sustained, phenomenological critique of traditional, dualistic ontology. In its place, it develops an original, integrative ontology based on lived experience which is faithful to "the earth," and which is expressed in an ever deeper circle of becoming. Two nonhuman animals (snake and eagle—arguably anthropomorphized) offer both the best understanding of this circle, and its most poetic expression: "'O Zarathus-tra,' the animals said, 'to those who think as we do, all things themselves are dancing: they come and offer their hands and laugh and flee—and come back. . . . Everything dies, everything blossoms again. . . . The center is everywhere.'"[19] Yet the traditional human/nonhuman hierarchical opposition is, at best, only partially resolved. Further, the man/woman hierarchical opposition remains firmly in place, despite the symbolic inte-gration of female and male power in the prologue's image of the snake wound lovingly around the neck of the soaring, circling eagle. Eco-femi-nist insights are certainly needed here to help dislodge such longstanding phallocentrism. As well, "environmentalism" can offer a far more posi-tive, nonanthropocentric and nonhierarchical way of including nonhu-man animals in a philosophical text. It can also develop a fuller description of what it means to remain true to "the earth." *Thus Spoke Zarathustra* suggests implicitly that the earth is not simply synonymous with nature understood as forests, mountains, caves, seas and lakes, and nonhuman animals. Yet it remains unclear to what extent humans and culture constitute part of the earth. Nietzschean and environmentalist perspectives can thus be reciprocally enriching.

Over the past decades, environmentalists have consistently focused more on Heidegger than on any of the other phenomenologists, and there is by now a considerable body of environmentalist literature dealing with his work. Consequently, I propose to focus directly on three aspects of his thought which are particularly important for environmentalism: the ques-tion of "values," the meaning of thinking, and the significance of lan-guage. The concept of values constitutes the very core of environmental ethics. Over the years, a number of environmentalists have argued that nature has intrinsic value and that nonhuman animals therefore have inherent rights, which humans must respect. In his "Letter on Human-ism," Heidegger criticizes the division of thinking into disciplines and branches, such as "physics," "logic," or "ethics." He asserts that this frag-mentation signals the cessation of genuine thinking. Instead, humans circle endlessly around themselves. Heidegger goes on to critique the very notion of values: "It is important finally to realize that precisely through the characterization of something as 'a value' what is so valued is robbed of its worth."[20] Heidegger's point here is that valuing something—no matter how positively—subjectivizes it, instead of letting it be. By valuing it, we reduce it to an object for our estimation. Heidegger's critique suggests that despite all claims to the contrary, "environmental ethics" is unavoidably anthropocentric. If Heidegger is right, environmentalists accomplish precisely the opposite of what they intend when they seek to establish the integrity of nature by arguing that it has "inherent" or "intrinsic" value. Moreover, it may be misguided to encourage interdisciplinarity to counteract the narrowness of discipline-oriented thinking. Again, if Heidegger is right, such an approach simply masks the fragmentation of thinking.

It is worth pondering whether so-called environmental issues require an approach that is entirely different, and more original than disciplinarity or interdisciplinarity. What Heidegger means by "original thinking" is helpful here. In his "Memorial Address," Heidegger calls such genuine thinking "meditative," and contrasts it with the dominant mode of thinking. Calling the latter "calculative thinking," he traces its rise to the seventeenth-century scientific-philosophic revolution in major concepts. (As is well known, Descartes played a key role in bringing that revolution about.) Heidegger describes "calculative thinking" as a reductionistic, coercive, means/ends-oriented thinking. It is concerned with productivity, efficiency, utility, management, regulation, planning, prediction, and control. Calculative thinking attacks and grasps an operationally defined "reality" and regards language as merely a container for its preoccupations. Heidegger acknowledges that such thinking has its place; but he is concerned that it has become the predominant way of thinking and may soon be the sole way of thinking. He notes that "[t]he world now appears as an object open to the attacks of calculative thought. . . . Nature becomes a gigantic gasoline station, an energy source for modern technology and industry."[21]

"Calculative thinking" is actually thoughtless and oblivious of Being—which withdraws, leaving humans "rootless" and "homeless." By contrast, "meditative thinking" is profoundly thoughtful and receptive to Being. It dwells in the nearness of Being, where humans are truly "rooted" and "at home." As "the thinking of Being," meditative thinking is nonmanipulative and noncoercive. It lets Being and beings be; and this "letting be" involves profound care and concern. Such thinking is not a matter of having ideas or constructing theories—nor is it a particular act or series of acts. Rather, it is an entire disposition and way of living which, full of thought and heart, heeds Being's call. Such heart-full, thought-full thinking cannot, of course, be coerced or willfully begun, because it is itself noncoercive. Ultimately, it comes to us as a gift from Being. It is up to us to "step back" from our thoughtless ways of thinking so as to "prepare the ground" for this gift, just as a farmer prepares the soil but cannot force the seed to grow. Such receptivity opens us to nature's meaning and mystery. Meditative thinking lets the unspoken Truth of Being come to language; and "[l]anguage is the house of Being" insofar as it shelters the Truth which Being discloses. Such authentic language is the "home" in which we thoughtfully dwell.[22] Already decades before his "Letter on Humanism" and "Memorial Address," Heidegger emphasized the crucial importance of language, claiming that "the power of language" distinguishes us "from stones, plants, animals, but also from the gods." He cautioned that "words and language are not wrappings in which things are packed for the commerce of those who write and speak. It is in words and language that things first come into being and are. For this reason the misuse of language . . . destroys our authentic relation to things."[23]

For environmentalism, Heidegger's meaning of thinking and of language is particularly important at this time, as is his emphasis on wonder and mystery. Given the increasing extinction of plant and nonhuman animal species, the rapid disappearance of habitats (including old-growth forests), the growing mass of pollutants, the acceleration of global warming, and all the other pressing environmental issues, environmentalists may well feel increasing pressures to "do something," and to wrap environmentalist concerns in the prevailing, "calculative" way of speaking. Heidegger emphasizes that succumbing to such pressures brings even greater estrangement from Being, and the destruction of any authentic relation with nature. Instead, it is essential to cultivate receptivity to Being—all the more so, given the contemporary preoccupation with commodification, control, and the quick fix. There can be no "fix" for environmental issues. Rather, there must be a radical change in humans' relation with Being. As I noted earlier, such a transformation cannot be willed—but it can be thoughtfully prepared. A first step lies in recognizing that thought and language are internally related, and that they involve an entire way of living. In the first part of this chapter, I drew attention to some eco-feminists' concerns about the erasure of nature's alterity through the use of such representations as "home." These eco-feminist insights can make an important contribution to Heideggerian phenomenology by questioning Heidegger's use of tropes, such as: "home," "homeland," "homecoming," "homelessness," "at home," "house," "neighbour," "shepherd," "farmer," "rootedness," "rootlessness."[24] Could it be that these representations (of Being, of its relation to humans, and of humans' relation to Being) erase Being's alterity? Despite his intentions and claims to the contrary, it may be that Heidegger's tropes subjectivize Being and make his phenomenology anthropocentric. Further, environmentalists can question Heidegger's claim that the power of language distinguishes humans from other beings.

In *The Visible and the Invisible* (which he was writing at the time of his death), Merleau-Ponty draws on Heidegger in emphasizing that "what is primary is Being." Merleau-Ponty describes it as "a wave of Being," and as a "wild" or "brute" Being, whose "wild meaning" is expressed in a "language [which] is everything since it is the voice of no one, since it is the very voice of the things, the waves, and the forests."[26] "Intercorporeity" weaves everything together, because everything participates in the "the flesh of the world." Merleau-Ponty points out: "Where are we to put the limit between the body and the world, since the world is flesh?"[27] The body is a "living bond with nature," and body and world intertwine and "embrace." The natural and cultural "planes" can no longer be distinguished here, since nature is flesh, and "even the cultural rests on the polymorphism of the wild Being." Merleau-Ponty stresses that Being's meaning is "absolutely different from the 'represented' . . . [and that] none of the 'representations' exhaust . . . the wild Being."[28] "The flesh is . . . an 'element' of Being," in the sense in which one "used to speak of water, air, earth, and fire" as elements. Thus the flesh is not mind, matter, spirit, or substance; nor is it any union or combination of these. Merleau-Ponty emphasizes that there is no name in any philosophy for this element of Being which radiates everywhere, dissolving the God/man/creatures cleavage and the I/other problem (which Merleau-Ponty calls specifically "Western"). Instead of hierarchy and bifurcation, there is reciprocal embrace ("Ineinander") within polymorphic Being. Analyses that attempt to "unravel" or "disentangle" Being merely render it "unintelligible," says Merleau-Ponty.[29]

In his earlier books, *The Structure of Behavior* and *Phenomenology of Perception*,[30] Merleau-Ponty undertakes a detailed examination of such traditional analyses and shows how their "objective" thinking distorts all being-in-the-world, including that of insects. Intellectualist and empiricist approaches employ this thinking, which finds its crassest expression in positivistic science. The latter attempts to reduce and to reify the dialectic of being-in-the-world into a meaningless collection of inert objects observed by an unsituated spectator-manipulator. At issue, once again, is a fundamentally flawed, dualistic ontology. Merleau-Ponty overturns that ontology in describing the inherently meaningful structure of all behavior, be it that of insects, humans, or other animals. The fundamental intentionality of behavior makes retention of the traditional ontology untenable, and rules out any division of "reality" into different types, or different orders, of beings—such as "physical," "vital," and "mental." Instead, Merleau-Ponty insists humans must recognize that nonhuman animals are existences participating in a shared, intrinsically meaningful world. In *Themes from the Lectures at the Collège de France 1952–1960*, Merleau-Ponty points out that we forget our own source and support in espousing an objectivist concept of nature and pretending to be disengaged observers. Moreover, qualitative differences in organisms emerge through rearrangements that resume and transfigure "already latent activities." Thus "one cannot conceive of the relations between species or between the species and man in terms of a hierarchy," says Merleau-Ponty.[31] Rather, "all corporeality is already symbolism," and the human body is "a metamorphosis of life."[32]

In *Phenomenology of Perception*, Merleau-Ponty describes in detail the ambiguous, dialectical movement through which the lived human body and the perceived, preobjective world come-into-being. This movement forms an ongoing, prepersonal "dialogue" underlying all reflection and objectification. Merleau-Ponty shows that this "dialogue" is irreducible, and that the lived body is not a shell housing a Cartesian pure consciousness. All consciousness is thoroughly corporeal. There is thus no realm of thought or subjectivity that is distinct from bodily being, and to which others would have no access. Merleau-Ponty shows that, instead, there is an intrinsic relationship between thought and the body, and between ourselves and others. World, others, and body-subject intertwine in a continual dialectic of intercorporeal intentionality and worldly solicitation. This marvelous, ambiguous "dialogue" ceaselessly brings-into-being a web of multiple, inseparable meanings which "speak" directly to the body. In describing this prereflective movement, Merleau-Ponty comes to realize that "[i]t is by the flesh of the world that in the last analysis one can understand the lived body."[33] As already indicated, he accordingly deepens his description by introducing "universal flesh" as an "element" of a "brute" or "wild" Being, whose "wild meaning" cannot be captured in representations.

Merleau-Ponty thus not only provides the most detailed critique of the traditional dualistic ontology, but he also offers a highly original, nondualistic ontology in its place. His critique includes a very comprehensive examination of traditional approaches to nonhuman animals (in *The Structure of Behavior*). Further, based on that critique he develops an alternative, transdisciplinary, nonreductionistic, nonanthropocentric description of nonhuman animals, and of nature in general. In doing so, Merleau-Ponty preserves the fundamental alterity of nonhuman animals and nonhuman nature. In describing universal flesh as an element of a wild Being whose meaning is irreducible to representations, Merleau-Ponty respects Being's alterity without reinstating a dualistic ontology. He creates "a positive semantic space" of the sort Berman is calling for. (Of course, one might still question the adequacy of the term "wild.") All this can supply environmentalists with a comprehensive ontological and phenomenological foundation for an environmental ethics. Both Merleau-

Ponty's critiques of objective thinking and his new ontology support environmentalists' call for a radical change in our perception of ourselves and the world. Moreover, Merleau-Ponty's phenomenological descriptions can contribute to bringing about such a fundamental paradigm shift. As well, his detailed, transdisciplinary descriptions of lived experience lend credibility to environmentalists' claims regarding the primacy of lived experience. Merleau-Ponty's marvelous description of a language that is "the very voice of the things, the waves, and the forests," can implicitly caution environmentalists against slipping into jargon and slogans.

"Environmentalism" can also contribute to "Merleau-Pontian" phenomenology. For example, a phallocentric bias emerges in the description of lived sexuality in *Phenomenology of Perception*; and like Nietzsche and Heidegger, Merleau-Ponty is oblivious to possible connections between the subjugation of nature and the subordination of women. Once again eco-feminist insights can call attention to these shortcomings and suggest ways of rectifying them. Further, environmentalism is concerned with concrete, environmental problems that develop over time. In light of this, environmentalists are well positioned to question Merleau-Ponty's a-historical descriptions of the lived body. They may thus question whether an a-historical description is an abstraction and a distortion of concretely lived experience. In addition, eco-feminists can critique Merleau-Ponty's attempt to describe universal structures of bodily experience. They can argue that the alleged universality of structures and seeming gender neutrality of the body are mystifications. As well, environmentalists can stress the need for a more comprehensive consideration of what "nature" means. They can also critique Merleau-Ponty's neglect of nature's "dark side."

Finally, environmentalism can draw attention to the inherent limitations of a purely descriptive approach. In reflecting on Heidegger, I noted the importance of withstanding pressures to provide a quick fix for environmental problems. Nietzsche's, Heidegger's, and Merleau-Ponty's phenomenological descriptions show that such environmental problems arise from a fundamentally flawed ontology and involve an entire way of life. The question at hand is whether descriptive critiques and the development of new ontologies suffice, given the evident urgency of the environmental problems. Of course, there cannot be any "recipes" for action, and it would be misguided to try to supply them. Nonetheless, there is perhaps a need to go beyond description to a thoughtful discussion of how one might best respond to the timely concerns raised by environmentalists.

In conclusion, I suggest that phenomenology and environmentalism have much to offer each other. Today, the distinction between these two is perhaps somewhat artificial, since many phenomenologists also consider themselves to be environmentalists. In reflecting on how their phenomenological research informs their environmentalism, and how their environmentalism informs their phenomenological research, they initiate an open-ended, mutually enriching dialogue between these two endeavors.

Notes

1. See, for example: Arne Naess, "The Shallow and the Deep, Long-Range Ecology Movement. A Summary," *Inquiry* 16 (1973), 95–100; Erazim Kohák, *The Embers and the Stars: A Philosophical Inquiry into the Moral Sense of Nature* (Chicago: University of Chicago Press, 1984); Bill Devall and George Sessions, *Deep Ecology: Living as if Nature Mattered* (Salt Lake City: Gibbs M. Smith, Peregrine Smith Books, 1985); Alan Drengson, "Fundamental Concepts of Environmental Philosophy: A Summary," *The Trumpeter* 2, no. 4 (Fall 1985), 23–25; Naess, "The Deep Ecological Movement: Some Philosophical Aspects," *Philosophical Inquiry* 8, no. 1–2 (1986), 10–13; Michael Zimmerman, "Philosophical Reflections on Reform vs. Deep Environmentalism," *The Trumpeter* 3, no. 4 (Fall 1986), 12–13; Warwick Fox, "Post-Skolimowski Reflections on Deep Ecology," *The Trumpeter* 3, no. 4 (Fall 1986), 16–18; Naess, "Self-realization: An Ecological Approach to Being in the World," *The Trumpeter* (Summer 1987), 35–42; David Abram, *The Spell of the Sensuous: Perception and Language in a More-Than-Human World* (New York: Vintage Books, 1996); Carolyn Merchant, *The Death of Nature: Women, Ecology, and Scientific Revolution* (New York: Harper & Row, 1980); Freya Mathews, "Relating to Nature: Deep Ecology or Ecofeminism?" *The Trumpeter* 11, no. 4 (Fall 1994), 159–66; Val Plumwood, *Feminism and the Mastery of Nature* (New York: Routledge, 1991); Robert Sessions, "Deep Ecology versus Ecofeminism: Healthy Differences or Incompatible Philosophies?", *Ecological Feminist Philosophies*, ed. Karen J. Warren (Bloomington: Indiana University Press, 1996), 137–54; Val Plumwood, "Nature, Self, and Gender: Feminism, Environmental Philosophy, and the Critique of Rationalism," *Ecological Feminist Philosophies*, 155–80.
2. Tzeporah Berman, "The Rape of Mother Nature? Women in the Language of Environmental Discourse," *The Trumpeter* 11, no. 4 (Fall 1994), 173–78.
3. Catrina Sandilands, "Political Animals: The Paradox of Ecofeminist Politics," *The Trumpeter* 11, no. 4 (Fall 1994), 167–72.
4. Neil Evernden, *The Social Creation of Nature* (Baltimore: Johns Hopkins University Press, 1992), 121.

5. Mathews, "Relating to Nature: Deep Ecology or Ecofeminism?" 164.

6. Ibid., 165.

7. Evernden, *The Social Creation of Nature,* xii, 15, 16, 132.

8. See also Evernden, *The Natural Alien: Humankind and Environment* (Toronto: University of Toronto Press, 1985), 124–28, 140.

9. The following are examples of some attempts simultaneously to make the classic phenomenologies more accessible and to show their relevance to "ecological issues": Evernden, *The Natural Alien: Humankind and Environment*; Carol Bigwood, *Earth Muse: Feminism, Nature, and Art* (Philadelphia: Temple University Press, 1993); and David Abram, *The Spell of the Sensuous: Perception and Language in a More-Than-Human World.*

10. Friedrich Nietzsche, *Thus Spoke Zarathustra,* in *The Portable Nietzsche,* trans. and ed. Walter Kaufmann (New York: Penguin, 1976), 307. To accord with the German text, I have removed Kaufmann's italicizations.

11. See, for example, *Thus Spoke Zarathustra,* in *The Portable Nietzsche:* "On the Gift-Giving Virtue," 190; "On Priests," 204; "The Wanderer," 265; "On Old and New Tablets," 321; "The Last Supper," 397; and "On the Higher Man," 402.

12. See, for example, *Thus Spoke Zarathustra,* in *The Portable Nietzsche,* 128–31, 218, 360, 367, 439.

13. Ibid., 430.

14. "On the Thousand and One Goals," *Thus Spoke Zarathustra,* in *The Portable Nietzsche,* 171.

15. "On the Afterworldly," *Thus Spoke Zarathustra,* in *The Portable Nietzsche,* 145. For a less favorable interpretation of this and of *Thus Spoke Zarathustra* as a whole, see Carol Bigwood, *Earth Muse,* 75–96.

16. See, for example, *Thus Spoke Zarathustra,* in *The Portable Nietzsche:* "Zarathustra's Prologue," 122–23; and "The Other Dancing Song" 336–40.

17. Ibid., 160–66, 211–15, 217, 237, 280, 298, 370, 402.

18. For a fuller discussion, see Monika Langer, "The Role and Status of Animals in Nietzsche's Philosophy," *Animal Others: On Ethics, Ontology, and Animal Life,* ed. H. Peter Steeves (New York: State University of New York Press, 1999), 75–92.

19. *Thus Spoke Zarathustra,* in *The Portable Nietzsche,* 329–30.

20. Martin Heidegger, "Letter on Humanism," *Basic Writings from* Being and Time *(1927) to* The Task of Thinking *(1964),* ed. David Farrell Krell (New York: Harper & Row, 1977), 228. See also 195–96, 221, 232.

21. Martin Heidegger, "Memorial Address," *Discourse on Thinking,* trans. John M. Anderson and E. Hans Freund (New York: Harper & Row, 1966), 50.

22. Heidegger, "Memorial Address," *Discourse on Thinking*, 43–57; and "Letter on Humanism," *Basic Writings from* Being and Time *(1927) to* The Task of Thinking *(1964)*, 193–94, 196, 199, 217–19, 222–23, 228, 236, 239, 242.
23. Heidegger, *An Introduction to Metaphysics*, trans. Ralph Manheim (New York: Anchor, 1961), 69, 11.
24. Heidegger, "Letter on Humanism," *Basic Writings from* Being and Time *(1927) to* The Task of Thinking, *(1964)*, 199, 217–19, 221–22, 239.
25. Maurice Merleau-Ponty, *The Visible and the Invisible: Followed by Working Notes*, ed. Claude Lefort and trans. Alphonso Lingis (Evanston: Northwestern University Press, 1968), 251.
26. Ibid., 136, 168, 200, 155.
27. Ibid., 141, 144, 138. See also 250, 267.
28. Ibid., 27, 138, 271, 274, 253.
29. Ibid., 139, 147, 142, 274, 221, 268. Merleau-Ponty's working notes indicate he planned to make explicit our "kinship" with animality, and to describe "the man-animality *intertwining*" (see 168, 274).
30. Merleau-Ponty, *The Structure of Behavior*, trans. Alden L. Fisher (Boston: Beacon, 1967); *Phenomenology of Perception*, trans. Colin Smith (London: Routledge & Kegan Paul, 1962).
31. Merleau-Ponty, *Themes from the Lectures at the Collège de France 1952–1960*, trans. John O'Neill (Evanston: Northwestern University Press, 1970), 63–69, 99, 83, 97.
32. Ibid., 98, 128.
33. Merleau-Ponty, *The Visible and the Invisible*, 250 (see also 168).

CHAPTER 7

Back to Earth with Reflection and Ecology

DON E. MARIETTA, JR.

Environmental ethics requires an ontological commitment. Even though several different systems of metaphysics seem to provide a suitable philosophical background for environmental ethics, and the major metaphysical schools do not seem to entail any particular system of ethics, I am uneasy about neglecting metaphysics in the study of environmental ethics. I will explore in more detail the nature of the ontological commitment which I believe is necessary, but the main element in this commitment is a philosophical anthropology which holds that humans are a part of the system of nature. It is a holistic metaphysics, but it must be a critical holism that subjects to careful scrutiny any claims regarding the relationship between humans and the rest of the system of nature.

By referring to an ontological commitment, I do not mean to imply that this is an arbitrary acceptance of an ontology simply to undergird the demands of environmental ethics. The holistic ontology stands in its own right. The rightness of the ontology is a discovery, not a decision. My path to the justification of this ontology was primarily through existential phenomenology, especially that of Maurice Merleau-Ponty.[1]

Even though environmental philosophy that stresses the involvement of humans in the system of nature and produces an ethic of responsibility to nature was not well developed in their time, the existential phenomenologists found in Edmund Husserl's work an approach to human consciousness and experience that lays a groundwork for environmental thought. It is through a phenomenological type of reflection that I was led to see that the oneness of the human person and the rest of the system of nature is discovered, not invented. In phenomenological reflection on the most original, most primal, and least theoretically structured awareness of the world, what I call concrete reflection, a sharp division between the self and an environment is not present. Instead we find a unity of self and the nonself, the so-called subject and object.

Merleau-Ponty criticizes the "objectivistic ontology" that we inherited from Descartes, an ontology that maintains a doubting of human experience, holding it suspect, often dismissing it as subjective. He directs us to a reflection on "that primordial being which is not yet the subject-being nor the object-being."[2]

Reflection on the primordial (or primal) awareness of the world shows two things important for the development of environmental philosophy. One is the unity of this experience. As we describe the world reflected upon, we see that we do not paint our picture of the world by a kind of intellectual pointillism. We do not receive bits of unrelated sense data. Experience does not give us a "pure sensation," an "atom of feeling." We are aware of matters in context, what Merleau-Ponty called "the upsurge of a true and accurate world."[3]

Our perception of whole contexts in concrete reflection enables us to move from the particular to the general, and it provides a context for seeing the connection between description and explanation. The horizon of the matters reflected on is flexible. It can focus narrowly on an object in its more immediate context, or it can see the matter in a much wider context, a context in which other similar things can be attended to. With attention to memory, this broader context incorporates naming and grouping of things. Since we see some things as associated with other things, including seeing some as causally related to others, an element of explanation enters our reflection. At this point, we must be careful not to let preestablished schema override our attention to the matters themselves. A critical attitude toward interpretive schema and a frequent return to the matters themselves is an important difference between concrete reflection and abstract, intellectualizing reflection.

The second important observation about our awareness of the lived world is that there is no separation of factual information from meaning and value. Merleau-Ponty describes the primordial lived world as charged with meaning. Recognition that an object has certain value for us, such as its being attractive, can come before recognition of its physical qualities. This has implications for ethics that we will indicate later.[4]

A truly individual self that is achieved through separation from other persons and the world about us is not discovered in reflection on our primal experience of world, the world experience that some existential phenomenologists refer to as the pre-thetic, the awareness before conscious reflection has separated matters into various kinds and categories.

We find this separated self when we engage in what Merleau-Ponty called "intellectualist analysis." This is the sort of thinking that is at home in a Cartesian world, the world of separated subjects and objects. Within this mode of reflection we make qualities of which we are aware in concrete reflection on our most primal experience into mere elements of consciousness; whereas, Merleau-Ponty says, a quality so discovered is not an element of consciousness but "an object for consciousness." Intellectualist analysis draws us away from reflection on the world as it is given to us, "and we construct perception instead of revealing its distinctive working; we miss . . . the basic operation which infuses significance into the sensible."[5] Thus we make the mistake of attributing to "judgment" what is actually in experience.

Merleau-Ponty was critical of the way science creates a limited and artificial worldview. He said science "makes its own limited models of things; operating upon these indices or variables to affect whatever transformations are permitted by their definitions, it comes face to face with the real world only at rare intervals."[6] He comments on Einstein's rejecting as "psychology" intersubjective experience of simultaneous events. He said, "This is to postulate that what is is not *that upon which we have an openness,* but only *that upon which we can operate.*" This is one example of the problems in physics and psychology resulting from the subject/object distinction.[7]

We can still reflect on the primal oneness of experience in the kind of phenomenological reflection I call "concrete reflection," in contrast to intellectualized abstract reflection. In concrete reflection we find that our bodies are not just objects in the world, but that they are, as Merleau-Ponty described it, "the vehicle of being in the world." The body is not detached, as an object, from the self, the subject. The experience of one's body does not support the separation of subject and object. Merleau-Ponty said that having a body is "to be involved in a definite environment, to identify oneself with certain projects and be continually committed to them."[8]

From the perspective that concrete reflection gives, a problem is seen in talk about the environment, a residue of Cartesian separation of the mind-self, the subject, from the environing object. We might do well to qualify our notion of the world as an environment. In one sense, the world is something around us, to be sure, but it also passes into and through us making us part of itself. We live a natural environment more than we live in it. Two people working side by side do not have exactly the same environment because they are not exactly the same in the ways they live the environment. My colleague who steps out of the building as I do exclaims, "What a gorgeous day!" I am polite about it, but to me it is oppressively hot. The environment is not something that begins where our skins end. Paul Shepard uses a graphic metaphor to refer to the unity of humans and the natural world. He says the human skin is "like a pond surface or a forest soil, not a shell so much as a delicate interpenetration."[9]

This is the holistic ontological commitment which I believe necessary for sound environmental philosophy. So much are we a part of the natural world that even speaking of environment can enter a conceptual wedge into our thinking. Why do I speak of this view as an ontological commitment? Why not just call it an ontology? I speak of a commitment, in the first place, in recognition that other people arrive at the realization that humans are part of nature through studies that have been different from mine. In the second place, I speak of commitment to stress that this must be a moral commitment to holism, not just an intellectualistic concept. Mere intellectual assent to an ontological doctrine is not the commitment I believe necessary. An environmental ethic will not be adequate if it is an abstraction that does not engage a person's thought and feeling and result in the adoption of a way of living.

The Big Pictures

The metaphysical commitment of environmental philosophers has often been expressed in big pictures, analogies that make the place of humans in the natural system vivid and graphic. These pictures were often those of biologists and ecologists, the pictures that were used to make their conceptual models understandable and attractive. A few philosophers have gone directly to traditional metaphysics to undergird their ethics. George Sessions's appeal to Spinoza's metaphysics,[10] other people's use of other classical and recent philosophers, and the use of theology to support stewardship approaches are examples of this use of metaphysics, but the use of analogies, big pictures to show the reasonableness of the ethical demands, have dominated the discussion. Such conceptual notions as community, kinship between humans and other living things, diversity, and stability made both the scientific theories and the ethical demands clearer to people who had little grasp of the technical principles of ecology. One did not need to know how plant species help define a wetland to respond to the claim that we humans are part of a community.

I do not wish to make light of the value of the big pictures nor to suggest that they will not continue to be of value, not only in environmental education of the public, but in our thinking about our planet and our responsibility to it. We need to recognize, however, the dangers involved in our use of the pictures. Such concepts as community and stability have been vulnerable to attack. There was an attack on moral grounds, which first engaged our attention. Now we must respond to attacks on scientific grounds.

The moral questioning of the holistic pictures, such as that of community, come from the fear that holism will overrule the demands of individualistic humanistic ethics. Aldo Leopold's description of the land community, together with his belief that the role of humans should be that of being plain members and common citizens of that community, seemed to threaten the rights of individual persons. Leopold's moral criterion, "[a] thing is right when it tends to preserve the integrity, stability, and beauty of the biotic community. It is wrong when it tends otherwise" seemed to subordinate all moral concerns to duty toward the natural environment. Arne Naess's concept of "biospherical egalitarianism" and Paul W. Taylor's "life-centered ethics," which holds that human beings have no moral superiority to other animals,[11] were taken as threats to all human concerns. Leopold did not advocate harsh measures to preserve the stability of the natural system, and Naess incorporated concern for justice and freedom within the human community in his "deep ecology." Taylor greatly qualified his concept of equality between humans and nonhumans. This moderation did not alleviate the fears of holism, nor should it have done so if the logical conclusion of holism is rejection of humanistic ethical concerns—which thinkers of our day are not ready to accept, but at which thinkers in the future might not blanch.

Humanistic moral philosophers, whose primary concern was freedom and justice in the human community, have opposed social and political forms of holism, such as those which sacrificed the good of individual citizens to the power of the state. An environmental holism might be more threatening than political holism. It might call on humans to sacrifice themselves for the good of the natural environment. Several philosophers saw environmental holism in just this light. William Aiken thought that the practical implications of holism were "astounding, staggering," because of the threat to rights of individuals. Tom Regan wrote that "what holism gives us is a fascist understanding of the environment." Marti Kheel called ecological holism "totalitarian."[12]

Is environmental holism the threat some people have thought? I have argued elsewhere that the moral problems with the big pictures comes from several misuses of concepts that were developed as conceptual models by biologists.[13] The main mistakes were exaggeration, reductionism, and excessive abstraction.

Exaggeration should be the easiest of the faults to identify and avoid. It should be obvious that Francis Thompson's often quoted lines:

thou canst not stir a flower
Without troubling of a star

greatly exaggerate the interrelatedness of things in the system of nature. There is not a scintilla of evidence that picking a flower disturbs even the nearest stars. Picking a whole bouquet of flowers would have no astronomical significance. It might be claimed that an attitude of such reverence for nature would have a good effect on human conduct, but the ways I have seen the poem quoted seemed to be making claims, not about beneficial attitudes, but about the interrelatedness of things, even though fostering propitious attitudes might have been the ultimate objective of the discourse.

In the Victorian era Tennyson expressed a romantic sort of holism in a little poem.

Flower in the crannied wall,
I pluck you out of the crannies,
I hold you here, root and all, in my hand,
Little flower—but if I could understand
What you are, root and all, and all in all,
I should know what God and man is.

This is the sort of sentiment that probably makes most people think, "Oh! Wow!" Even though I have not been a logical positivist for many years, even decades, my reaction to the poem is "Ouch!" Not only is the claim about knowing what God is subject to frontal and flank attacks on theological grounds, which does not need to concern us here, but the claims it makes about knowledge of the nature of humans are highly dubious. I cannot imagine any knowledge of a flower, even if it is of "root and all," which would put out of work all psychologists, sociologists, anthropologists, physiologists, and all the other people who are studying humanity. The exaggeration of romantic holism is so obvious that we should have no trouble with it.

There is a danger in an exaggerated notion of the unity of all nature that makes it necessary for us to be careful. Frederick Ferré points out the need for an ontology that recognizes external relations as well as internal relations. A perfectly unified world (such as a world with internal relations only) would make experience of a coherent world impossible. External relations are necessary for "coherence in dynamic balance with adequate openness to experience." Ferré shows that freedom and creativity require external relations, but with external relations alone all properties would become "bare particulars" in a "conceptual vacuum."[14] Our ontology must not exaggerate either unity or divergence. We must accept the sense in which the world is "out there" without thinking of the world as an alien system of which we are wholly independent.

The moral objections to some of the pictures and concepts employed by environmental philosophers seem to have been caused by the reductionism suggested by the way the models were presented. As I explain elsewhere,[15] the reductionism is a logical flaw. It fails to take into account important features of the world, especially important aspects of being a human person. With the avoidance of the reductionism, the community model will not have the moral implications that disturbed a number of writers.

The abstraction involved in the way some of the big pictures were presented was a result of getting too far removed from the ecological data. When the big pictures went too far beyond the actual data about organisms in natural systems and the ways they are interrelated, the abstraction became a problem. Not only do such abstract pictures go hand in hand with the reductionism that causes moral concern, but the abstract pictures are subject to attack from within science. This is what must engage the attention of environmental philosophers now. Recent papers show that philosophers are attending to this important concern.[16]

The conceptual models employed by scientists have been useful as ways to show the relationships between separate bits of data. They have provided a unifying framework and indicated areas that needed exploration. They indicated which experiments would be significant and how data from the experiments should be interpreted. Some of these models were beautiful, even awesome, products of human creativity. The conceptual models used by biologists and ecologists were helpful in environmental education. They became great houses of the mind. It is not to be wondered at that people could become attached to certain big pictures. What a shame it is, then, that some of these wonderful pictures have to be abandoned, or at least remodeled, but that has been the fate of conceptual models through the history of science. It is important that our metaphysical achievements and moral insights not become captive to an outmoded picture.

We would be making a mistake if we continued using the familiar pictures as though the theories of Raymond Lindeman, Charles Elton, Frederic L. Clements, and Eugene P. Odum were accepted by all biologists. Patch dynamics, hierarchy theory, and chaos theory cannot be ignored. I think it would also be a mistake to throw up our hands and give up the effort to make sense of the natural world. The newer approaches to biological research need to be studied with care. New approaches to a science are not always doing what old approaches did in another way. The newer approaches to biology suggest a breaking away from holism, but this may be as much a matter of technique as of theory. Newer approaches are sometimes adopted because they are manageable. Research with a discrete base of data has its attraction. In some research, that which cannot be computerized becomes invisible. It may take a while for the full implications of the new approaches to ecology to become apparent.

Do we need to wait until biological approaches sift themselves out before we can continue with environmental ethics? I do not think we need to wait. If we wait for biological theory to settle down for a period of centuries, or even generations, we might wait forever. The point, I believe, is that we must not be locked in to one big picture. Our job is to do philosophy, not to do biology, and we must work along with the biology that biologists do.

Can we abandon the concept of one biotic community? It has been important to us, and we would regret its loss, but we could settle for separate biotic communities. We have used the concept of human community, which we think we understand, to throw light on biotic communities. There are human communities, but does the concept of one total human community explain much about human behavior? If the science of population biology becomes dominant in biology, it would hardly destroy the notion of community, any more than a "population sociology" would destroy the notion of human communities.

If we are going to use the notion of community in environmental ethics, we need to think more carefully about the concept. Thinking in terms of range, and acknowledging certain limitations of community, might help. Do we need to think of one inclusive biotic community to explain our duties to Earth? I believe we should be so well grounded in our metaphysics and ethics that the big pictures can be used when they serve us well, even as we are ready to abandon them or accept changes in them as necessary.

The Ontological Commitment

The metaphysics that I think basic to environmental ethics is a critical holism. In what senses is it holistic, and in what senses critical? It is holistic in that it acknowledges that humans are part of the system of nature. Our being parts of the natural system does not take away those aspects of human life that may belong to humans alone. Talk of biospherical egalitarianism and of humans being morally equal to other animals should be carefully qualified. Humans are able to move from one part of the world to another, unlike the frog who lives in the pond in which it was born, and in which it lives more effectively than we could. How are we equal? We can use moving vans and airplanes, and we can think great thoughts and have aesthetic experiences, but all this does not take us out of the system of nature. Are we equal to other creatures? We must be realistic about what we are; we are not just apes who wear shoes, but we are no more able than the ape to transcend the biological realities that affect our lives. We can overcome some natural limitations and natural dangers. Some of us could not read this book or hear what people say to us without means by which humans have avoided some of the effects of being creatures of nature; some of us would be dead now without the benefits of human medicine and surgery; but we must beware letting these things make us too proud. We are part of this natural system, and the recognition of our ontological status is necessary for sound environmental ethics.

This holistic understanding of our place in the system of nature is our basic ontological commitment. How does our holism become a critical holism? It is not a critical holism if myths, poems, fables, or even big pictures that were once part of accepted biological theory hold us captive. Our holism is critical when we are flexible enough in our understanding to keep on studying biology. Our holism is critical when new developments in biology do not threaten it. Why should they threaten it? The particular way the interactions that occur in natural systems is described is unlikely to cut the ground from under the fact that we are natural beings.

One type of metaphysics that is employed in support of protection of the natural environment might seem incompatible with my claim that our basic ontological commitment is that we are a part of the system of nature. Does the theological basis for a stewardship position acknowledge that humans are a part of nature? There are several things to say about this. First, we must avoid seeing theology as an intellectual monolith. There are theological positions that do not deny that humans are parts of the natural system. Christian and Jewish theology is not always dualistic. I remember years ago reading a theologian, I believe it was Archbishop Temple, who called psycho-physical dualism "Descartes' *faux pas*." In graduate school I learned that the Hebrew Bible does not reflect a dualistic view of the human person. It may be that most theists profess belief in a dualistic view of humans according to which the real person is a soul and not part of the world, but the numbers are not important. The point is that the religionists who are environmentally aware and concerned can keep their religious faith and also accept the holistic ontological commitment. Even within a dualistic perspective, the human body is part of nature, and religionists need not be unconcerned about human bodies.

If a person takes an extreme version of dualism, and holds as James Watt, a former Secretary of the Interior, did that humans should not be

concerned about the natural environment, it is obvious that this metaphysical position does not provide an adequate basis for environmental
ethics.[17] What of a dualist who holds that we should protect the natural
environment simply because God demands stewardship, basing the stewardship on an authoritarian divine command ethic? Is this person's dualism an adequate basis for environmental ethics? I would have to say it is
not. I do not think I am just being tendentious in saying that such an ethic
is not an environmental ethic. It derives duties toward the environment
from religious principles of long standing in some religious communities,
but these principles are not environmental principles. The principle is the
same whether the command is to shun the worship of idols or to avoid
cutting down forests. Unless the moral importance of the environment
itself contributes in some way to the basis for the ethic, the ethic may
govern use of the environment, but it is not on all fours with ethical
approaches in which values in nature or our being a part of nature undergirds the demand that nature be protected. There are parallels in other
kind of ethics. An ethic that is not related to the nature of sexuality, but is
only a matter of obeying a deity who forbids certain practices, can hardly
count as an ethic of sexuality. An ethic that forbids on divine authority
some practice, such as slavery or murder, but is not related to an anthropology, would hardly be a humanistic ethic.

Can an ethic dealing with the environment, but without an ontological commitment such as holism, be an adequate ethical guide? People
with such beliefs might act as good stewards, but I would not want to
entrust the keeping of Earth to them. Their commitment to the natural
world seems too much a matter of happenstance. These stewards do not
have a firm enough basis for earthkeeping. Is this the situation of most
religious people who are working to protect Earth? I do not think it is. I
believe most religious environmentalists know they are parts of the
system of nature. Creedal statements which support a dualism that would
make earthkeeping optional do not seem to have an overwhelming
impact on most believers. Stewardship for most religionists, I believe, is
an environmental ethic.

Ontology and Ethical Commitment

How is our ontological commitment related to our environmental ethics?
Without going into the detail with which I treat this matter in *For People
and the Planet* and elsewhere,[18] I will give a sketch of my approach. The
first thing to note is that I do not try to derive an ethic from ecological

knowledge through deductive argument. The "is/ought" dichotomy holds within its own domain, which is that of logical entailment. Our ontological commitment does not entail an ethic. What is the relationship? The best way to see the connection, I believe, is to begin with phenomenological reflection. This is not the abstract and analytical sort of reflection, which sorts through things and places them in previously acquired, and usually unquestioned, categories. It is a reflection that seeks to describe our awareness of the world with as little presupposition as possible. As we have seen, Merleau-Ponty described this approach as finding the world there for us, not only in its physical qualities but also with its values. We perceive matters in the world as good, ugly, beautiful, or frightening as soon as, or in some cases before, we take note of sizes, shapes, and colors.[19]

The importance of this for ethics is that there is no "is/ought" impasse in this reflection on the world. The relationship between the way the world is seen and our recognition that some things have value, on the one hand, and our sense that some things ought to be and some not, on the other, is not a matter of entailment. It is not derived by logical argument. There is a sort of directness and immediacy in matters as reflected on.

Does this reflection show that the values perceived and the obligations felt are correct? Does it show us what we should do? No, of itself it cannot do this. The way matters are discovered to be related in one's world experience might be mistaken. Even phenomenological reflection can be influenced by previous beliefs and commitments. What then is the value of this kind of reflection? The value is in seeing that there is no sharp division between physical aspects of the world and the social aspects, and there is no sharp division between these qualities and values and a sense of obligation. The properly sharp distinction between fact and value in logical reasoning is not a wall that continues down into the core of our awareness of the world. This should tell us that trying to deal with facts, values, and obligations in terms of logical reasoning is not necessary and will be futile. Once we have separated facts from values in an abstract kind of reflection, we will not be able to bring them together again successfully. We will have put them in a context, logical reasoning, which has rules and procedures that do not allow the restoration of the primal unity of physical, social, valuational, and volitional aspects of our world.

How are we to make sound judgments about our values and obligations? If we cannot argue logically—that is, deductively and inductively—what can we do? I do not think we need to accept a subjectivistic or emotivistic understanding of moral judgment. I do not believe we must accept an untestable intuitionist approach. We can examine and evaluate

our volitions and sense of moral obligation even without reliance on
logical argument. One tool we can use in examining our moral beliefs is
intersubjective verification. We have become accustomed to verifying factual claims intersubjectively. This is the necessary basis for examining factual claims. There is no possibility of a purely objective perception of
worldly matters; that is, perception that is not affected at all by the human
observer. What we can have is a high degree of intersubjective agreement.
We have little trouble in using intersubjectivity in respect to the physical
qualities of things. We use intersubjective verification in respect to social
aspects of the world, even though this may be a little more difficult. We
have not used intersubjectivity in seeking to know values and moral
duties as much as we can and should. Intersubjectivity cannot give us
logical certainty, but if we insist on logical certainty, we are pursuing a
will-o'-the-wisp. Demanding certainty is not only futile, it is harmful,
since it leads people to reject the degrees of knowledge available to us in
regard to physical, social, and valuational aspects of our lives.

Intersubjectivity is not the only tool we have for evaluation of moral
beliefs, and it should be used in conjunction with two other means of
evaluation: recognition of fittingness and criticism of individual worldviews. This chapter does not allow for detailed description of these two
aids to evaluation. They have been described in *For People and the Planet*.
Let me point out here that fittingness has long been employed in ethics. I
do not claim that a sense of fittingness will always give adequate guidance. That is one reason for using fittingness in conjunction with other
means of examining beliefs.

Individual worldviews incorporate a wide-ranging and continually
changing body of beliefs, attitudes, values, and commitments. The influence of these world views in perception and the formation of belief and
attitudes and the acceptance of values can best be grasped by phenomenological analysis. The worldview of a person is critically important in
that person's thinking processes, both cognitively and effectively. Worldviews can also be a source of errors in perception, thinking, and feeling.
That is why it is important to evaluate a personal worldview in terms of
how it was developed, its inclusiveness, its having a reasonable level of
consistency, and other factors. An ontological commitment is a significant
part of a worldview.

Where then does this take us? We have seen that at least a minimum
metaphysical belief, an ontological commitment which acknowledges
that humans are part of the system of nature, is necessary for developing
a sound environmental ethic. This ontological commitment is not dependent on any particular biological conceptual model. We can go along with
the shifts in big pictures that it is reasonable to expect.

We have also seen how our ontological commitment functions in the making of moral decisions. A degree of ambiguity in our perception and understanding of the world, and uncertainty in our moral judgments, are some things we must face. It would be a mistake to try to remove the ambiguity and uncertainty by adopting principles and procedures that could do a great deal of harm and lead us away from decision procedures that are adequate and may be as good as we can acquire. We do not need simplicity and certainty bought at a very high price. Adopting a metaphysical scheme that explains everything neatly but is difficult to believe would not be a helpful step. We can have a basic metaphysical position that does not call for great credulity. To guide our moral thinking, we already have more tools at our disposal than we have been using.

Replacing the big pictures with concrete reflection will enable us to avoid being saddled with the failure of a picture science has outgrown. These pictures have guided and inspired environmentalists for decades, but it would be a mistake to rest our case on any one of them. The pictures have been subject to criticism on various grounds all along, so we should not be surprised if a picture turns out to reflect the ecological thinking of yesterday. I do not think we must consign these pictures to the fires. They might still suggest important issues to us, as well as continue to inspire us, but we should not treat them as classics we cannot touch. We may need to review some of the pictures, while others might better go into the scrapbook, if not the scrap pile. The point is that changing or even losing the big pictures need not be a defeat for us. I do not think that environmental ethics is at the end of its road. It may need to proceed more carefully as it becomes a mature discipline, but that is all to the good.

Notes

1. Environmental philosophers have paid more attention to Heidegger than to other existential phenomenologists, but note Monika Langer, "Merleau-Ponty and Deep Ecology," in *Ontology and Alterity in Merleau-Ponty*, ed Galen A. Johnson and Michael B. Smith (Evanston: Northwestern University Press, 1990), 115–29, 192–97; also Joseph Campisi, "Maurice Merleau-Ponty's *Phenomenology of Perception* and Its Contribution to a Naessian Philosophy of Ecological Harmony" (unpublished paper: Duquesne University Department of Philosophy).
2. Maurice Merleau-Ponty, *The Visible and the Invisible*, trans. Alphonso Lingis (Evanston: Northwestern University Press, 1968), 106, 183;

also *Themes from the Lectures at the College de France, 1952–1960*, trans. John O'Neill (Evanston: Northwestern University Press, 1970), 65–66.

3. Maurice Merleau-Ponty, *Phenomenology of Perception*, trans. Colin Smith (New York: Routledge, 1962), 3–5, 35, 53, 67–68.

4. Merleau-Ponty, *Phenomenology of Perception*, 4–5, 21, 24, 52.

5. Merleau-Ponty, *Phenomenology of Perception*, 5.

6. Maurice Merleau-Ponty, *The Primacy of Perception*, ed. James E. Edie (Evanston: Northwestern University Press, 1964), 159.

7. Merleau-Ponty, *The Visible and the Invisible*, 18, 22–23.

8. Merleau-Ponty, *Phenomenology of Perception*, 82, 198–99.

9. Paul Shepard, *The Subversive Science: Essays toward an Ecology of Man* (Boston: Houghton Mifflin, 1969), introduction.

10. George Sessions, "Spinoza and Jeffers on Man in Nature," *Inquiry* 20, no. 4 (Winter 1977): 481–528.

11. Aldo Leopold, *A Sand County Almanac* (London, Oxford, and New York: Oxford University Press, 1949), 204, 216, 224–25; Arne Naess, "The Shallow and the Deep, Long-Range Ecology Movement: A Summary," *Inquiry* 16 (1973), 95; Paul W. Taylor, "The Ethics of Respect for Nature," *Environmental Ethics* 3 (1980), 211–18.

12. William Aiken, "Ethical Issues in Agriculture," in *Earthbound*, ed. Tom Regan (New York: Random House, 1984), 269; Tom Regan, *The Case for Animal Rights* (Berkeley: University of California Press, 1983), 372; Marti Kheel, "The Liberation of Nature: A Circular Affair," *Environmental Ethics* 7 (1985), 135–49.

13. "Environmentalism, Holism, and Individuals," *Environmental Ethics* 10, no. 8 (1988): 251–58. (Reprinted in *Environmental Ethics: Divergence and Convergence*, ed Susan J. Armstrong and Richard G. Botzler [New York: McGraw-Hill, 1993] and in *Environmental Ethics: Concepts, Policy, and Theory*, ed. Joseph R. Des Jardins [Mountain View, Calif.: Mayfield, 1998].) See also *For People and the Planet: Holism and Humanism in Environmental Ethics* (Philadelphia: Temple University Press, 1994), chapter 3.

14. Frederick Ferré, "Internal Relations, External Relations, and the Foundation of Environmental Ethics," conference paper for a research symposium sponsored by the Adelaide R. Snyder Professorship in Ethics, Center for Advanced Research in Phenomenology, Inc., and the Department of Philosophy, Florida Atlantic University.

15. See note 13.

16. Donald Worster, "The Ecology of Order and Chaos," *Environmental Ethics* 14 (1990): 1–18; Karen J. Warren and Jim Cheney, "Ecosystem Ecology and Metaphysical Ecology: A Case Study," *Environmental Ethics* 15, no. 2 (Summer 1993): 99–116; J. Baird Callicott, "On Warren

and Cheney's Critique of Callicott's Ecological Metaphysics," in *Environmental Ethics* 15, no. 4 (Winter 1993): 373–74.

17. See the discussion of Watt in Marietta, *For People and the Planet*, 19.
18. "Reflection and Environmental Activism," in *Environmental Philosophy and Environmental Activism*, ed. Don Marietta and Lester Embree (Totowa, N.J.: Rowman & Littlefield, 1995), 79–97.
19. Merleau-Ponty, *Phenomenology of Perception*, 4–5, 21, 24, 52.

II

New Directions in Eco-Phenomenology

CHAPTER 8

The Primacy of Desire and
Its Ecological Consequences

TED TOADVINE

Environmental ethicists are invariably led to construct a philosophy of nature, since the question of whether anthropocentrism is a sound basis for environmental policy rests on the plausibility of attributing intrinsic value to nature. Thus runs the dominant line of reasoning in Anglo-American environmental circles, and the battle lines are drawn by implication: either humans project values on an objective and valueless factual world, or nature enjoys some valuable and/or valuing status in its own right. Recent trends seem to favor the latter direction, toward a philosophy of nature that, on the rebound against earlier anthropocentric views of "man-apart-from-nature," insists on inserting the human subject within a continuum of value originating within the ecosystem or the natural organism itself.[1] But perhaps this movement toward a continuity with nature, a homogeneity or kinship between the human and the natural, is wrongheaded. This problemmatic tendency is also apparent in recent phenomenologically oriented approaches to environmental philosophy, for example, in recent attempts to establish a kinship of the human and the natural on the basis of Merleau-Ponty's phenomenology of corporeality and later ontology of flesh. Is environmental ethics best served by adopting this "humans-as-a-part-of-nature" paradigm? Or, to pose the question theoretically rather than practically, is a perceived teleological continuity between humans and nature a suitable basis for attributing value? And perhaps we should throw our net wider still: Is the question of "intrinsic value" the right question?

The intrinsic value of nature becomes an issue within a worldview that conceives culture and nature dialectically; the naturalization of culture and the culturization of nature are simply modalities of this dialectic. But perhaps the possibility of an ethical response to nature lies with the impossibility of trimming its claws for adoption as our sibling or household pet. Perhaps, as I will suggest here, an ethical response to nature becomes possible only when we are faced with the *impossibility* of reducing it to the homogeneous, the continuous, the predictable, the perceivable, the thematizable. What is called for is not a new philosophy of nature, but an ethics of the impossibility of any "philosophy" of nature. The basis for such "impossibility" is phenomenological, but in a way that stretches this method, perhaps to the breaking point. As resources for an "impossible phenomenology" of nature, I will draw on analyses of corporeality, desire, and flesh in Schopenhauer, Sartre, and Merleau-Ponty. What I develop here is by no means a complete view, but has two aims: first, to suggest that the current "kinship" view is neither satisfactory nor our only alternative in providing an ethical ground for the relation with nature; and, second, to indicate the direction in which an alternative "phenomenology of the impossible" could be developed.

Beyond the Dialectic of Intrinsic Value

J. Baird Callicot and Holmes Rolston, III, occupy dialectical poles in the intrinsic value debate. "From the scientific point of view," Callicot asserts, "nature throughout, from atoms to galaxies, is an orderly, objective, axiologically neutral domain." A sound environmental ethic should, on Callicot's view, adopt this scientific perspective, with the consequence that "value is, as it were, projected onto natural objects or events by the subjective feelings of observers. If all consciousness were annihilated at a stroke, there would be no good and evil, no beauty and ugliness, no right and wrong; only impassive phenomena would remain."[2] Callicot holds that this state of affairs does not exclude intrinsic value; it merely requires that we understand this notion in terms of the projection of the subjective observer, such projections being explainable in "Humean-Darwinean" fashion (Callicot, 162).

While Callicot is content to return to a Humean empiricism, Holmes Rolston seems to favor a teleological interpretation of nature drawn straight from Aristotle. What science shows us, Rolston argues, is that "the organism is a spontaneous, self-maintaining system, sustaining and reproducing itself, executing its program, making a way through the world. . . . Something more than physical causes, even when less than sentience, is operating within every organism. . . . [This] is the modern equivalent of what Aristotle called formal and final causes; it gives the organism a telos, or end, a kind of (nonfelt) goal."[3] As an "axiological, evaluative system," this living individual *is* an intrinsic value. But our duties do not stop at the individual, since such evaluative activity can be attributed to species and even ecosystems. The "fundamental unit of survival," and therefore of duty, is the ecosystem, in which "order arises spontaneously and systematically."[4] Consciousness and self-consciousness are the products of the evaluative telos of ecosystem evolution. There is no "dumbfounding epigenesis" of values at the human level, Rolston retorts to Callicot, since human subjectivity as an evaluative system is merely the evolutionary perfection of evaluative processes at work in life's deepest substratum.[5]

Rolston avoids making any experience or sentience of nature a mainspring of his ethics, but his aim is still the construction of a clockwork nature, a whole within which the gears of human activity can mesh. Rolston offers us a "mental image" of nature not unlike Leopold's biotic pyramid, and perhaps motivated by the same ethical presupposition: that "we can be ethical only in relation to something we can see, feel, understand, love, or otherwise have faith in."[6] Rolston and Leopold both adopt what Don Marietta has called the "person-as-a-part-of-nature model," a model of human-environment relations that stresses "kinship with our fellow creatures in the world" and a sense of "belonging to a [natural] community."[7] While this position is certainly preferable to the man-apart-from-nature view that saturates the history of philosophy and Western culture, there is another option that is at least hinted at in Rolston's discussion. In the course of denying that value arises only with the human valuer, Rolston notes that "[s]omething from a world beyond the human mind, beyond human experience, is received into our mind, our experience, and the value of that something does not always arise with our evaluation of it" (Rolston, 94). Perhaps nature's value, if value is the word, should be sought in this "something" that is beyond the human mind and experience. How might such a something be characterized?

A first answer is offered by Neil Evernden, who argues for an idiosyncratic experience of nature as unpredictable, nonhomogenous, and noncontinuous—in his phrase "Nature-as-miracle."[8] Despite its theological ring, nature-as-miracle is the farthest thing from the kind of "natural law" approach seen in Rolston. Through a social psychoanalysis of nature, Evernden discloses the culturization of nature that operates hand-in-hand with the naturalization of culture.[9] "Every social group," he contends, "has had a conception of nature which it uses in maintaining its own internal stability" (Evernden, 154–55). "Wilderness," for instance, as others have argued, may well be a Western concept.[10] "Nature-as-object" is Evernden's label for the perspective, paradigmatically illustrated by

Callicot, that reduces nature to axiologically neutral raw material. Such a view is made possible, he argues, by the "rise of humanism and the notion that the individual human is the only authority and the only source of value and meaning" (Evernden, 157). Accordingly, nature becomes the "lowest common denominator of perception," an assumption at the heart of modern democratic society and modern science since Bacon and Leibniz.

But this nature-as-object view gives rise to a countermovement, a pendulum swing toward the popular environmentalism of nature-as-self, the view that postulates a kinship relation between humans and the larger ecosystem. Evernden mentions "deep ecology" as an example of such a view, and I would argue that Leopold, Rolston, and Marietta belong to this camp as well.[11] But, if Evernden's characterization is correct, nature-as-self is just as much a dialectical construction as was the nature-as-object view it hoped to unseat, which is perhaps why we cannot avoid recognizing the anthropomorphic and even romantic overtones of a return to holistic oneness with nature conceived as an organized and productive telic system.[12] As Kant has already shown us, natural inclinations toward one's neighbor may lead to happiness, but they are an insufficient basis for duty.

Evernden offers an illuminating alternative to this dialectic between nature-as-object and nature-as-self: the idiosyncratic experience of nature to which each of us, as an individual, is privy is itself contrary to the laws of nature with which we are indoctrinated. If nature, within the context of the dominant nature-as-object view, is homogenous and continuous—as it must be for consistent causal relationships to be established—then there can be "no pockets of resistance, no surprises" (Evernden, 160). As "heirs of Descartes . . . we all know nature to be a continuous and predictable phenomenon" (161). But this complex abstraction, stripped of all subjective qualities, bears no relation to our individual, unique experience of nature—which, as itself contrary to the "laws of nature" so conceived, can only be described as "miraculous." By overcoming Whitehead's "fallacy of misplaced concreteness," perhaps we can return to a "direct experience" of nature in which "the 'laws of nature' do not always apply" and "heterogeneity cannot be entirely exercised" (162). Despite our enormous investment in the nature-as-object perspective, Evernden holds out the possibility for an alternative "return to the things themselves": it might be, he suggests, that "nature-as-miracle, some experience that transcends the normal understanding and holds it temporarily in abeyance so that the personal awareness of the living world is restored, is a prerequisite to any real change in the awareness of individuals and therefore also to a change in the conceptions of nature in popular culture" (162–63). This idiosyncratic experience would foreswear not only the attempt to control nature, but also the desire to establish a kinship relation with it: such an experience would, instead, be brought up short with wonder before the inexplicable and unpredictable; it would take a turn from economics and politics into metaphysics.

While Evernden's alternative is illuminating, it is also problematic. First, one may well ask what guarantees that this option bypasses the hegemony of culture-nature. Evernden may be headed toward a "phenomenology of the life-world," but the criticisms of any return to an original, prediscursive lived experience of nature are well known.[13] But this is not the criticism I wish to pursue here. My question is this: even if one can access this idiosyncratic experience—the *idios kosmos* of the dreamer or the madman rather than the *koinos kosmos* of rational discourse—in what sense is such a nature thinkable or expressible? Can a "miraculous" experience be described in any language, whether mundane or transcendental? Can it be subjected to imaginative variation? And, following on this question, is the turn toward metaphysics truly the exemplary path for the grounding of an ethical imperative? Evernden's "alternative" quickly begins to look like a retreat into noumenality. Before we make up our minds on this question, however, it will be useful to consider another, similar undertaking: Schopenhaur's investigation of the "World-as-Will."

The World-as-Will and Desire

Modeled on the Kantian phenomenal world, Schopenhauer's world-as-representation is constrained by the forms of space and time and the category of causality.[14] Since representations form a closed causal system, all phenomena are subject to the "principle of sufficient reason": every appearing thing can be explained sufficiently by its causal relationships with other things. The body, for Schopenhauer, is one among many representations; but it is more than this, as our experiences reveal it to be animated by an "inner mechanism"—namely, the will. The body as it is "in itself," transcendentally, is disclosed through our corporeal experience of pain, pleasure, and especially desire. It remains the case, nonetheless, that our concepts and the forms of space and time cannot be extended to the noumenal realm; therefore, the in-itself will of the body cannot be individuated from Will as such. Since "theoretical egoism" is, on Schopenhauer's view, absurd, the conclusion follows that every phenomenal object—all mundane nature—is paralleled by a transcendental nature—namely the Will—that is beyond the human categories of causality, unity, or difference.

The transcendental world is accordingly the World-as-Will, and the human will is the highest manifestation or species of this more general form of will. The recognition of this transcendental "unity" with all things is central to Schopenhauer's philosophy: one is led to recognize, Schopenhauer writes,

> [the] same will not only in those phenomena that are quite similar to his own, in men and animals, as their innermost nature, but continued reflection will lead him to recognize the force that shoots and vegetates in the plant, indeed the force by which the crystal is formed, the force that turns the magnet to the North pole . . . all these he will recognize as different only in the phenomenon, but the same according to their inner nature. He will recognize them all as that which is immediately known to him so intimately and better than everything else, and where it appears most distinctly is called *will*. . . . It is the innermost essence, the kernel, of every particular thing and also of the whole. It appears in every blindly acting force of nature, and also in the deliberate conduct of man, and the great difference between the two concerns only the degree of the manifestation, not the inner nature of what is manifested. (WWV I, 181–2/110)

Schopenhauer recognizes that the term "will" is an unhappy necessity, since its referent is not to be understood in terms of human psychology, that is, as a matter of rational motives and explicit intentions; in fact, Schopenhauer considers using the term "force," but he finally prefers the dangers of the anthropomorphic interpretation to those a natural-scientific interpretation in terms of physical causality would introduce. Still, since will is outside the world of phenomena, it cannot be said to engage in willing for any reason or to have any *telos*; rather, it is groundless, and its groundless striving is characterized by an apparently aimless and endless struggle. The will can be compared, Schopenhauer tells us, to an "unquenchable thirst," a need or lack that stands at the origin of all worldly suffering: "The basis of all willing," he writes, "is need, lack, and hence pain, and by its very nature and origin it is thereby destined to pain" (WWV I, 458/312). Since the will operates blindly, its various manifestations are at variance with themselves, resulting in the apparent struggle between forms of life and the operations of nature. The harmony of the whole extends only to the continuation of the whole as a manifestation of will.

What deserves our attention in Schopenhauer's work is the attempt to ground a transcendental perspective in a worldly ("immanent") experience, precisely the experience of corporeal desire. What begins here as a phenomenology of desire falls short when it is transformed into a metaphysical claim about the noumenal realm; but this failure and its motivations suggest another direction that such a "phenomenology" might take. Rather than understanding Schopenhauer's method as a failure to acheive the noumenal, we can read it as a positive articulation of the motivations and directions of a phenomenology of desire—a phenomenology that, in its struggle to account for the *resistance* to desire, is forced into an analysis of what exceeds our experience while, in an inexplicable fashion, remains within it or interrupts it.

Two of the problematic moments in Schopenhauer's account can be read as clues to this alternative account of desire: first, his troubles mediating between mundane and transcendental perspectives, reflected in the problematic status of the term "will"; and second, his determination of desire as lack or need. The troubles of mediation are methodological: what is the motivation for extending our phenomenal concept of will to the noumenal realm? Even granting some sort of "direct access" to an initself corporeal "experience," the subsumption of human will under a general category of noumenal will extends the powers of reason beyond their acceptable sphere of operations. What works in Schopenhauer's favor are his compelling descriptions of will in natural phenomena: something strikes us as more-than-physical in the growth of the plant or the crystal, and yet we know without a doubt that this something is excluded in principle from causal accountability. Clearly Schopenhauer is motivated by the same insight driving Rolston's reference to "something beyond experience" and Evernden's search for the inexplicable. But the troubles of naming this unnameable cannot be underestimated; the contradictory requirements of a transcendental language in this case are perhaps not unlike those Fink unravels in Husserl's attempts to motivate the transition to transcendental consciousness from a mundane perspective.[15] Schopenhauer's account of desire operating on two different planes cannot explain the resistance of things: Is desire mundane, transcendental, or somehow a mediation between the two? What could the World-as-Will lack, and hence for what could Will be the desire?

We can reinterpret Schopenhauer's project along the lines of a phenomenological inquiry into corporeality, setting aside the Kantian framework and retaining what he has in common with those strains of contemporary phenomenology that work to unearth a stratum of experience neither reducible to nor completely accessible to consciousness. Rather than seeing the problem of mediation as a methodological defect, we might elevate it to the status of methodological pivot: the analysis of experience is precisely what allows us to feel the boundaries of what

experiential analysis can illuminate. This approach would read Schopenhauer as a precursor to Merleau-Ponty's own attempts to encounter the
philosopher's shadow—or, in Plato's words, his "shade," since what is at
stake is precisely a philosophical revalorization of the inescapability of the
corporeal.[16] On this reading, Schopenhauer oddly brings together Rolston's intuition of a striving in nature with Evernden's emphasis on discontinuity. Of course, none of this explains why we should continue to
speak of nature in terms of desire, especially if nature is the unnameable
and the unpredictable, or why such desire would be best understood in
terms of need or lack. But if we continue along Evernden's lines, we might
put the problem this way: what would a desire be like that is neither the
attraction of similars (Plato), nor of opposites (Hegel)? To evaluate the
role of the body and of desire in an "impossible" phenomenology of
nature, the meaning and method of which we have yet to determine, we
must look further for an account of desire.

An Impossible Phenomenology of Desire

Merleau-Ponty's earliest works present themselves as a direct attempt to
undercut the internal/external value dualism we saw earlier in the debate
between Callicot and Rolston. Perception, conceived as a dialogue
between a sensing body and the sensible thing, is implicitly normative in
both directions simultaneously. Merleau-Ponty explains this dialogue in a
characteristic passage:

> The sensor and the sensible do not stand in relation to each other
> as two mutually external terms. . . . [I]t cannot be held that one
> acts while the other suffers the action, or that one confers signif-
> icance on the other. . . . [A] sensible datum which is on the point
> of being felt sets up a kind of muddled problem for my body to
> solve. I must find the attitude which *will* provide it with the
> means of becoming determinate, of showing up as blue; I must
> find the reply to a question which is obscurely expressed. And
> yet I do so only when I am invited by it, my attitude is never suf-
> ficient to make me really see blue or really touch a hard surface.
> The sensible gives back to me what I lent to it, but this is only
> what I took from it in the first place.[17]

The thing calls to me, poses a question to my body, which in perceiving
accommodates this demand and in a sense makes the demand itself possible. Sensible meaning happens, then, at the conjunction of body and
world in perception. But in Merleau-Ponty's early works, this orientation

and the event of meaning are internal to the perceptual event; it is the very structure or Gestalt of the perceived which disseminates normativity. In this sense, Merleau-Ponty's *Structure of Behavior* comes very close to offering a worldly teleology of the organism not so distant from Rolston's[18]— and this is not surprising given Merleau-Ponty's reliance on such works of Gestalt psychology as Kurt Goldstein's *The Organism*.[19] But, strictly speaking, what calls to us from the thing cannot be reduced to the in-itself structure of a physical factum, as Merleau-Ponty himself brilliantly demonstrates; nor can this call itself be perceived. Although it is the dialogue with the thing that makes perception possible, that opens the horizon of the perceptual field, the call to which our body responds is itself an imperceivable. The call of the visible is itself invisible, revealed only as a kind of invisible obverse of the visible itself, the obverse that makes vision possible. This recognition on Merleau-Ponty's part only becomes thematic in his later works, where he writes less of a dialogue between sensor and sensible than of an intertwining of the "flesh" of the body with the "flesh" of the world. With the introduction of the notion of "flesh," the "call" of the visible takes on a decidedly sexual overtone. Here, conversation becomes intercourse; the intertwining of all flesh is described as a primordial "promiscuity" or "coupling," and the self-enfolding of flesh is a narcissistic invagination.[20]

It is too often overlooked that Merleau-Ponty's notion of flesh has its roots in Sartre's analysis of desire in *Being and Nothingness*. Sartre's brief comments there concerning the nature of flesh shed light on Merleau-Ponty's attempts to join flesh with desire in his later work. For Sartre, desire is a clogging of the For-Itself by its own facticity; that is, desire is subjectivity's impossible attempt to submerge itself into the plane of being. He writes that

> there is a world of desire. . . . [T]o perceive an object when I am in the desiring attitude is to caress myself with it. Thus I am sensitive not so much to the form of the object and to its instrumentality, as to its matter. . . . In my desiring perception I discover something like a *flesh* of objects. My shirt rubs against my skin and I feel it. What is ordinarily for me an object most remote becomes the immediately sensible; the warmth of air, the breath of the wind, the rays of sunshine, etc.; all are present to me in a certain way, as posited upon me without distance and revealing my flesh by means of their flesh.[21]

For Sartre, this is merely a passing comment on the way to an analysis of interpersonal desire, my attempt to seduce the other into becoming flesh by first reducing myself to a fleshy stratum. But the dialectic of desire is, of course, a failure for Sartre, since the For-Itself can never truly submerge into the In-itself; and therefore, the experience of the world's flesh is a limit experience—or, strictly speaking, an impossible experience.

Whereas Sartre denies any possible mediation between self and world, such mediation is the focus of Merleau-Ponty's later ontology; thus, his analysis of desire might be said to pick up where Sartre's ends. Already in *Phenomenology of Perception*, Merleau-Ponty had spoken of a "coition of our body with things," but in the earlier work this "coition" is a complementary union or communion of self and world (PP 370/320). The interpretation of the desirous relationship within flesh as a kind of monistic narcissism seems motivated by the same tendency—a tendency toward homogeneity and continuity; in fact, Merleau-Ponty himself often speaks of a "kinship" of the body with things.[22] But what is interesting for our present purposes is another tendency: that which finds a certain invisibility at the heart of the visible, namely the "blind spot" of phenomenology (VI 300/247).[23] My suggestion is that a phenomenology of this blind spot, the experience of what cannot, strictly speaking, be experienced, is the key to desire.

An experience of the impossible—whether we name this impossible the miraculous, the In-Itself, the blind-spot, or brute being—is, strictly speaking, an impossible experience. A phenomenology of the impossible experience is an impossible phenomenology. This is more than woolly word play: Even Merleau-Ponty had difficulty extricating himself from an interpretation of the other as a modification of the self and of the perceptual field as an horizon of the "*Ich kann.*" Phenomenology is a description of *possible* experience, an articulation of the world in terms of *possibilities*, my own or another's. But the experience of the world as flesh is not an experience of anyone's possibilities; it does not open an horizon—it is not a modality of consciousness, nor even of a perceiving corporeality. The "call" of the outside is not something perceivable, not something conceptualizable, not something experiencable. And yet just such an im-possible experience motivates Rolston, Evernden, Schopenhauer, Sartre, and Merleau-Ponty, an "experience" of the "same" exteriority that Blanchot and Levinas describe as the "murmur" and "rustling" of the *Il y a*, the "there is."[24]

The *Il y a* names that "existence without being" that resists my labor in the elements, the rustling of the night that rings in the insomniac's ears, the sound that one hears in the absence of sound. As such, the *Il y a* is, strictly speaking, imperceivable. And yet, it is not nothing, though it impinges on the margins of our awareness only as what cannot be elucidated, brought to sense, or transformed into a theme. In this sense, the *Il y a* escapes phenomenology while being indicable only on the basis of phenomenology. It is equally, as Paul Davies notes, "a contribution to ontology that ruins ontology."[25] I contend that readers of Merleau-Ponty who, like David Abram,[26] strive to reconcile his later ontology to a kinship-with-nature position fail to account for his appropriation of the phrase *Il y a*.[27] What is the role of *Il y a* in an ontology of narcissistic flesh? I suggest that the *Il y a* is the soil of the desire and resistance animating what is otherwise a monistic ontology: *Il y a* is the invisible that cannot, in principle, be brought within the sphere of the visible.

The *Il y a* is a more radical version of what Evernden called the miraculous, or what Schopenhauer called the Will. But the *Il y a*, like the Heideggerian Earth, withdraws from perception or from presence. It opens the space of perception by calling for the response of our bodies, but it remains on the hither side of that opening. A philosophy of nature, in the worldly sense, takes place within the opening that the *Il y a* discloses, as does traditional metaphysics. While it may be true that philosophy begins in wonder, precisely that same wonder Evernden expressed in the face of the miraculous, the *Il y a* remains exterior to the curious glance or the questioning thought. Even so, the *Il y a* is not an "absolute other," but is the other side of the perceivable and thinkable; it is the call that gives rise to sense. Perceiving and thinking are a response to this call, even while they are directed to the world's opened horizon. If the image of a dialogue can be retained, the dialogue with the exterior can only be a dialogue with what is outside of sense, the insensible. Desire is this contact with the exterior, an immersion into the *Il y a* that is in excess of perception or "sensible" contact. In desire, we heed the call of what cannot strictly speaking be thought or sensed. Desire is not, therefore, a need or lack to be filled, but is itself a response to the insensible. This excess insensible is the impossible that withdraws before the opening of the world.

Granted, the *Il y a* is not nature as we usually conceive of it: it is neither wilderness, nor animals and plants, nor an ecosystem striving for diversification. But that it is none of these things is precisely the point. The *Il y a* is a "wild" or "brute" being, being as it shows itself in the impossible limit experience or which withdraws from the opening of the world or of subjectivity. There is an opacity of my body as a desiring being which subjectivity cannot penetrate, just as there is an ecceity and resistance of matter which cannot in principle be comprehended or brought into the circuit of language. It is not my suggestion that we should formulate an ethical code to respond to this brute being, which is neither plausible nor necessary: the world is already open, which means that we have always already responded to the call, we are already along the way of perception and thought. But if we are seeking the fundamental basis of an ethical response, that basis cannot be worldly; it cannot be within the dialectic of culture and nature, or at the level of perception and thought. The basis for responsiveness is in the call of a more radical Outside. Nature in this radical sense is, if anything, the refusal of the hegemony of perception, language, and thought; it is the "pocket of resistance" and the unpredictable par excellence.[28]

If the call for a response proceeds from that which recedes in opening the world, then an ethics of nature cannot be developed on the basis of kinship, continuity, or homogeneity; ethics can be derived neither from a philosophy of nature nor from a metaphysics. The "value" of a nature that lies outside the dialectical system of nature-culture cannot be anything like the "intrinsic value" most environmental ethicists are seeking. This is not to deny the necessity of traditional ethical inquiry or practical activism, but simply to suggest that the attempt to ground such an ethics on a metaphysically homogenous substratum be displaced by a phenomenology of the impossible—that is, by an attentiveness to the resistance of what cannot be thought or perceived, to the opacity of a wild being that circumscribes our concepts and percepts. It is at the margins of our experience, in the desirous response of our flesh to the *Il y a*, that we are confronted with a wildness with which we can never come face to face.[29]

Notes

1. I have adopted the expressions "man-apart-from-nature" and "humans-as-a-part-of-nature" from Don E. Marietta Jr., whose use of the masculine and gender-neutral expressions is intentional. See Marietta, *For People and the Planet* (Philadelphia: Temple University Press, 1995), especially the first chapter.
2. J. Baird Callicot, "On the Intrinsic Value of Non-Human Species," in *The Preservation of Species: The Value of Biological Diversity*, ed. Bryan G. Norton (Princeton: Princeton University Press, 1986), 156.
3. Holmes Rolston, III, "Environmental Ethics: Values in and Duties to the Natural World," in *Ecology, Economics, Ethics: The Broken Circle*, ed. F. Herbert Bormann and Stephen R. Kellert (New Haven: Yale University Press, 1991), 79.
4. Rolston, "Environmental Ethics: Values in and Duties to the Natural World," 88, 90. To be precise, Rolston does not ascribe *intrinsic* value to ecosystems, since they do not have value "for themselves." Rather, he coins the new phrase "systemic value" to capture what he has in mind. See Rolston, 92.
5. Rolston takes even more direct aim at Callicot's view, concluding that "the valuing subject in an otherwise valueless world is an insufficient

premise for the experienced conclusions of those who respect all life" ("Environmental Ethics: Values in and Duties to the Natural World," 94).

6. Aldo Leopold, "The Land Ethic," in *The Sand County Almanac* (New York: Oxford University Press, 1949), 214.

7. Marietta, *For People and the Planet,* 13, 21, 28. Rolston's foreword to Marietta's book seems very agreeable to this line of thought.

8. Neil Evernden, "Nature in Industrial Society," in *Cultural Politics in Contemporary America,* ed. Ian Angus and Sut Jhally (New York: Routledge, 1989), 151–64.

9. As an example, consider Judith Butler's exemplary discussion of the cultural constitution of "natural sex" as a prediscursive and nonpolitical foundation underlying gender (*Gender Trouble* [New York: Routledge, 1990], 7).

10. This claim is made quite powerfully in Ramachandra Guha's widely anthologized essay, "Radical American Environmentalism and Wilderness Preservation: A Third World Critique," *Environmental Ethics* 11 (1989), 71–83.

11. I may be extending the notion of nature-as-self beyond the characterization offered by Evernden, but not without cause—as I hope to have established by indicating that each of these views plays on a certain notion of kinship or continuity between the human and the natural.

12. As Donald Worster reports in his interesting essay "The Ecology of Order and Chaos" (*Environmental History Review* [Spring/Summer, 1990], 1–18), scientific ecology has also developed a suspicion of the holism and teleology implied by the traditional concept of "ecosystem." Don E. Marietta Jr.'s chapter in the present volume seems intended, in part, as a response to the kinds of concerns Worster identifies.

13. For a sense of these criticisms, see Kate Soper, "Nature/'nature'" and Neil Smith, "The Production of Nature," both in *FutureNatural,* ed. by George Robertson et al. (London: Routledge, 1996), and Steven Vogel, "Nature as Origin and Difference: On Environmental Philosophy and Continental Thought," *Conflicts and Convergences,* ed. by Linda Alcoff and Merold Westphal, SPEP Supplement to *Philosophy Today* 42 (1998), 169–81.

14. Arthur Schopenhauer, *Die Welt als Wille und Vorstellung,* 2 vols. (Cologne: Könemann Verlagsgesellschaft mbH, 1997); *The World as Will and Representation,* 2 vols., trans. E. F. J. Payne (New York: Dover, 1969). Cited hereafter as WWV, with German preceding English pagination.

15. See Eugen Fink, "The Phenomenological Philosophy of Edmund Husserl and Contemporary Criticism," in *The Phenomenology of Husserl: Selected Critical Readings*, ed. R. O. Elveton (Chicago: Quadrangle, 1970), 73–147, esp. 142–44.

16. See my essay "Leaving Husserl's Cave? The Philosopher's Shadow Revisited" in *Merleau-Ponty's Reading of Husserl*, ed. Ted Toadvine and Lester Embree (Dordrecht: Kluwer Academic Publishers, 2002).

17. Maurice Merleau-Ponty, *Phénoménologie de la perception* (Paris: Gallimard, 1945), 247–48; *Phenomenology of Perception*, trans. Colin Smith (London: Routledge & Kegan Paul, 1962; rev. 1981), 214. Cited hereafter as PP, with French preceding English pagination.

18. Merleau-Ponty, *La structure du comportement* (Paris: PUF, 1942); *The Structure of Behavior*, trans. Alden Fisher (Boston: Beacon, 1963).

19. Goldstein, *Der Aufbau des Organismus* (The Hague: Martinus Nijhoff, 1934); *The Organism* (New York: Zone Books, 1995).

20. The following are only a few characteristic passages: *Le Visible et l'invisible* (Paris: Gallimard, 1964), 155, 158, 189; *The Visible and the Invisible*, trans. Alphonso Lingis (Evanston: Northwestern University Press, 1968), 115, 118, 144. [Cited hereafter as VI, with French preceding English pagination.] Rudi Visker offers an interesting analysis of these sexual motifs in his "Raw Being and Violent Discourse: Foucault, Merleau-Ponty, and the (Dis-)Order of Things," in *Merleau-Ponty in Contemporary Perspectives*, ed. Patrick Burke and Jan van der Veken (Dordrecht: Kluwer Academic Publishers, 1993), 109–29.

21. Jean-Paul Sartre, *L'Être et le néant* (Paris: Gallimard, 1943), 442; *Being and Nothingness*, trans. Hazel Barnes (New York: Philosophical Library, 1956), 392.

22. See, e.g., VI 176/133, 182/138.

23. Cf. VI 308–309/255.

24. See, for instance, Levinas's discussion of this term in his and Blanchot's usages, as well as the contrast with Heidegger's "es gibt," in *Ethics and Infinity*, trans. Richard Cohen (Pittsburgh: Duquesne University Press, 1995), 45–52. From this discussion, one might conclude that the "murmer" of the *Il y a* is an inversion of the traditional notion of the "music of the spheres."

25. Paul Davies, "A Linear Narrative? Blanchot with Heidegger in the Work of Levinas," in *Philosophers' Poets*, ed. David Wood (London: Routledge, 1990), 42.

26. David Abram, *The Spell of the Sensuous: Perception and Language in a More-Than-Human World* (New York: Vintage, 1996). See also my "Naturalizing Phenomenology," *Philosophy Today* 43, SPEP Supplement (1999): 124–31; and "The Organic and the Inside-Out: Alterity in

Abram's Eco-Phenomenology," in *Interrogating Ethics*, ed. James
Hatley and Christian Diehm (forthcoming).

27. The phrase "*Il y a*" appears throughout *The Visible and the Invisible*: see
VI 59/36, 65/41, 119-120/87, 130/95, 134/98, 171/129, 238/184,
249/196, 256/203, 206/259, 208/262, 214/267, 221/274, 292/239,
304/250, 313/260.

    Robert Bernasconi has noted that Merleau-Ponty probably bor-
rowed this phrase from Levinas or Blanchot (see "One-Way Traffic:
The Ontology of Decolonization and Its Ethics," in *Ontology and
Alterity in Merleau-Ponty*, ed. Galen Johnson and Michael Smith
[Evanston: Northwestern University Press, 1990], 73). But, to the best
of my knowledge, the significance of the phrase in Merleau-Ponty's
ontology and its relation to the use by Levinas and Blanchot has
never been explored.

28. This interpretation of *Il y a* and its promise for environmentalism is
also explored in my "In Wildness Is the Refusal of the World: Gerald
Bruns's Reading of Maurice Blanchot," presented at the 1998 meeting
of the Society for Phenomenology and Existential Philosophy
(Denver, Colo.).

29. An earlier version of this chapter was presented at the 1998 meeting
of the International Association for Environmental Philosophy
(Denver, Colo.).

CHAPTER 9

Phenomenology on (the) Rocks

IRENE J. KLAVER

"Athos, how big is the actual heart?" I once asked
him when I was still a child. He replied: "Imagine
the size and heaviness of a handful of earth."[1]

Humanity has become a major earth-shaping force—acknowledged
even by the United States Geological Survey. We radically change
our future, our past, the future of our past. "Evolution itself" almost dis-
appeared in a layer of black slick when an oiltanker, latest mammoth of
cultural selection, ran aground on the Galápagos rocks, spilling tons of
diesel fuel into the archipelago's waters. Iguanas, giant land tortoises,
miniature penguins, flightless cormorants, they all held their breath for a
week: could this be the last selection nature/culture had in store for them?
As in a Greek drama, it was up to the winds to decide—but where
Agamemnon could placate the winds by offering Iphigenia to them, there
was no king of cormorants to sacrifice his daughter on the beach. They
were well disposed to Darwin's living museum, anyway, and did not
wash the oil ashore. Of course, this was just an "incident," an "accident,"
but, given the ever-increasing volume of commodity transportation in a
global economy, the word "risk" turns increasingly into a euphemism for
inevitability. The effects of the presence of mankind are pervasive and
ubiquitous; modernity has established itself solidly as globality. With a
global culture and a global economy spanning the planet with worldwide
webs, multinationals, mass media, and mass migrations, the earth seems
to have turned into a human-dominated world. Globalization is often
viewed through the critical light of the Frankfurt School's critique of mass
culture and seen as a homogenizing force, dulling the imagination
through commodification and obliterating cultural and natural specificity,

155

effecting a general uprootedness—if not disappearance—of cultures and species. However, without underestimating the eroding force of unbridled transnational corporate rule—legitimized by WTO, IMF, World Bank, and NAFTA—it has been global Internet networking that has created a most forceful global alliance of local communities to counter the destructive policies of a global market.[2] Globalization is far from a simple phenomenon. Furthermore, anthropologists, such as Arjun Appadurai, have shown convincingly how many cultural traditions have undergone a revival through incorporating international cultural elements and how local identities have been reinterpreted in terms of cultural globalization. Appadurai speaks in this context of "vernacular globalization" and contrasts the expected scattering and demise of cultures with a "globalization of differences," a revitalization in new connections.[3] Thriving communities of hindus in Houston, sikhs in California, in short: global processes *create* as well as displace regional distinctiveness.[4]

Also in the realm of environmental awareness, globalization, I want to suggest, has not resulted solely in uprootedness, but has also brought us down to earth. Confronted with the global effects of human doings, we experience the fragility of natural constellations and hence our own vulnerability. Where, for writers such as Bill McKibben, the global effects of humanity inaugurate the "end of nature," I want to claim that in our global world, nature is more alive than ever. Undeniably there are huge problems, with potentially devastating consequences for many ecological communities, including ourselves. But no longer does the earth appear as simply a stage for history. On the contrary, nature is increasingly experienced as an intrinsic constitutive part of our lives. It has acquired relevance, and the earth has turned into a field of significance. For the first time in history, nature is entering the political domain as a serious presence instead of a taken-for-granted background. The Greeks made a distinction between "simple natural life," common to all living beings, *zoê*, and a "qualified life," a "particular way of life," proper to an individual or a group, *bios*. The first realm was for the home. Only the second one was at play in the political realm of the *polis*. Giorgio Agamben calls the "entry of *zoê* in the sphere of the *polis*—the politicization of bare life as such—the decisive event of modernity."[5]

Indeed, more than ever nature is contested terrain. At the same time, as William Cronon emphasizes, "This silent rock, this nature about which we argue so much, is also among the most important things we have in common. . . . It is, paradoxically, the uncommon ground we cannot help but share."[6] Sharing this uncommon ground means realizing that nature is intertwined with culture. Just as the new vernacular global cultures subvert the very definitions of what it is to be local and global, the definitions of the cultural and the natural are also subverted. The realism versus constructivism debate has turned obsolete. There is no nature "out there" as radical other—either to be reduced to utilitarian value or to be revered because of its intrinsic value.[7] Neither is nature a sheer social construction, a blank slate, waiting for us to give it meaning and value. This chapter is about the coconstitution of nature and culture, the circulating reference between them, as Latour calls it.[8]

Michel Serres links this awareness of intertwinement between nature and culture to globalization: "What was once local—this river, that swamp—is now global: Planet Earth. . . . At stake is the Earth in its totality, and humanity, collectively. . . . Global history enters nature; global nature enters history: this is something utterly new in philosophy."[9]

As Appadurai does for cultural phenomena, I would want to bring natural phenomena into the dynamic relation of "vernacular globalization." Serres's local river that has turned global should be seen, experienced, and treated locally at the same time. This is an especially fruitful way to analyze restoration projects. One has to address them at multiple scales.

Furthermore, what Serres called "something utterly new" was in fact already intimated by Husserl in his 1934 essay "Origin of the Spatiality of Nature," in which he posited the intrinsic relation between world possibility and earth basis. Merleau-Ponty developed this intertwinement further. Like Serres, he brings time and space, history and geography together: "In fact it is a question of grasping the *nexus*—neither 'historical' nor 'geographic'—of history and transcendental geology, . . . which I will have rediscovered by my analysis of the visible and the flesh, the simultaneous *Urstiftung* of time and space which makes there be a historical landscape and a quasi-geographical inscription of history." And he ends with staking out the "fundamental problem: the sedimentation and reactivation."[10]

It is precisely this dynamic between reactivating the sedimented and the sedimentation of activity that I see as the guiding thread for contemporary phenomenology interested in the natural world. The reappearance of the material realm as *indépassable* or "un-get-around-able" (after a period of—at least philosophically speaking—deconstruction of "presence") is not a returning of a "simple presence," but of a presence that finds itself located in different dynamic relations. Such are the relations between nature and culture, and those between the sedimented and the reactivated. Discourses about material and natural phenomena are often seen and practiced as a search for foundation or stability in times of change. I will show that a "return" to material constellations—even in the shape of the supposedly most stable element or realm, namely, stone—

cannot be understood as a simple foundational counterweight to a relativity born of a decentered subject. Neither can it serve as a grounding in a time of movement, as a stability in fluctuation. Rather, it should be seen in the dynamics of *both* these terms, that is, in the very interaction between sedimentation *and* reactivation.

This renewed focus puts phenomenology in its traditional form on the rocks: a philosophy of primordial constitution based on intentionality of the subject gives way to a thinking in terms of *co*-constitution and a so-called operative intentionality. Both were already intimated in Husserl's later works when he opened the door to intersubjectivity and spatiality. Both were explicitly explored by Merleau-Ponty in his thinking of flesh. And both come to full play in contemporary Continental thought insofar as it takes matter seriously.

I will concretize the intricate relation between nature and culture, and specifically the contribution of contemporary Continental thought to this theme, through what seems the most indifferent and impervious to us, the world of stones. Even that which seems the most stable is never simply given but is always culturally articulated, often in most paradoxical ways, revealing that, in a variety of practices, the earth enters our worlds.

On the Rocks

Last summer we hiked Montana's mountains, set camp at the glacial lake of Many Winds. The next day was perfectly still, and we walked to a big granite rock outcrop that overlooked the water—calm basin protected at three sides by steep rocky slopes. We sat down and talked, as we have done for the last years, about "Philosophy on the Rocks." The title of this chapter is taken from these discussions, in these kinds of places. As always, our words wander peaks and crevasses. The more the others lean toward grace and the sacred, the more I hear myself defending the clumsy and the everyday. But however different our views might be, we keep finding each other in feeling the wind touching our skin, the gradient of the mountain hastening our heartbeat.[11] Our voices calm down and we doze off, comforted by the warmth held by the granite. Suddenly at the westside slope an immense boulder crashes through the silence and rolls downhill, its echo bursting through the valley, stirring the placid water. We are stunned. There was no wind, no goats. Astoundingly, a big stone was on the move by itself, inserting itself in our discourse, leaving us silent, awestricken. Our guest, Dexter, wrote a poem about it. I wrote this chapter, which was already in the making. And then there is our larger project of "Ethics on the Rocks." But we all know that no one will ever be able to convey the roaring of this rock on that quiet summer day. The other's presence was suddenly present but remained utterly other.

By rolling downhill the stone rocks our world. It inserts itself into our dialogue, "speaks up," audibly. But all this is only possible because it *was already* part of our world, albeit latently so. We—and now I include *it*, as well—participated in the same space/place. At the moment it rolls down, our little club of philosophers becomes part of its world. We sense its being-in-the-world. At that moment the place has become *consciously* shared with . . . a rock.

Stones Surfacing

When famed Jesse James was finally killed, his body was buried in the backyard of the Missouri family homestead. The place soon became a site of pilgrimage, and people started to take stones from the gravesite home with them. His mother, Zerelda James, who had always denied that her boys, Jesse and Frank, were train robbers, and who had paid a high price for them—she lost her youngest child and her left hand during a police raid on her home—turned loss into business. Noticing people took stones from the grave, she sold the rocks to the visitors. Soon all the stones were gone, and she wheeled in more from elsewhere and dumped them on the grave, which transformed them into . . . , yes, into what? Into commodities, memorabilia, symbols, sacred objects, things to hold on to? All of the above. And more than that? Stones, handfuls of sedimentized earth, petrified hearts, leaving circles in the water when they sink to the bottom of the lake.

During the past fifteen years, earth and stones have surfaced in a variety of discourses. In humanities disciplines, many works have appeared with references to stones and earth in their titles: *The Writing of Stones, Back to Earth, Stone, Earth Matters, Flesh and Stone,* and *The Song of the Earth,* to name only a few. Similarly, literary works include *Teaching a Stone to Talk, The Stones Cry Out,* and *The Gift of Stones.* If we see these wide-ranging works as part of themes such as place, landscape, and nature, we could clearly speak of an explosion of new interest in a basic material realm.

How to understand this phenomenon? Enterprising and inventive as Zerelda James might be, her act only works because there is already a world in place, spun around her son, in which it has significance: the world of the mystique of the outlaw, the one who operates at the other side of the law, in the shadow of civilization. Zerelda furthers this world, as the stones keep the presence of her absent son alive. In various ways, the stones have touched his existence—they were part of the place he grew up, they rested on his grave—and now they put people in touch with their hero-outlaw. The stones have acquired a significance through a vicarious reference to Jesse James. As funerary objects they carry a promise of a permanent reference, replacing the absence of the dead with the presence of a seemingly lasting and meaningful memorial object.

Similarly, the fact that stones-the earth-nature enter into intellectual or cultural discourse has to do with the fact that there is a "world in place." And the writing furthers this world. What is this world? What field of significance is in play? Doubtlessly, there is still an element of fascination with the "outlaw" at work. That is, a romantization of nature as the other, the wild, the shadow of civilization. But there is also a growing awareness of the natural world as an intrinsic and constitutive part of the human world. Paradoxically, but not surprisingly, this is related to the experience of the fragility of the natural background. And, in and through that fragility, the stage itself becomes an actor in the play—revealing that in fact it had been an active participant all along, but never recognized as such. That is, it was usually taken for granted.

Philosophical discourse should take "account of its own presentness" in order, as Foucault argues, "to find its own place, to pronounce its own meaning." By determining "a certain element of the present" that elucidates "what this present is," one can come to a so-called ontology of the present.[12]

We see in Foucault's "ontology of the present" the same paradox that Arjun Appadurai captured in his notion of "vernacular globalization." Where "ontology" refers to "suprahistorical structures of being," the "present" refers to the particular event of a "here and now." By juxtaposing the two concepts into one term, Foucault draws the incompatibility of an ontology of the present into an oxymoronic tool that brings both concepts into play when it comes to understanding a phenomenon. Jean-Luc Nancy makes a similar move in describing the world as "the infinite resolution of the finite," as does Judith Butler when she speaks of an "ongoing cultural articulation of universality."[13] All try to grasp how these opposite movements arise in one and the same move, continuously shaping and readjusting each other's borders in a constitutive tension. Merleau-Ponty called these movements "sedimentation and reactivation" and determined their relation as the most "fundamental problem."[14] Navigating Scylla and Charybdis, an ontology of the present always brings its ontology into reactivation, its present into sedimentation, both in one and the same movement and moment.

A persistent theme such as the interest in natural/bodily/material phenomena readily qualifies for such an "element of the present." What ontology will appear in and through this theme? I want to argue for an ontology of im/permanence, incompatibility, and boundary.

Im/permanence

Stone endures, bears weight, withstands the elements. Egyptians, Hebrews, the Mesopotamians, early Native Americans, they all entrusted markings, signs, messages, pictures to the rocks: petroglyphs, hieroglyphs, holy cuttings, cuttings in stone. The specific materiality of stones invites certain cultural articulations and predisposes certain practices. With an endurance and a temporality overarching our own, they are witnesses of times beyond us, long ago, far in the future, witnessing what happened and what is to come. They are messengers of other times, themselves painted and carved with messages, traces of other civilizations, cultures long gone.

On the same stones that throats were cut, kings were coronated. Stones are memorial reminders of the past; they are silent witnesses. They witness as well the law of God/Yahweh as the law of Nature. Sentinel stones watch over what happens. Some are sacrificial stones, stones on which to slit throats of goats, lambs, or Joseph K.—who in Kafka's *The Trial* is accused, judged, and condemned, in an unintelligible judicial practice. Heads are put on a stone—at ground level, ground zero—and the red-brown iron in the victim's blood leaves the stones stained. In 1996, after 740 years, the mythical stone on which Scottish kings were coronated was returned from England to Scotland. In a solemn ceremony, the stone crossed the river in a black car, flanked by slow-walking men, as in a funeral. This did not occur because of geological evidence that Scotland was once part of North America instead of England, but because of developments in the unification of the European Community that resulted in larger autonomy of regions vis-à-vis the nation state. Even that which was once thought to be stable moves. Tectonic plates are moving, inch by inch. But that the crisis in the Middle East will eventually dissolve by the African plate crunching into the Eurasian one does not resolve the Middle East conflicts of this moment nor absolve us from dealing with them.

Incompatibility: This Rock, Called Peter

In a phenomenology of rocks, the rock itself appears a paradox. Stones often articulate liminal experiences, borders, moments of transition. Their stability and weight makes them serve equally well as symbols of foundation and instruments of torture.

Christ already knew. He called the one who would betray him three times, Peter, from *petrus*, Latin for rock. Peter, the Rock on which he would found his Church.[15] Any act of naming is formative as well as performative: it sets a boundary and effectuates a norm. The act of founding on a rock invokes permanence and projects stability. The betrayal is what Spivak calls an "enabling violation." It allows for disobedience, disruption, a rearticulation of the law of the father. A "defence of the authentic," outside the betrayal, is as Žižek indicates "the most perfidious mode of its betrayal: *there is no Christ outside Saint Paul*; in exactly the same way, there is no 'authentic Marx' that can be approached directly, bypassing Lenin."[16]

The town Lone Rock was named for a massive piece of sandstone in the Wisconsin River that had been a landmark for early river raftsmen known as "The Lone Rock." The people used and cut the rock for the foundations of their homes. When all the foundations were laid the rock was gone.[17] This is a symbolic example of the versatility between what is foundational and that which is supported undermining itself.

Boundaries

Especially in moments or places of change, stones are invoked, placed as markers of transition. In different historical and cultural moments, stones are "turned," taken up differently. In the very turning, sense arises, happens, shows itself, materializes. Gravestones are tributes as well to the ones who are gone as to the ones who stayed and those who will come. What stones *are* depends on how they surface and are inscribed in a certain culture, history. And how they surface in a certain discourse depends on how they are. The question is where do we enter this circularity. That is a matter of where a certain sedimentation is reactivated.

Stones are common boundary objects. A boundary stone does not limit one property against another, but marks a transition. Boundaries are places where different entities, different modes of being, different ontological domains, meet, interact with each other, give and take from each other—places of heterogeneity and diversity that call for negotiation, or translation. Translation is facilitated by so-called boundary objects.[18] These have different meanings in different social worlds, but are robust enough to maintain a common identity across sites. As vehicles of translation they are crucial for developing and maintaining coherence across and within worlds, maximizing both the autonomy of and the communication between heterogeneous worlds. To carry a stone home from Jesse James's grave or from the Petrified National Forest is to hold on to a conversation with another world. It is a reference to the absent other. In their very presence, rocks symbolize the presence of the absent. The absence is signified by the presence of the stones, they refer to something gone. Wheeled into Jesse James's gravesite, these most simple pebbles turned into a world.

As boundary objects, stones have a long tradition in marking transitions, often symbolizing passages to other realms. They are places of coming and going. In the case of the gravesites, the stones symbolize, in their apparent stability, the boundary between life and death. With their larger-than-life solidity and permanency, they are invested with an intention to give immortality to the dead.

Boundaries are not places where things stop, but where they begin. They do not preexist, but materialize in certain practices. They are generative. As Donna Haraway simply puts it: "Objects are boundary projects."[19] These material invitations into liminal experiences incite a rethinking of the relation between meaning and matter. How are they intertwined? In which ways do they translate into each other? Meaning matters, not necessarily in the sense that it is important—that depends, that judgment is still hanging (*pendere*)—but meaning always *matters*, because it participates in materiality. Similarly, materiality insofar as it is experienced is experienced as meaning. As Jean-Luc Nancy says concisely: "The world is the infinite resolution of sense into fact and fact into sense." Or, as he states elsewhere, the world "is structured as *sense*, and reciprocally, *sense* is structured as *world*." That is, "the sense of the world" is a tautological expression.[20] To say "the world is sense" instead of the "the world has sense" is a major shift in philosophy, if not philosophy's end in its traditional sense of preposturing or proposing a world of sense. There is no separate world of sense through which we interpret the world. The end of such a world of sense opens, as Nancy says, "the praxis of the sense of the world." What does such a praxis look like? How, for example, do stones "work" in culture? How does culture work in and with and through them?

Stones are always culturally articulated. Because of larger forces that operate in any given culture—or circumstance, or event—certain things are done with/to stones. They are the passive activity of matter. Or there is an activity of matter that operates through us, through cultural manifestation. Exchanges take place on the borders where they touch. But only where and when they touch do they materialize into borders, in the very exchange of their touch. The border does not exist before the touch, similarly the touch does not exist without the border. The border is doubled

by being approached from two sides, and, at the same time, it is constituted as one. The border between the abstract and the concrete, between
the particular and the universal, is the location where the abstract *is* the
concrete, the concrete *is* the abstract, the particular *is* the universal, and
the universal *is* concrete. All these relations, that are in fact always movements, occur at the border. Reactivation turns into sedimentation and sedimentation into reactivation. At the border, coconstitution and operative
intentionality take place.

Ultimately the ontology we looked for earlier is an ontology of the
being-with, in Nancy's sense, that is, a being in common instead of a
common being. Being-with as a being-in-common means that different
forces are operating on each other in an unpredicted way.

Operative/Operant Intentionality

At the end of "Origin of the Spatiality of Nature," Husserl emphasizes
that human history is not accidentally situated on the earth, but that the
earth, as "primitive home-place" or as "ark of the world," precedes every
"world possibility." Human and all other life gains its constitutive force
from the earth, which is "coconstitutive of its own being."[21]

This coconstitution is a furthering of Husserl's thoughts on different
modes of constitution that he started to develop in *Ideen II*, where he
explicitly acknowledges a mode of "pretheoretical constitution" (*vortheo-
retischen Konstituierung*) of the "pregivens" (*Vorgegebenheiten*).[22] These
samples of "preconstitution," together with other moments in Husserl's
work, such as coconstitution in the articles on spatiality, show that constitution can no longer simply be relegated to consciousness grasping content as an exemplification of an essence. For Merleau-Ponty these
moments reveal that Husserl is equally attracted by the "haecceity of
Nature as by the vortex of absolute consciousness." Husserl, however,
never systematically developed any theses about this relationship. This is
the "unthought-of" in Husserl that Merleau-Ponty himself takes up. As he
states, it is "into this interval that we must try to advance," because there
is "undeniably something between the transcendent Nature, naturalism's
being in itself, and the immanence of mind, its acts and its noema."[23] And
he further specifies his own task as developing "the *fungierende or latent*
intentionality which is the intentionality within being."

Merleau-Ponty is well aware that his move is "not compatible with
'phenomenology,' that is, with an ontology that obliges whatever is not
nothing, to *present* itself to the *consciousness*."[24] Precisely this kind of "old"
Husserlian phenomenology is put on the rocks; namely, the phenomenol-

ogy that in reaction to the causal determinism of naturalism took consciousness as its primary focus. For Merleau-Ponty, however, intentionality is no longer the mind's grasping the essence. Nor is it a causal force of nature that works in us but without us. Rather, "to 'understand' is to take in the total intention . . . the unique mode of existing expressed in the properties of the pebble, the glass or the piece of wax, in all the events of a revolution, in all the thoughts of a philosopher."[25] This "total intention" or operative intentionality is intrinsically related to the fact that "constitution becomes increasingly, as Husserl's thought matures, the means of unveiling the back side of things that we have not constituted."[26] The "transcendental field has ceased to be simply the field of our thought and has become the field of the whole of experience, and . . . Husserl trusts the truth which we are *in* from birth and which ought to be able to contain both the truths of consciousness and the truths of Nature."[27] "It is a question of recognizing consciousness itself as a project of the world, meant for a world which it neither embraces nor possesses, but toward which (*vers lequel*) it is perpetually directed."[28]

Once I picked up a quite inconspicuous brown-yellowish stone in the Pryor Mountains of Montana. It looked like a big pebble and only caught my attention because of its perfect smoothness. It looked like silk. Later I learned the different fields of significance. It was a gastrolite—a stone from the stomach of the dinosaur. Like chickens, dinosaurs grind their food in their stomachs—the same idea, only with bigger stones. Some prehistoric indians had made a tool of it—laying smooth in the hand. And now it lies on my desk, holding my books open. For all three parties involved—and doubtlessly many more—the stone was encountered and taken up in a world. The same "properties of the pebble" that Merleau-Ponty talked about, elicited, in the togetherness with different beings, different constitutive effects, different operant intentionalities. Swallowed by a dinosaur, it ground up food in a stomach; picked up by an early hominid, it turned into a hammer; and found by me, it is an object of wonder lying on a desk.

Taken for Granite

"We took her for granite," a student wrote about his mother. This brilliant mistake renders the intended meaning more poignantly than the correct spelling would. The hard/rock/granite quality resonates what it means to be underestimated, not valued, taken for granted: it touches the core of one's being, the bedrock of one's existence. Furthermore, "taking someone for granite" implies that she is supposedly capable of enduring anything, without feeling or orientation herself, that is, hard as granite. Only her absence reveals how much she was present. Before that, she was "just there," as any good foundation is. As we saw at the beginning, earth itself has a long history of being a world not taken seriously into account: granite taken for granted. That is, until invisible veins turn into hairlines. First cracks crawl through the stone. Then a huge slab thunders down the mountain. This does not just happen. For a long time forces have been operating: processes of weathering—freeze and thaw. Culminating in this undecidable moment in time when "wood becomes stone, peat becomes coal, limestone becomes marble. The gradual instant."[29]

Granite was Goethe's favorite, because you could find it at the highest mountain top and in the deepest layers of the earth. He calls it *Ur-Gestein*; "primal stone," the prefix *Ur* denoting primal, original, the very first—a little word reaching for the ultimate origin of things. In his *Theory of Colours*, he qualifies a similar polarity, but now between light and darkness, as *Urphänomen*.[30]

In Weimar, the wall of Goethe's small sober bedroom is decorated with only two posters. One displays the different geological time periods as conceived by the English geologist Lyell. Next to it is a poster about *Ton-Lehre*, a study about scales of sounds. That is all. Stones and sounds. Elemental presences. Next to the bedroom is the library with a considerable stone collection of some 18,000 pieces. Goethe made some little-known but substantial contributions to the natural sciences, for which he was honored by having a mineral named after him: Goethite. Despite this illustrious reference, goethite is a most unassuming mineral, just an amorphous, earthy lump. However, as the most stable iron compound on earth, it is one of the most ubiquitous mineral species, and therefore an important ore. Most iron-rich minerals will alter to goethite over time. Since rust consists mainly of goethite, weapons and tools used to end up as goethite.[31]

The earthy form of goethite is ochre, colorful red and orange, used since early prehistory to decorate bodies and cave walls. Neanderthals covered their dead with ochre. So did the Clovis Paleo Indian people. Their leaf-shaped flint spearpoints, bone tools, all are colored ochre. And so were their bodies, as testify red earth silhouettes around the bones of the dead. Flesh and skin gone—its red coloring seeped into the earth, long ago—all that is left is a red silhouette. Early humans made extensive use of the color red. They made the earth worldly through the color of blood and hot burning fire.

Some eight miles north in the woods of Weimar lies Buchenwald—its lush forests a favorite spot for the cultural elite of Goethe's time to spend a leisurely Sunday. In this tradition, only the best of the SS were stationed close to Weimar. Buchenwald, with its exploitable clay and limestone deposits, was a perfect building site. Prisoners cleared the forest and built roads and a concentration camp. One tree was ordered to be left standing, an old oak, a tree with symbolic value for the Nazis. This particular one was even more special; it was "Goethe's Oak," as he used to sit under it.[32] The limestone quarry next to the camp was the most brutal work place. The limestone was processed in deliberately primitive ways, quarried and crushed bare-handed. After all, according to Heinrich Himmler, the commander-in-chief of the SS, Jewish people were *Urstoff alles Negatives* ("primary matter of everything negative").[33]

Now the place is empty, stratified with heaps of black stones, tributes of memory. Some are stretched out in long patterns, memorializing the presence of barracks. Others are heaped together. Black boulders are silent witnesses of crushed shoulders.

> I couldn't turn my anguish from the precise moment of death. I was focused on that historical split second: the tableau of the haunting trinity—perpetrator, victim, witness. But at what moment does wood become stone, peat become coal, limestone become marble? The gradual instant.[34]

> *Stones, rocks—all of the above and more than that.*

Notes

I want to thank Tammy Clewell for her extensive comments on an earlier version of this paper and J. Baird Callicott for his meticulous editing of most of the text—any oddity left is my responsibility.

1. Anne Michaels, *Fugitive Pieces* (Toronto: McClelland & Stewart, 1996), 113.
2. NAFTA and similar trade agreements have already been used succesfully to overrride national environmental health laws. See David Wood, "The International Campaign against the Multilateral Agreement on Investment: A Test Case for the Future of Globalisation," *Ethics, Place and Environment* 3, no. 1 (March 2000): 25–45, specifically 29.
3. Arjun Appadurai, *Modernity at Large: Cultural Dimensions of Globalization* (Minneapolis: University of Minnesota Press, 1996), 7, 10–11.

4. John Agnew made this point already in the eighties in *The United States in the World-Economy: A Regional Geography* (Cambridge: Cambridge University Press, 1987); see specifically p. 94.
5. Giorgio Agamben, *Homo Sacer: Souvereign Power and Bare Life*, trans. Daniel Heller-Roazen (Stanford: Stanford University Press, 1998), 1–4.
6. William Cronon, "Introduction: In Search of Nature," in *Uncommon Ground: Toward Reinventing Nature*, ed. William Cronon (New York: Norton, 1995), 56.
7. See also J. Baird Callicott, "La nature est mort, vive la nature," trans. Marc Saint-Upéry, *Écologie Politique* (Summer 1993): 73–90.
8. Bruno Latour, "Circulating Reference," in Latour, *Pandora's Hope: Essays on the Reality of Science Studies* (Cambridge: Harvard University Press, 1999), 24.
9. Michel Serres, *The Natural Contract*, trans. Elizabeth MacArthur and William Paulson (Ann Harbor: University of Michigan Press, 1995), 4.
10. Maurice Merleau-Ponty, *The Visible and the Invisible*, trans. Alphonso Lingis (Evanston: Northwestern University Press, 1968), 258–59.
11. Thanks to my mountain partners Tom Birch, Jim Cheney, and Anthony Weston.
12. Michel Foucault, "Kant on Enlightenment and Revolution," trans. Colin Gordon, in *Foucault's New Domains*, ed. Mike Gane and Terry Johnson (London: Routledge, 1993), 12–18.
13. Jean-Luc Nancy, *The Sense of the World*, trans. Jeffrey Librett (Minneapolis: University of Minnesota Press, 1997), 5, 152–55; Judith Butler, "Universality in Culture," in *For Love of Country: Debating the Limits of Patriotism*, ed. Joshua Cohen (Boston: Beacon, 1996), 51.
14. Maurice Merleau-Ponty, *The Visible and the Invisible*, 259.
15. Matthew 16:18.
16. Slavoj Žižek, *The Fragile Absolute* (London/New York: Verso, 2000), 2.
17. Text from the sign at Brace Park. I owe this reference to Anthony Weston.
18. Susan Leigh Star and J. R. Griesemeier develop this term in "Institutional Ecology, 'Translations' and Boundary Objects: Amateurs and Professionals in Berkeley's Museum of Vertebrate Zoology, 1907–39," *Social Studies of Science* 19 (1989): 387–420.
19. Donna Haraway, "Situated Knowledges," in Haraway, *Simians, Cyborgs, and Women: The Reinvention of Nature* (New York: Routledge, 1991), 201.
20. Jean-Luc Nancy, *The Sense of the World*, 155, 8–9.
21. Edmund Husserl, "Foundational Investigations of the Phenomenological Origin of the Spatiality of Nature," trans. F. Kersten, in

Husserl: Shorter Works, ed. P. McCormick and F. Elliston (Notre Dame: University of Notre Dame Press, 1981), 228–31.

22. Husserl, "Foundational Investigations of the Phenomenological Origin of the Spatiality of Nature," 228; Husserl, *Ideen zu einer reinen Phänomenologie und phänomenologischen Philosophie. Zweites Buch*, Husserliana, vol. 4, ed. M. Biemel (The Hague: Martinus Nijhoff, 1952), 5; *Ideas Pertaining to a Pure Phenomenology and to a Phenomenological Philosophy. Second Book.*, trans. R. Rojcewicz and A. Schuwer (Dordrecht: Kluwer Academic Publishers, 1989), 7.

23. Merleau-Ponty, "The Philosopher and His Shadow," in *Signs*, trans. R. McCleary (Evanston: Northwestern University Press, 1964), 166.

24. Merleau-Ponty, *The Visible and the Invisible*, 244.

25. Merleau-Ponty, *Phénoménologie de la perception* (Paris: Gallimard, 1945), xiii; *Phenomenology of Perception*, trans. Colin Smith (London: Routledge and Kegan Paul, 1962), xvii–xviii.

26. Merleau-Ponty, "The Philosopher and His Shadow," 180–81.

27. Merleau-Ponty, "The Philosopher and His Shadow," 177.

28. Merleau-Ponty, *Phénoménologie de la perception*, xiii; *Phenomenology of Perception*, xvii.

29. Anne Michaels, *Fugitive Pieces*, 140.

30. Erich Heller, *The Disinherited Mind: Essays in Modern German Literature and Thought* (London: Bowes & Bowes, 1952), 23.

31. See "Goethite," in Martin Holden, *The Encyclopedia of Gemstones and Minerals* (Michael Friedman, 1999), 121.

32. With Baroness von Stein; see Joseph Roth's last poem (1939): "Goethe's Oak in Buchenwald," in Sabine and Harry Stein, *Buchenwald: A Tour of the Memorial Site* (Buchenwald Memorial, 1993), 33.

33. Daniel Goldhagen, *Hitler's Willing Executioners* (New York: Knopf, 1996), 412.

34. Anne Michaels, *Fugitive Pieces*, 140.

CHAPTER 10

Natural Disasters

CHRISTIAN DIEHM

When Plato looked at the night sky he saw two distinct sorts of things. One he called the "divine class" of created beings, the fixed stars which moved in their orderly procession across the heavens, movers whose motion was never errant and whose courses never strayed.[1] The other he dubbed "the wanderers."[2] Against the background of the heavenly order of divine lights there appeared those luminaries whose movements seemed to work counter to such orderliness, stars whose progress was somehow regressive, "retrograde," celestial bodies that were ill at ease, stars that were noticeably unstarlike, *asters* that were dis-asters. Like Plato, Emmanuel Levinas is no stranger to disasters. For him the disaster is written on the face of the other; it is the wandering destitution of the other who is exposed to violence, prone to being pushed off course or sent backwards into retrograde movement; it is the mortality of the other that expresses the "Thou shalt not kill" of ethics and calls me to responsibility. But who speaks this first commandment? Levinas clearly thinks that such disastrousness is present in the human face, but can it be found on faces other-than-human? Is it visible on the "face of the earth"? Is it written in the stars?

If this were nothing more than a question of *destruction*, the answer would be simple enough. More than half of the earth's forests are gone, and they continue to be leveled at the rate of sixteen million hectares per year, accompanied by an anthropogenic extinction rate nearing one thousand times the natural or "background" rate.[3] The domestic picture is no brighter, as countless billions of "live stock" are marched through slaughterhouses each year to meet the changing dietary demands of increasingly affluent human populations.[4] Insofar as these activities directly involve other-than-human beings, we can certainly say that they destroy

171

"nature," but would Levinas call such destruction *disastrous*? If for him "the disaster" is fundamentally an *ethical* category, can disasters *ever* be "natural"?

Much of Levinas's writing appears to answer these last questions in the negative; it is a self-proclaimed humanism, sometimes silent about, and at other times apparently quite hostile to, the possibility that anything other-than-human could be called "the other."[5] Such resistance forces one to wonder what Levinas's thought could possibly contribute to an environmentalism seeking to respond to current environmental crises by saying something more than the platitude that nature is a valuable resource. But is a Levinasian contribution entirely out of the question?

If there is a bright spot in Levinas's work for such environmentalism, it lies in the fact that Levinas has a healthy philosophical uncertainty about all of this, occasionally hesitating before answering the question of who the other is. When asked about the faces of animals, for example, he admits that he is unsure how to respond, going back and forth about the faces of dogs, and saying of snakes that "I don't know if a snake has a face. I can't answer that question."[6] One could, of course, take the absence of a definitive answer here as an indication that these others have failed to impress themselves upon Levinas, but it may be more fruitful to ask why it is that he does not immediately reply in the negative. Why, that is, do such others give him pause? And why, despite proclamations of the priority of the human face and of ignorance regarding the faces of animals, does he nevertheless feel that there is something "disquieting" about the death of *any* living being, claiming that such annihilation is fundamentally different from "the destruction of a form or a mechanism"?[7]

The Nudity of the Flesh

It is my suspicion that Levinas waivers on the question of others who are other-than-human because he remembers well his own philosophical principles. He is quite aware that it is his own work that cautions against reducing alterity to simple difference, against reducing *the* face to *a* face, to something thematic or comprehended. The face is not the color of eyes or skin, and alterity does not consist in the relative differences between hair styles, bone structures, the wrinkles in foreheads or the snubness of noses. As Levinas puts it, "[t]he other must be received independently of his qualities, if he is to be received as other. If it weren't for this . . . then the rest of my analyses would lose all their force. The relationship would be one of those thematizable relations that are established between objects."[8]

If we take a moment to think about this idea—an idea absolutely fundamental to Levinas's work—it should strike us that its logic is one of inclusion rather than exclusion, and that it should not immediately exclude other-than-human others. If there are no specific differences that make an other an *alter*, if the other is not *autrui* because of the qualitative differences between our faces, then how is it possible to say that *any* specific differences form the basis for an exclusion of the other's face? I am not using the phrase "specific differences" here in an arbitrary way, either, for it is precisely the differences between humans and other species that I have in mind when asking this question. If the face of the African is no less "face" than the face of the European or the Latino (and others); if the face of the woman is no less face than the face of the man or the hermaphrodite (and others); if the face of the child is no less face than that of the adult or elder (and others); if all these faces with all their nearly infinite differences are not in any way limited by these differences in their power to face me, then how on earth do the differences between these faces and the faces of others whose differences mark them as nonhuman drown out the call that emanates from their faces? What does biological "nonhumanity" have to do with one's status as *other-than*-human?

Levinas of course expresses the thought that the alterity of the face should not be reduced to qualitative differentiation by describing the face as "nude," where nudity means transcendence and the escape of the other from assimilation into my horizons of understanding.[9] But it seems to me that there is another sense of nudity at work in the texts of Levinas, a nudity that is in a sense less abstract, a nudity that is a mortality "in person," "in the flesh." This sense of nakedness is not only the nakedness of the face without cultural adornment, but is that nudity of the other that "shows in the cracks of the mask of the personage, or in his wrinkled skin."[10] Nudity in this sense refers to the exposure to wounds in the flesh, an "extreme exposure . . . as to a shot at 'point blank' range."[11]

Point blank. Like someone with a gun to the head, or a knife to the throat. Like someone who gets shot down in cold blood, from behind, from the side, from above or below. Like a body torn through by a bullet, sliced open. Nudity here means exposure to the most immediate violence, the violence that afflicts the flesh of the body, like the bullet that is aimed at a corporeal weak spot, an Achilles' heel that is not just a face but a possibility of corporeality itself—a body that is always at point-blank range.

We are proposing, therefore, that the nudity of the *visage* is the nudity of the body frail and indigent, a face whose skin is exposed to the cold, wrinkled with age, or gnawed through by disease. And although Levinas does not often stress this point, he makes note of it with more frequency than one might expect. One particularly poignant example is found in the interview entitled "The Other, Utopia, and Justice," where Levinas is asked if all human others are to be considered "face," or if there are some faces that do not make their claim upon me: "But is every man that 'other' man? Is there not sometimes a desertion of meaning, faces of brutes?" Levinas is sure to emphasize in his reply that for him "the word *face* must not be understood in a narrow way." He then proceeds to discuss how Vassily Grossman, in *Life and Fate*, describes people waiting in line to send letters and packages to loved ones arrested for political crimes, and how each person is able to read "on the nape of the person in front of him the feelings of hope and misery." His interlocutor then interjects, saying "[a]nd the nape is a face . . . ," at which point Levinas remarks that "Grossman isn't saying that the nape is a face, but that all the weakness, all the mortality, all the naked and disarmed mortality of the other can be read from it. He doesn't say it that way, but the face can assume meaning on what is opposite of the face!"[12]

Thus although the phenomenal face may be a privileged location for encountering the other's mortal cry for aid, the face is by no means restricted to the area of the body above the neck and beneath the hairline. The eyes may very well be, as Levinas says, "the most naked part of the human body,"[13] but they are, nevertheless, naked with that corporeal nudity of which they are nothing more than a focal point.

Convulsions

What, then, is this power that the naked body has to "face" me? If the nudity of the other is the destitution of the body exposed, the gravity of the body that has fallen from the heavens, then what we are describing under the heading of "face" is the possibility of a distinct sort of reduction, the disastrous reduction of health to sickness, of heroic strength to mortal weakness: the possibility that the corporeal star that today is shining will tomorrow (or maybe just a little later today) have its lights snuffed out.

Levinas, unlike Plato who seems to have enjoyed talking about beautiful young bodies most of all, has never shied away from the ugly possibilities of the *corpus*. In *Existence and Existents* he had already caught sight of the fact that the position in which the corporeal subject finds itself involves effort and fatigue, suffering and forsakeness, the "humbling" of the existent by the forces that dominate it.[14] *Time and the Other* focused closely on the misery and destitution of materiality, and laid emphasis on "the pain lightly called physical" in an attempt to describe an experience in which the subject "finds itself enchained, overwhelmed, and in some

way passive."[15] Such passivity is described in the late essay "Useless Suffering" as "more profoundly passive than the receptivity of our senses. . . .
In suffering, sensibility is a vulnerability, more passive than receptivity;
an encounter more passive than experience."[16] Suffering involves "the
impossibility of fleeing or retreating"[17] from one's situation, the inability
to escape one's suffering or to go about one's business as usual. Accordingly, suffering marks the "dialectical reversal" of materiality,[18] the point
at which the body, which is usually the mute support of one's existence
and visible perhaps only on the fringes of one's life, becomes an unignor-
able intrusion into and disruption of the subtle mastery that one exercises
over things. To suffer is to be denied the possibility of self-forgetfulness
and of living with the carefree ease of enjoyment; it is to be forced to
occupy oneself with oneself, to be inescapably drawn into oneself. The
existent that suffers is not exalted but crushed by its own weight: unable
to maintain the vertical position of *Homo erectus* the suffering body dou-
bles over, convulsing.

　　In itself, phenomenally, there is something gratuitous about suffering; it announces the absurdity of an existence that includes pain,
anguish, and death. As Camus so simply and eloquently described it in
The Myth of Sisyphus, the experience of suffering and fatigue can readily
reveal that life "is not worth the trouble,"[19] or, as Levinas has it, that life
is "an enterprise without issue and always ridiculous."[20] But Levinas's
insight is to discern in the suffering of the other a different sort of mean-
inglessness, one which has ethical significance. There is, he finds,

> a radical difference between *the suffering in the other*, where it is
> unforgivable to *me*, solicits me and calls me, and suffering *in me*,
> my own adventure of suffering, whose constitutional or congen-
> ital uselessness can take on a meaning, the only one of which suf-
> fering is capable, in becoming a suffering for the suffering . . . of
> someone else.[21]

The other's suffering, like all suffering, is indeed an absurdity, but absurd
in the sense that it strikes me as an absurd cruelty that is unjust and unjus-
tifiable, unwarranted, "for nothing." That is, I do not witness the other's
suffering without being moved; I cannot help but think that it is not necessary. Put another way, my response to the other's suffering is not to note
the ridiculousness of the being that suffers only to die, but to be moved
by the apparent gratuitousness of the pain.

　　Consequently, it is the suffering of the other that initiates the "ethical
perspective of the interhuman."[22] The other's exposure to wounding in
the flesh, which is still like a trap in which the existent is caught, is

nevertheless something that beckons across the shores of the body to me. In this way the "evil of suffering" which is its "extreme passivity, helplessness, abandonment and solitude" is "also the unassumable, whence the possibility of a half opening, and, more precisely, the half opening that a moan, a cry, a groan or a sigh slips through—the original call for aid, for curative help, help from the other me whose alterity, whose exteriority promises salvation."[23] Levinas even goes so far as to say, in a comment that demands special emphasis, that "this attention to the suffering of the other" can be "raised to the level of the supreme ethical principle."[24]

Before proceeding, several qualifications of this discussion should be made. First, we should make it clear that the argument is not that there is never any point to pain or hardship, that there is never what John Caputo calls an "economy of pain and suffering" in which "short-term suffering may . . . belong to long-term flourishing."[25] Rather, the point is that the suffering of the other is something that troubles me even when it seems to make sense or to have some purpose behind it. No matter how strong my belief in the future benefits that the other stands to gain from present misery, such misery still strikes me and commands my attention, demands my concern—as in the case of the "suffering of innocents" in which, regardless of my faith in God or the future, I must question the legitimacy of children's agony, or, more accurately, have my faith called into question by the apparent cruelty of a God or a history whose best designs include the torment of children.

Next, although the term "suffering" typically refers to some sort of consciousness of one's physical or psychic states, Levinas's understanding of *souffrance* does not appear to be restricted in this way. In "Useless Suffering" he discusses the suffering of "beings who are psychologically deprived, retarded, impoverished in their social life and impaired in their relation to the other [*autrui*]—that relation in which suffering, without losing anything of its savage malignancy, no longer eclipses the totality of the mental and moves into a new light, within new horizons." Despite the fact that these horizons "remain closed to the mentally deficient," this does not silence the cries that emanate from their flesh, for it remains that I am exposed to the afflictions of their mortal bodies even if they are not.[26] Suffering, then, is not equivalent to "pain": the flesh that suffers is not only the flesh that is conscious of its suffering, or that knows it has been wounded. And it is certainly not only the flesh of an other that can be responsible for my own, for even those who are, like beasts, "impoverished in their social life and impaired in their relation to the other" can nevertheless appeal to my responsiveness from the depths of their naked skin.

Finally, although Levinas's descriptions of the suffering of the other seem to take as their starting point experiences in which the other is in immediate distress, it is not the case that ethics arises only at the sight of blood. What this "phenomenology of suffering" allows us to catch sight of is something like an a priori structure of the body, a possibility that inheres in the flesh of every body. To say that materiality harbors the potential for a "dialectical reversal" is to indicate that needs can go unmet just as easily as they are sated, that bodies can be denied what they depend on or have things "turn ugly." We are thus referring to the *exposure* of the body to violation and degradation, the naked indigence that is perhaps best expressed by the term *vulnerability*. Such vulnerability is not an ability or capacity, not an activity, but is instead an inability or an incapacity, the passivity of the body that is structurally destitute, of necessity "capable" of being laid low, of being incapacitated. Vulnerability denotes a possibility that exists wherever flesh exists, but a possibility that is, properly speaking, not a possibility but an impossibility—the im-possibility of in-vulnerability. As soon as there is flesh there is exposure. Hence when Levinas claims that ethics begins in the encounter with the other's suffering, or that the "supreme ethical principle" is my responsibility for the suffering of the other, he is referring to a responsibility that arises in the proximity of the naked destitution of the other's exposure to wounds, the point-blank contact with the nudity of the flesh.

These reflections, which have been thoroughly inspired by and, hopefully, faithful to Levinas, allow us to understand the centrality of the body in his conception of ethics, a point that is sometimes clouded by his preoccupation with discussions of the face. We are in the position, that is, to grasp what Levinas means when he says that the face is a body frail and indigent, for we have shown that the calling into question of the same by the other is the vulnerability of the I to the vulnerability of the other, the susceptibility of my flesh to the wounding of the flesh of the other; it is a substitution for the other in which the exposure of the body of the other to its own disastrous possibilities becomes something for which I myself am responsible. *Face*, therefore, refers to the power of the poverty and exposure of the other to call me into question, the power that the frailty of the body of the other has of calling for my assistance. What summons me to responsibility is the expressive mortality of the naked body, the cry which is the groaning or whimpering of the body exposed, a sound more like a death knell than the harmony of the spheres.

The expressivity of the face is, then, a *carnal topography* in which I read the commandments written on the surfaces of the flesh, a *corporeal topology* in which the body is the place from which the *heteros* speaks the *nomos*. The prohibition against violating the point-blank exposure of the other—the "Thou shalt not kill"—is engraved on wrinkled skin, like an alarm that warns me to be careful or a sign that signals to me the presence of an other who needs me to respect the fragility of the vulnerable body.[27] Such signals constitute the expressivity of the other's "whole sensible being" that Levinas mentions,[28] signals that do not have to be *spoken*—or even come from beings that have the potential to speak—for me to receive them, for even those who are socially "deficient," or "impaired" in their relations with others, "speak" with the authority of the vulnerable flesh, voicing the silent expression that emanates from the body exposed to violence.[29] And this means, if we recall the question about the "faces of brutes" to which Levinas was responding above, that even the most "brutal" faces are still faces! The face of the brutal one does not quit its status as face because the face of the brute is not disembodied, because it faces me from the contours of the flesh, because it is a prohibition that appeals to me from the depths of the skin exposed to violence, even when that skin is beastly.

Who Suffers? Life and Exposure

If we have shown that it is the nudity of the body that faces me, that the exposure and vulnerability that we are calling the "suffering" of the other in its uselessness calls out to me, then the question of *who* the other is is not Who speaks? but Who suffers? Levinas sometimes seems to favor the former version of this question, but it is the latter that is definitive for him: if attention to suffering is the "supreme ethical principle," then Who suffers? is, so to speak, the supreme ethical question. This question calls for an answer, but we should be careful with our response. Levinas's tendency is to say that it is the human being who suffers, but when he says that he is unsure about the faces of snakes, or of dogs, or when he has the intuition that all living things somehow "matter," he indicates that perhaps the corporeal topology of ethics is more than an anthropology. What would it mean to say that every living body suffers, that all living beings have a face? To reply to this question, certain observations that are lacking in Levinas's work must be made, for here it is a matter of trying to understand the sort of alterity that is proper to living things, a topic Levinas left largely unexplored. Let us take a moment then to consider these other-than-human beings, to try to hear what, if anything, they are saying.

In a collection of essays published in 1966 under the title of *The Phenomenon of Life*, Hans Jonas attempted to give "an 'existential' interpretation of biological facts." Jonas's work was animated in part by the suspicion that there were substantial "anthropocentric confines" that existential philosophy had yet to overcome, and that a "new reading of the biological record" could perhaps lead us outside the boundaries set by the

humanistic philosophers of existence.[30] His reflections take as their starting point an analysis of metabolic activity, which is one of the most distinctive characteristics of living organisms. By means of metabolization
the organism is constantly engaged with its environment, having the
matter by which it is constituted continually replaced with new material
drawn from its surroundings. As Jonas puts it, "the material parts of
which the organism consists at any given moment are for the analytic
observer only temporary contents, whose own identity does not coincide
with the identity of the whole they pass through." And it is through the
metabolic exchange that the functional identity of the whole is maintained; the whole "sustains its own identity by the very fact of foreign
matter passing through its spatial system."[31]

What is of particular importance to us is the manner of this exchange,
for "material alteration" is not something unique to organisms. Rocks, for
example, as well as streams, and even the "waves" that form when
streams pass over rocks, all undergo material changes, but the metabolic
changes of which we are speaking are of a different sort. The organism
will, at various times and to varying degrees, encourage or inhibit the
material exchanges in question, acquiring what is needed and resisting
what is not necessary for the maintenance of its functional identity. Thus
regulating and directing the metabolic process, the organism does not
simply "undergo" change but actively participates in its changing, a point
that can be expressed by saying that the organism is a *selective* system.[32] If
we were to insist, as some physicists and environmental philosophers do,
on saying that the organism is, like the wave, a temporary result of a
material or energy flow, we would have to say that it is a temporary result
that works to make its appearance less temporary.[33]

Through its metabolic activities, therefore, the organism breaks from
a state of sheer material continuity with its environment; it establishes
what Holmes Rolston, III, refers to as a "careful, semi-permeable boundary" around itself, a "border" across which the metabolic exchange takes
place.[34] Subsequent to, or contemporary with, such separation, the organism can take in nutrients and thus, on the basis of the break in material
continuity, it is able to counter or resist forces of material decay. But the
metabolic activity that frees the organism from its environment and which
translates into its ability to preserve its somatic integrity, is at the same
time a task that is demanded of it. That is to say that the organism's ability to selectively appropriate material from its surroundings is an activity
that it *must* perform; the organism is in constant need of the environment
from which it distinguishes itself. Jonas calls this the organism's "dialectical relation of needful freedom" to its material surroundings: by virtue
of its metabolic activity the organism stands in contradistinction to its

environment, but nevertheless requires that same environment for its continued existence.[35] Far from severing the bonds between organism and world, freedom both inaugurates them and stamps them with life's peculiar urgency.

With the appearance of organismic life, the dimensions of exteriority and interiority emerge simultaneously. Via its relative discontinuity with its environment, the organism is open to the exterior: freed from the world, the living being is at the same time directed toward it, turned toward its surroundings as that to which it is vitally related.[36] At the same time, the outward directedness of need involves some dimension of inwardness, "imbuing all encounters occurring within its horizon with the quality of felt selfhood, no matter how faint its voice."[37] Whether one calls such inwardness feeling, receptivity, or responsiveness in relation to stimuli, the organism's selective engagement with what is exterior implies some degree—possibly "infinitesimal"—of inward sensitivity or "awareness." In being turned towards what is other than itself, organismic life is likewise turned toward itself, for "only by being sensitive can life be active."[38]

It is important to note that the boundary between inside and outside, between organism and world, is dynamic and fluid rather than static and fixed. The somatic integrity of the organism is formed in communication with what is other, through a process of constant response and adaptation that integrates the environment into the body and reintegrates the body into the world. In the relation of the living being to its surroundings, there is spontaneity and creativity, adaptability and flexibility, a productive interplay between interior and exterior. But in this interplay there is also a definite tension, a situation in which the boundary between inside and outside is capable of being pushed to the point of breaking. This tension is due in part to the fact that the organism, as a selective system, stands in need of select aspects of its surroundings, which is to say that it requires specific environmental conditions to perform the activities by which it sustains itself, and the presence of these conditions cannot be guaranteed. This is the basic principle noted by Darwin, who himself found it in the work of Malthus: in a materially finite world, living things are exposed to material scarcity.[39] Additionally, and in contrast to Malthusian scarcity, the tension between organism and world signifies an exposure to excess, something that can be seen when we reflect on the fact that the boundary between the organism and its surroundings must remain permeable. Such permeability entails vulnerability, for that which is permeable cannot be impenetrable. Here we discern a sort of "overexposure," the organism's inability to fend off, once and for all, the forces that threaten to overwhelm and overtake life itself. In all of this, we find that the organism can be challenged by both deficiency and excess, presented with circumstances to which its responses are inadequate, conditions to which it cannot creatively adapt, at which point the relation between organism and environment ceases to be productive and becomes destructive, issuing in decay, corruption, and failure. Hence the corporeal boundary established by the organism is fluid but not absolutely so; it is flexible but not infinitely malleable. Intimately bound up with the myriad possibilities of life is the possibility of death.

Rolston encapsulates some of these thoughts in a general formulation, saying that "[b]iology requires preserving the identity of selves, articulated from other selves, in an environment with which the self must be in constant exchange."[40] In this way we are able to say, without denying the broader systemic relations known to the ecologist as *symbioses*—mutualism, commensalism, or parasitism—or entering into debates surrounding the possible philosophical implications of these relations, that the horizon opened by need is, minimally, a horizon of self-concern, an openness to experience in terms of self-maintenance. Being, understood as being alive, is appropriately, although partially, characterized as being-for-itself.

Gravities, Disasters

Stepping back from these analyses, we find that we are now able to respond to the question that we have continued to ask Levinas, which is the question of *who* the other is. If this question is Who suffers? where by "suffering" we understand the vulnerability of the other that puts into question my powers of appropriation and violence, then the preceding description of organismic life provides us with the answer: every body does. Everybody is the other.

Everybody is the other. This statement has a dual meaning, just as the term "alterity" does for Levinas. In the first place it refers to the idea that living bodies are sites of vital activity, focal points around which networks of selective relations are found, and sites of sensitivity or receptivity by virtue of which such relations are established and maintained. The positions occupied by living bodies are, in principle, positions which I cannot myself occupy, centers of vital experiences not directly experienceable by me. But the sites where life is found are not fortresses, they are castles in the sand, positions that are lightly plotted in pencil, erasable. As soon as the body takes its stance at a distance from its environment, that distance is capable of being traversed, of falling under siege, and hence every body's "strangeness" is at the same time destitution, naked vulnerability.

This is the twin aspect of alterity that occupies so much of Levinas's work, the nudity that calls to me from the surfaces of the flesh, from "wrinkled skin." Thus it is not only the other human being who appeals to me. The other-than-human being is also a mortality, a gravity, and my encounter with the other-than-human body is not the neutral observation of an other that stands in vital relation to its surroundings, but takes place as the proximity of an other whose exposure and need call out to me, the troubling proximity of every body that stands poised on the threshold of death.

Despite appearances, all of this is not as foreign to Levinas as one might think. He has never denied the neediness of living beings, or that living things can be properly described as beings who exist "for themselves." His preferred manner of expressing this thought is to say that there is a *conative* dimension among living things, a claim that does not signal a return to Aristotelianism but is instead drawn from the work of Darwin, who viewed life in terms of the "struggle for existence."[41] Referring to the "persistence in being," or what he more frequently calls the *conatus essendi*, Levinas states that "[t]hat's Darwin's idea: the living being struggles for life. The aim of being is being itself."[42] This is in fact a point that had been made in *Existence and Existents*, where Levinas briefly noted the agreement between contemporary philosophy and the biological sciences of the nineteenth century regarding the relation between existents and their existence. "Hitherto," he wrote, "a being was taken to have been given existence by divine decree, or to have it by virtue of its very essence. . . . The new and fundamental idea is that this belongingness is the very struggle for life."[43] Living beings, therefore, "strive" to be, existing in the tension between being and nonbeing, engaging in the struggle that beings whose existence has no divine guarantee must endure to maintain their tenuous hold on life. And although Levinas tends to miss, misunderstand, or misdescribe the way in which such precarious striving "faces" me, he is not entirely ignorant of this point, either. In a statement that may appear shocking to his readers, he says that his "conception of the face is a certain way of expressing philosophically what I mean when I speak of the *conatus essendi*, the effort to exist which is the ontological principle."[44] The face refers to the *conatus*! This means, considering that the ontological principle is, by Levinas's own admission, the principle of life itself, that the ethical resistance of the face is found wherever there is life, that any body that strives or struggles is a mortal body, forsaken and destitute, capable of suffering, of being laid low, of becoming a disaster, and that these disasters weigh on me.

Of course, that Levinas may have implicitly recognized the significance (or signifyingness) of other-than-human others does not mean that he always kept such others clearly in view. In fact, as we noted at the outset, his tendency is to push other-than-human beings to the periphery, to place them in the margins. It takes a philosophy that is attentive to the other-than-human to allow us to catch sight of what Levinas apparently saw but failed to take seriously, to bring others who are other-than-human to the fore. But it also takes a philosophy that is sensitive to the ethical dimension of the encounter with alterity to keep us mindful of the exigencies that are an inescapable part of our being in the world with others. It is on this latter point that Levinas's thought is particularly instructive, working to ensure that we do not forget these responsibilities, calling us to remember that we are accountable to all those lives that flicker once, and then disappear.

There are countless natural disasters. If Levinas has a contribution to make to environmental philosophy, I would venture to say that it is as simple and powerful as this. It is not astronomy. Its sights are set lower than that, pulled down by so much gravity. Such gravity is not only a property of the human body, but of every body that appeals to me from the depths of its need and draws me in. The tenderness of the flesh calls to me from every direction, from above where the crow flies to below where the mosses and ferns carpet the forest floor, from across the shore where the otter and kingfisher make their homes and from behind where the white oak on which I rest extends its body above and below me, from right beside me where my friend sits and from right in front of me—point blank. So many obligations! A world inhabited by countless vulnerabilities, all of whom demand accountability, is a world in which it is easy to feel pulled apart by all the sufferings, all the gravities of all the bodies that cry out.

Ours is a world riddled by disasters, human and otherwise.

Notes

1. *Timaeus*, 40a.
2. *Timaeus*, 38c.
3. These statistics are taken from recent issues of the Worldwatch Institute's annual *State of the World* reports (New York: Norton).
4. For an excellent introduction to the issue of "animal agriculture," see Jeremy Rifkin, *Beyond Beef: The Rise and Fall of the Cattle Culture* (New York: Penguin Books, 1992).
5. For a discussion of why this is the case, see Adriaan Peperzak, "Technology and Nature," *Beyond: The Philosophy of Emmanuel Levinas* (Evanston: Northwestern University Press, 1997), 131–44. For a more sharply critical analysis, see Part I of Silvia Benso's *The Face of Things: A Different Side of Ethics* (Albany: State University of New York Press, 2000).
6. Alison Ainley, et al., "The Paradox of Morality: An Interview with Emmanuel Levinas," trans. A. Benjamin and T. Wright, *The Provoca-*

tion of Levinas: Rethinking the Other, ed. R. Bernasconi and D. Wood (London: Routledge, 1998), 172.

7. Emmanuel Levinas, *God, Death, and Time*, trans. Bettina Bergo (Stanford: Stanford University Press, 2000), 37.

8. Emmanuel Levinas, *Entre Nous: Thinking-of-the-Other*, trans. Michael B. Smith and Barbara Harshav (New York: Columbia University Press, 1998), 80.

9. Levinas writes that the "nakedness of the face is an extirpation from the context of the world, from the world signifying as a context" (*Entre Nous*, 57).

10. Emmanuel Levinas, *Collected Philosophical Papers*, trans. Alphonso Lingis (Dordrecht: Martinus Nijhoff, 1987), 167.

11. *Entre Nous*, 145.

12. *Entre Nous*, 231–32.

13. Emmanuel Levinas, *Difficult Freedom: Essays on Judaism*, trans. Sean Hand (Baltimore: Johns Hopkins University Press, 1990), 8.

14. "But human labor and effort presuppose a commitment in which they are already involved. We are yoked to our task, delivered over to it. In the humility of the man who toils bent over his work there is surrender, forsakeness. Despite all its freedom effort reveals a condemnation; it is fatigue and suffering." From Emmanuel Levinas, *Existence and Existents*, trans. Alphonso Lingis (The Hague: Martinus Nijhoff, 1978), 31.

15. Emmanuel Levinas, *Time and the Other*, trans. Richard A. Cohen (Pittsburgh: Duquesne University Press, 1987), 69, 71.

16. *Entre Nous*, 92.

17. *Time and the Other*, 69.

18. *Time and the Other*, 55.

19. Albert Camus, *The Myth of Sisyphus and Other Essays*, trans. Justin O'Brien (New York: Vintage, 1983), 5.

20. *Collected Philosophical Papers*, 138.

21. *Entre Nous*, 94, emphasis in original.

22. *Entre Nous*, 94.

23. *Entre Nous*, 93.

24. *Entre Nous*, 94.

25. John D. Caputo, *Against Ethics: Contributions to a Poetics of Obligation with Constant Reference to Deconstruction* (Bloomington: Indiana University Press, 1993), 29.

26. *Entre Nous*, 93.

27. As Caputo has it, the other "sends me certain carnal signals that warn me to proceed with caution" (*Against Ethics*, 213).

28. Emmanuel Levinas, *Outside the Subject*, trans. Michael B. Smith (Stanford: Stanford University Press, 1994), 102.

29. In "The Paradox of Morality" Levinas is asked whether or not it is "necessary to have the potential for language in order to be a 'face' in the ethical sense," and he begins his answer by saying "I think the beginning of language is in the face. In a certain way, in its silence, it calls you" (*The Provocation of Levinas*, 169).

30. Hans Jonas, *The Phenomenon of Life: Toward a Philosophical Biology* (New York: Dell, 1966), ix.

31. Hans Jonas, *Mortality and Morality: A Search for the Good after Auschwitz*, ed. Lawrence Vogel (Evanston: Northwestern University Press, 1996), 64. The first chapter of this work, "Evolution and Freedom: On the Continuity among Life-Forms," is nearly identical in theme to several of the chapters of *The Phenomenon of Life*, and I have taken the liberty of reading both texts together to present the ideas in this section of the chapter.

32. *The Phenomenon of Life*, 84.

33. For discussion of this issue see J. Baird Callicott, *In Defense of the Land Ethic: Essays in Environmental Philosophy* (Albany: State University of New York Press, 1989). Of particular interest are the essays "The Conceptual Foundations of the Land Ethic" (75–99) and "The Metaphysical Implications of Ecology" (101–14).

34. Holmes Rolston, III, *Conserving Natural Value* (New York: Columbia University Press, 1994), 168.

35. *The Phenomenon of Life*, 80.

36. As Jonas says, "'world' is there from the earliest beginning, the basic setting for experience—a horizon of coreality thrown open by the mere transcendence of want which widens the seclusion of internal identity into a correlative circumference of vital relationship" (*The Phenomenon of Life*, 84).

37. *Mortality and Morality*, 69.

38. *The Phenomenon of Life*, 84–85.

39. Charles Darwin, *The Origin of Species* (Oxford: Oxford University Press, 1996). For both Malthus and Darwin, this idea was linked to postulates regarding unchecked increases in species populations that would inevitably lead to such scarcity, which is why Darwin says of the famous "struggle for existence" that it is "the doctrine of Malthus applied with manifold force to the whole animal and vegetable kingdoms" (54).

40. *Conserving Natural Value*, 170.

41. See *The Origin of Species*, chapter 3.

42. *The Provocation of Levinas*, 172.

43. *Existence and Existents*, 23.

44. *The Provocation of Levinas*, 173.

CHAPTER 11

Taking a Glance at the Environment

Preliminary Thoughts on a Promising Topic

EDWARD S. CASEY

Everything that happens and everything that is said happens or is said at the surface.
—Gilles Deleuze, *The Logic of Sense*

The surface is where most of the action is.
—J. J. Gibson, *The Ecological Approach to Visual Perception*

Can things have a face?
—Emmanuel Levinas,
"Is Ontology Fundamental?"

We can be ethical only in relation to something we can see, feel, understand, love, or otherwise have faith in.
—Aldo Leopold, "The Land Ethic"

I

An ethics of the environment must begin with the sheer and simple fact of being struck by something wrong happening in the surrounding world. It is by noticing that something is out of joint—does not fit or function well—that a response is elicited and an action induced. Responsive action begins with what John Dewey called the "problematic situation." Unless this situation is apprehended in its very problematicity, it will remain noxious, troublesome, harmful. People will go on being persecuted and tortured, chemicals will circulate freely in the air, and food and water will be poisoned—unless attention is given to what is awry in these circumstances. Not that notice is enough; the full force of ethical action requires reflection and consultation: in a word, follow-through. But the first moment of noticing is indispensable; without this, nothing will happen, nothing will ensue.

In what follows I will examine this first moment of ethical responsiveness: the moment of the glance. My claim is that the human glance, meager as it seems to be, is indispensable for consequential ethical action. This is so despite the fact of its almost complete neglect by ethical theorists, who tend to find in it something merely trivial—at most, a predecessor to significant action but not part of this action itself. And yet it is of enormous significance, both in delimited interhuman settings and in the broader field of environmental ethics.

Beyond its special virtue as the opening moment of ethical action, there are several other contributions of the glance to ethical life:

1. The glance provides direct *access* to the other person: to his or her mood, thought, interest, attitude at the moment: what the other *feels* right now; this is crucial for ethics, since (as Scheler has argued) ethical values are conveyed by emotions as their "bearers" (*Träger*): to get a glimpse of a particular emotion is to gain a concrete sense of what ethical issue is at stake.

2. The glance catches a sense of *less manifest* aspects of the other, e.g., her darker thoughts; as when I glancingly realize that the other person is far more disturbed at a deeper level than her previous behavior may have indicated. Here the glance exercizes its penetrating power, its ability to go *under* the manifest phenomenon—yet without any interpretative activity on my part.

3. This is not to mention certain telltale *signs* which the glance picks up instantly and which may be pertinent to ethical activity: class, gender, race, way of dressing (betokening niche within class), even educational level; these are external indicators of the other person's identity, history, and present milieu; they are often (I don't say always) evident in a glance. When they are, they are immediately present to me in their delimited but sharp signification.

4. Not to mention, either, the *exchange of glances* that may be extremely relevant to ethical matters; in this dense dialectic, the other shows herself only insofar as she engages my glance with

hers; and it is the engagement itself, its duration and quality and direction, that becomes significant for ethical thought and action.

In these four ways—of which I here give only the most cursory descriptions—the glance can be said to *give witness* to the other: to testify to her or his compelling and demanding presence in the ethical field. It also *welcomes* that other into the same field of interpersonal relations.

Witnessing and welcoming are in effect the twin pillars of the ethical relation in the thought of Emmanuel Levinas. Despite his discerning discussion of this relation, Levinas nowhere attempts to spell out the exact ways by which these two basic actions are accomplished. I submit that they are realized in the four-fold way I have just outlined—the way of the glance. The glance fills the void left by Levinas's refusal to consider the precise means by which the ethical relation occurs. It is the missing member of any complete description of this relation.

II

The reason for Levinas's conspicuous neglect of the glance is not far to seek. It arises from his critique of perception as a form of knowledge, that is, as an act that takes a comprehensive and synoptic view of a given situation. Ethics, however, is not a matter of knowledge; no amount of knowledge of the Other (*Autrui*) will help one to become ethical in relation to that Other. Instead, the ethical is a matter of desire, and desire bears on what transcends the known or knowable. "Ethical witnessing," Levinas states, "is a revelation that is not [a matter of] knowledge."[1]

If this is the case, then any approach to the Other as an object of knowledge, as something thematized or thematizable, is bound to miss the ethical mark.

> I do not know if one can speak of a "phenomenology" of the face, since phenomenology describes what appears. By the same token, I wonder if one can speak of a look (*un regard*) turned toward the face, for the look is knowledge, perception. I think, rather, that the access to the face is ethical straight off.[2]

Levinas adds that "the best way to encounter the Other is not even to notice the color of his eyes"—or, for that matter, his nose, forehead, or chin.[3] Any such perceived feature of the face takes us down the primrose path of the knowable and the representable, and thus away from the true path of ethics, for "the Infinite does not show itself."[4]

This is a moment of double crisis. On the one hand, Levinas here departs from phenomenology—his discipline of origin—while, on the other hand, he denies any relevance of perception to the ethical relation as this is embodied in the face-to-face encounter. In short, he rejects a phenomenology of perception as playing any significant role in ethics. I hold, on the contrary, that such a phenomenology (and thus *all* phenomenology, as Derrida argues: "phenomenology . . . is always phenomenology of perception")[5] remains not just relevant to ethics but essential to it, both in its specifically human format and in its more extended sense as environmental ethics. And I will make my case on the basis of the unsuspected strength of the mere glance, which is as pivotal to the ethical dimension of the nonhuman environment as it is to that of the interpersonal situation.

Despite his outright denial of any place for perception (and thus for the glance as the vanguard act of perception), Levinas cannot consistently maintain this denial and ends by conceding a role for a certain form of perception. This concession is important: if perception can be seen to be integral and not adventitious to ethics *even within a Levinasian framework*, then the way would be open to a more comprehensive ethics of the environment that is perceptually based. To this end, I want to trace a revealing line of thought that emerges spontaneously in Levinas's discussions with Philippe Nemo.

In these conversations, Levinas speaks of the face as "a signification without a context," as "uncontainable" within the bounds of perception, as a "rupture" with perception, etc.[6] It follows that "one can say that the face is not 'seen' (*vu*)."[7] Yet later in the same interview, Levinas admits that "there is in the *appearance* of the face a commandment, as if a master spoke to me!"[8] Here I ask: How can there be an "appearance" (*apparition*) without a perception of that appearance? Perhaps perception, after all, is an ingredient in the relation to the face. But what kind of perception would this be—granting that "access to the face is not of the order of perception pure and simple, of intentionality that aims at adequation"?[9]

Let us call this impure and nonsimple perception (after Leibniz) *apperception*; that is, a subtle perception, a "petite perception" that precedes and in any case undoes the otherwise inveterate tendency of full-blown perception to objectify—to be a matter of knowledge, of comprehension and synopsis. My claim is that in our relations with the Other apperception is always already at work and that the primary form it takes is the glance, which in its mobile entrainment on surfaces does not consolidate into robust perception. Indeed, it deconsolidates obdurate objects; it no longer takes them to be well-formed substances with determinate edges and sides, definite volumes and weights, and so on.

III

The most insistent question now confronting us is this: *Where* is the ethical imperative? I am not questioning *that* there must be such imperativity, such a "sense of oughtness" (in Wes Jackson's phrase), for without it we would not be moved to act ethically in the first place. Ethics would be merely customary action: what most of us do for the most part. But ethics requires a sanction that is not reducible to commonalities of behavior nor to established normativities of conduct. Since this sanction is not determinable by sociological analysis—since it exceeds, and may go quite contrary to, what most people think is right on a given occasion, including the aptly named "moral majority" (in truth a distinct minority that would like to make itself the statistical majority)—it must be found somewhere else. But where is this?

Just as Heidegger posed the leading question Where is the work of art? (in "The Origin of the Work of Art"), so we must ask the same locatory question of ethics, especially an ethics of the environment. The Where precedes the What of determinate content—that is, what one should do in order to be ethical—as well as the How of how to apply the What: how to make it work or stick in a given circumstance. Even if it is true that the What and the How come first in the order of ethical *conduct*— we must know what to do and how to do it if we are to get anywhere at all in the moral life—a phenomenology of ethics must first ask where the source of the compelling power of the ethical is to be found.

In the history of Western ethics, there have been at least four major coherent answers to this primary question. The sanction or source of the ethical has been located in the Good, in God, in the spiritual Self, and in the Face. These in turn divide into two sets of answers: either the source of the ethical lies in something transcendent to the human—in the Good, as the ultimate object of knowledge, or in God as the final metaphysical or theological force—or in something intrinsically human: whether this be the spiritual self or the face. I set aside here the ancient and medieval moves to locate the seat of the ethical in the extrahuman: not because they are invalid or inconsequential but because they take us too far afield from finding an appropriate purchase for an environmentally based ethics. And I pass over Kant's effort to find the source of the ethical in the deep self which is as invisible as God or the Good.

The face, in contrast, is visible and thus directly accessible. As Levinas puts it in his 1951 essay "Is Ontology Fundamental?":

> It is not a matter of opposing one essence to another [e.g., freedom as opposed to determinism: whether in Kant or in Sartre].

It is above all a question of finding the place from where human beings cease to concern us exclusively on the basis of the horizon of being [as in Heidegger], that is, to offer themselves to our powers. The human existent (*l'étant*) as such (and not as an incarnation of universal being) can only exist in a relation where it is invoked [i.e., not just named]. The human existent is the human being, and it is as a fellow being (*prochain*) that human being is accessible. As a face.[10]

Significant here is Levinas's express effort to find a "place from where" (*la place d'où*) ethics can become possible without having to rely on the encompassing horizon of Being at stake in *Being and Time*, yet still be fully "accessible" to human beings in the course of everyday life. The point of access is found in the face—the face of the other, my "fellow being" or "neighbor" (as *prochain* may also be translated). The face punctures a hole in the Heideggerian horizon just as it penetrates the imposing edifice of the Kantian metaphysics of the spiritual subject. It has the right cutting edge for ethics to find its fulcrum in something very particular about the other person.

Levinas's achievement is to have located the force of the ethical in a feature of the actuality of the human subject, in its presence here and now in the ethical relation. The compellingness of the ethical, its where, is found in the face.

IV

If we are to pursue an ethics of the environment in the wake of Levinas, the pivotal question becomes: Where are we to find the equivalent of the face in the environing world? Just where is there a sense of oughtness that solicits, indeed compels, ethical comportment? Without this solicitation, we would not be drawn to *do* anything ethically efficacious. Human beings rarely if ever act from abstract principles, not from Kant's categorical imperative in its three formulations and not even from the Ten Commandments! (Which themselves, let us remember, were revealed to Moses at a particular place in the wilderness!) Where can we find in the other-than-human world the imperativity that being ethical requires? Is there anything like a face that commands us in the presence of nature?

It is quite remarkable that Levinas, who says very little about an ethics of the environment at any point, raises this very question in his 1951 essay: "Can *things* assume a face?"[11] He rejects the idea that such a face would be merely "relative to an environing plenitude."[12] The face must be grasped on its own terms, not in terms of a surrounding context. Yet, as Heidegger insisted, the very word for "environment" (*Umgebung* in German) emphasizes precisely the idea of something surrounding us, thanks to the fact that the prefix signifies "around" in English as well as German. Yet in such a highly ramified surrounding scene, it is difficult to locate anything with the force, much less the authority, of a face. It seems that either there is nothing like a face in the environment—as Levinas himself would doubtless have to conclude upon further reflection, given his stringent conditions of selfhood—or the face is all over the place: in which case, its meaning will be so diluted as to risk losing any ethical urgency. This is the kind of dilemma into which Levinas puts us, no less than Kant before him: either the face is strictly human (and then no ethics of the larger environment is possible) or it is part of a decidedly nonethical totality called "life" or "nature."[13] Otherwise put: ethics is human or does not exist at all. But this rigid choice gets us nowhere when we want to consider right and good action in the other-than-human world that includes us but much else of value besides.

What to do, then, in confronting this dilemma? One tempting move is to give up any search for a literal human face but still look for something human or humanlike in the environment as the hook on which to hang the hat of ethics. Levinas would be only too happy to enter into this search insofar as he rejects the literal face to start with—this is the very basis of his critique of the *perception* of the face as part of ethics—and insofar as he himself does not wish to confine the "face" to the front of the head.[14]

Could we not say that the whole natural world is like a body, the "world's body" (in John Crowe Ransom's memorable phrase), and that it is therefore capable of presenting a face to us? Perhaps—we shall explore a model not too distant from this later on—and yet this formulation entails the fatal flaw of anthropocentrism. The world's body thus conceived is parasitic on the human body. To generalize the human body, starting with its peculiar face, over the entire environment is only to indulge in an unremitting extension of humanism, making man indeed "the measure of all things." It is also to invite the insoluble problems occasioned by the analogizing called for in any such generalization, whereby we must effect a "pairing" (in Husserl's term) between our body and natural objects. Just as this act of *Paarung* is foredoomed as a model of how we know others who are different from ourselves, so it is futile when it (or any other kind of analogical inference) is invoked to explain how the world as a whole is similar to our own body, including its face.[15]

V

We need to make a new start to find the equivalent of the face in the environment. Instead of trying to locate this in a particular feature of that environment—its body or its mind, or in its sentience or its feeling (as in Buddhism or Whitehead)—we are better advised to look to a larger framework that does not borrow any of its basic traits from human beings. I refer to the environing *world* and, more particularly, to what I like to call the *place-world*. It is axiomatic that *every* entity of the environment, human or nonhuman, belongs to the natural world, and it belongs there in virtue of the particular place it inhabits. Thinking this way avoids invidious searching among species for priority in the ethical realm; it focuses on what all natural entities, including unspeciated ones, share: belongingness to the "place-world." Every entity, living or not, is part of this world, and therefore the ultimate ground of ethical force in the environment belongs properly to this world as a concrete, complicated nexus of places.

An imagined dilemma points to the rightness of this line of thought. Faced with the choice as to whether we would destroy a given member of a species or its habitat, we would surely prefer to save the habitat even if it meant sacrificing the animal. The value accrues not just to the larger whole but to the place-world in which certain animals flourish. Or to put the same point somewhat differently: whereas we value human animals primarily for what they are in each individual case (we can be face to face with only *one* Other at a time), we value animals not only for themselves (this we certainly do as well, as we know from the case of beloved pets) but also and ultimately for their belongingness to the place-world which they coinhabit. The source of the ethical commitment they inspire in us stems in good measure from our appreciation of the places to which they belong as coordinate members of the same habitat or territory.[16]

Another clue, this time from the history of language: *ethos*, the Greek word that lies at the origin of "ethics" and that signifies "character" in Attic Greek, first of all meant (in Homer's time) "animal habitat," for example, the place where wild horses go when they settle down at night. There is, then, a long line of thought that ties together ethics and place in the West.

Even if you will grant that place-worlds are the ultimate source of ethical force in the environmental field, you will rightly want something more specific to anchor the ethicity of the environmental imperative. Needed here is what Lacan would have called a *point de capiton*, an "upholstery button" that serves to pin down otherwise loosely fitting material. In the psychoanalytic field, a symptom plays this pivotal role; in it are condensed the repressed and repressing forces whose compromised conjunction constitutes a nodal point in the psychic field. Some such focal point, some concrete crux, is needed as well in the field of the environment if we are to locate not just the encompassing arc of environmental interpellation but the specific gravity of that same compellingness, its maxillary bite as it were. Where is this?

If we meditate on the place-world and look for its most characteristic and specific embodiment, we soon reach the *landscape* as that by means of which the place-world appears. Construing "landscape" to include cityscape, seascape, plainscape, mountainscape, skyscape, or whatever—any form of "placescape"—we find that it has two primary features: "layout" and "surface." *Layout* is J. J. Gibson's term for any coherent congeries of surfaces in the environment; in his own definition, it is "the persisting arrangement of surfaces relative to one another and to the ground."[17] It is the way in which various visual (and other) phenomena coconstitute an environment, its very extendedness. Layout also connotes the way in which a given environment provides opportunities to its inhabitants—opportunities that Gibson terms "affordances," remarking that "different layouts [offer] different affordances for animals."[18]

The place-world, then, comes across to us in terms of particular landscapes, and these in turn as layouts in our perceptual field—extended regions in which natural entities are not only located but afforded the chance to do various things, whether this be to build houses, pursue prey, or just to "vegetate" and stay put. But still more specifically the layout of the place-world, that is to say, the whole environment, is composed of *surfaces*. Not only is layout a matter of the arrangement of surfaces in relation to each other, but the very ground to which each of these surfaces relates is itself a surface: it is "the basic persisting surface of the environment."[19]

"Environment" itself, the most encompassing term of all, is in effect a concatenation of surfaces, since the "substances" of which it is composed present themselves only through surfaces, and the "medium" of the environment is imperceptible except in terms of particular surfaces (e.g., the edge of the wind as it moves across the Great Plains). Since a surface can be regarded as "the interface between a substance and [a] medium,"[20] it is the indispensable mediatrix between everything of import in the environment; it is never not present in the particular combinations of entities that make up the surrounding world. Everywhere we look, everywhere we feel and sense, we are confronted by surfaces: by their phenomenal properties (e.g., shape, color, size, etc.), their intersection, and finally their layout. They are the constituent units of every environment, starting with the animal *Umwelt*: "Animals," observes Gibson, "perceive surfaces and their properties, since animal behavior must be controlled by what the surfaces and their substances afford."[21] All the more is this true of plants and stones, which are even more fully affected, indeed dominated, by the surfaces around them. In their capacity to set forth the figure and texture of any given occupant of any given environment, surfaces act as sheaths for that environment, showing and specifying what would be otherwise mere perceptual flotsam and jetsam.

VI

Gibson says suggestively in a late essay on surfaces that "the perception of the [surface] properties of the persisting substances of the habitat is necessary if we are to know what they afford, what they are good for."[22] This points in the direction of the ethical, which allows us as well as commands us to be and do good in terms of what the surfaces of our immediate environment afford—what they are "good for." Although we are surrounded by surfaces,[23] we rarely pause to take note of what is special about them, especially not with regard to their role in ethical life. Yet if the glance is to play a role in ethics, then the perception of surfaces will be central in this life. For surfaces are precisely where glances alight: we glance at appealing or threatening, beckoning or off-putting surfaces. But what it is about surfaces that makes them so well suited for presenting ethical imperatives that concern the environment? Two things mainly: expressivity and simplicity.

At one level of analysis, surfaces show themselves to be eminently capable of *expressivity*, which is indispensable to those imperatives that call to us and stay with us. It is not just the face, or the whole body, that is expressive but surface as such. This is due to the fact that surfaces are capable of the kinds of variation that are important to expressivity. I think here of variations in pliability, elasticity, edgedness, extendedness, coloration, texture, and doubtless others: all of which, once coordinated, bring about expressivity in a given instance.[24] It is just because of this multiplicity of covariant factors that the full range of expressivity is possible, whether it is displayed in a face or a landscape. All the more so when it is a question—as it always is a question in an environmental layout—of several surfaces acting at once. Then we perceive their continual reconfiguration as surfaces meet and mingle, overlap and occlude each other, thereby increasing exponentially the possibilities for expressivity in the environment.

At a second level, a surface is able to hold together and present these diverse parameters precisely because of its own comparative *simplicity*. Consider the surface of a mirror or that of a window pane. It is its very smoothness, the lack of qualitative complication in such a surface, its transparency or its sheer reflecting power, that allows it to hold within its frame very complex objects and scenes. It is like a complemental ratio in what Gibson would call "ecological optics": the less complex the surface, the more complex the contents it can set forth, *on* the surface in the case of the mirror, *through* the surface in the case of the window pane.[25]

Given that surfaces facilitate expressiveness and that their very simplicity allows for the conveyance of environmental complexity, we have at hand a ready basis for their presentation of that which impels an ethics of the environment. This is *the direct presentation of environmental distress*. When I glimpse clearcutting on a mountain slope or the dumping of waste in a swamp or the ruination of soil on a farm, I am witnessing disorder in the environment. I am also witnessing *to* it: bearing witness already.[26]

When surfaces express environmental disruption, the natural order of things is not just complicated but trespassed and undermined. We witness a *corpus contra naturem*. By this, I do not mean merely a "freak of nature"—though this can be environmentally telling too, as in the case of birth defects caused by chemical pollution of underground water—but any feature of the layout that goes contrary to the natural order. Then, instead of an optical array that is well-ordered with regard to being and well-being, we are confronted with manifest disarray. What I have just called "distress" refers to any kind of environmental turpitude that is registered—expressively—in the surfaces of the layout inhabited by a given group of natural entities. This is not to deny that appearances on this surface may be misleading—especially when their full virulence is still masked—or ambiguous (e.g., a swarm of locusts devouring a field), but it is to emphasize that there is a great deal we can trust in our perception of environmental disorder: we can by and large rely on our "perceptual faith" as Merleau-Ponty calls it, or our "animal faith" in Santayana's term.[27] The signs of such disorder are telling something to us; they are expressing a wound to the ecosystem, a tear in its fabric, an illness in the landscape. To those who had eyes to see, the early effects of nineteenth-century industrialism in England and America were manifest in the country as well as in the city—as acute observers from Blake to Dickens, Thomas Cole to Thoreau all saw so poignantly.

Or let us say that these sensitive souls—ecologists of perception before there was any science of the subject—*apperceived* the destruction that was billowing in the air and poisoning the ground. So we, too, at the beginning of this New Millenium can apperceive the initial effects of global warming in such expressive elemental phenomena as changing weather patterns, whose persistently hotter surfaces we sense in our skins, and whose deadly effects are visible in the massive losses of sea otters and seals in the Pacific Ocean. I say "apperceive" in deference to our earlier discussion of glancing at the face of the other person. When I apperceive dis-ease in the environment, I attend to *where* it is located, in what *place*, and especially on which *surfaces* of that place. This is why the glance is so aptly invoked in this very circumstance: its pointed penetrating power allows it to go straight to where the problem is, like a hawk zeroing in on its prey. Or like a lance launched at its pinpointed target: *Ort*, the German word for place, derives ultimately from "tip of a spear": the glance, like a lance, is typically thrown at its target (as the French say, when we glance we "throw a blow of the eye": *jeter un coup d'oeil*). The target in landscape apperception takes the form of a particular place in the environment, a set of surfaces that betrays instantly the state of its health.

Analogues to this situation abound: the practiced medical doctor knows by a mere glance what her patient is suffering from, the painter knows by the briefest of looks what has to be added or substracted from his work, the poet to her text, the cook to the dish being prepared. The person familiar with his or her local environment—the farmer, the gardner, the landscape architect—can tell with similar swiftness if this environment is in trouble, and even if it is only starting to head for trouble. The place-world shows itself in its surfaces, as existing within its own normative parameters, geomorphic or evolutionary, agricultural or wild—or else as exceeding or undermining these parameters, as ill at ease with itself. The glance takes all this in without needing to pass judgment or to engage in reflection. A bare apperception, a mere moment of attention, is enough: *a glance suffices*.[28]

VII

A glance suffices not just to see distress and disorder. It also picks up the imperative to do something about that disarray. Here we take the crucial step from being *noticeable* to being *compelling*. Certain surfaces of the environment are noticeably in trouble, and we see this at a glance; but what about the ethical demand that we find a way out of that trouble? How can anything so stringent, so uncompromising, as this demand be a matter of mere surfaces and thus something that calls for just as mere glances? We might grant that the glance apperceives environmental problems quickly and accurately. But does it suffice to grasp the *imperative* to remedy the earth's maladies?

It does, but only if we single out one more factor in the distressed surfaces we notice. To be expressive and to be a comparatively simple foil to

the complexities of the environment are both essential to conveying difficulties happening in a place. But a certain *intensity* is also required: an
intensity *on* and *of* the very surfaces that draw our attention in the first
place. A pleasant and healthy landscape lacks intensity; it lulls us into the
pleasure of the beautiful. Only when a landscape is sublime does tension
arise. In this case (and in Kant's terms), the tension is between an imagination not able to comprehend the complexity of the scene and a reason
that claims to go far beyond it. In an environmental trauma, a different
but equally powerful tension between integrity and disturbance arises: a
tension whose intensity calls us to act and not just to spectate.

I once beheld the devastation wrought upon an entire slope of a
mountain to the east as I hiked up Cottonwood Canyon in the Crazy
Mountains in central Montana. My companion, David Strong, confirmed
my apperception: there had indeed been extensive clearcutting up there
for some time. In fact, he and others had filed suit with the United States
Forest Service for laxly allowing the sale of the land, without adequate
preliminary inspection, to the logging company that had effected the
depredations I was witnessing. From my bare glance at this scene of
destruction, I sensed the rightness of such concerted legal action, along
with another still more ambitious plan to have most of the Crazies per-
manently protected from logging. Nor did I need to have further evidence: the decisive and compelling evidence was before me, etched in the
distress of the land. The imperative for ecological action stemmed from
the intensity of the scene itself, its damaged surfaces speaking dramatically to my bare apperception: whole groves of trees had lost their right-
ful place in an aboriginal biotic lifeworld.

The clear-cut mountain slope was like a festering wound; it was a
scene of concentrated affliction. It presented itself as a *symptom* that draws
attention to itself rather than signalling something else in the manner of a
sign or symbol. As Freud said of symptoms in the context of psychoanalysis, "the symptom is on the agenda all the time."[29] It is always on the
agenda because it is at once painful and puzzling. In each of these ways,
a symptom is literally in-tensive, infecting the subject even as it conceals
its origins from this same subject. Of course, a symptom is also "overde-
termined"; it has at least several causes; it is part of a larger trans-subjec-
tive context. To interpret a symptom—and to relieve the patient's
suffering from it—is to advert to a more encompassing set of factors than
are presented in the symptom itself.

Just so, the clear-cut forest in central Montana was symptomatic on
both counts. On the one hand, it compelled attention on the basis of its
sheer disarray: not just the ugly stumps of cut down trees but the even more
ugly access roads that crisscrossed the landscape like so many razor slashes

on its upturned face. Whatever the profitability of the situation may be in
the eye of a logging company executive, there was undeniable disfigure-
ment in the land: the aesthetic join forces with the ethical in this scene of
destruction. My glance was drawn into the heart of its darkness. This is the
moment of pain that calls for alleviation by the appropriate action. On the
other hand, the same symptomatic suffering brings with it a profound puzzlement: Why this depredation? Why here? Why now? In pursuing this
puzzlement, I look to the larger picture. I become an ecoanalyst who won-
ders about the genealogy of the situation—not just its causes but also its
reasons. I consider history, social and political forces, and metaphysics.
(Metaphysics, if Heidegger is right that the Age of Technology is a certain
era of Western metaphysical thought in which the earth has come to be
regarded as "standing reserve" in a massive enframing action that regards
the earth as nothing but a resource to be exploited.) In this second moment,
I move away from the apperception of the immediate environmental
trauma; I undertake reflection and other cognitive and judgmental operations: my glance, which has catalyzed the entire experience, no longer suffices. The lambent lightness of the glance, combined with its compelling
disclosure, here gives rise to the spirit of gravity. An environmental imperative has precipitated reflective and responsible ecoanalysis, and perhaps
also (as in the case of my friend) effective political action.

I have been driven (again) to the idea of a symptom in an effort to
understand the peculiar intensity embedded in the clear-cut destruction
of an entire mountainside in Montana—an intensity that not just appalled
and angered me but that called out for action of the sort that my friend,
more forthright and knowledgeable than I, had taken: where I took in the
interpellation, he had acted on it in his actual conduct. But both of us
started with the same dismaying experience of a damaged landscape
whose intense call was located *in the environment*—not in "the moral law
within" (in Kant's celebrated phrase). The disruption and associated
intensity were out there in the land. They had their symptomatic existence
in a disturbed place-world—they drew our chagrined glances to themselves *there*—even if the larger causality lay elsewhere in the home offices
of the great paper companies of the Northwest and across the country in
the endless and mindless paper consumption of millions of ordinary
American citizens.

VIII

I have just been suggesting that intensity is the thin red line that links
glance, surface, and the ethics of the environment. It fuels the com-

pellingness of environmental imperatives. But we still have to grasp more fully what such intensity consists in. Granting that it cannot be measured by extensive magnitude, it nonetheless appears on surfaces that possess such magnitude. This means that it reflects the primary and especially the secondary qualities of extended surfaces.[30] Nevertheless, the intensity with which an environmental problem expresses itself is not just a matter of "too much," even if this can be a valuable indicative red flag: for example, too much sewage flowing into the marshland. In the presence of such undeniable givens, one stares the problem itself in the face; but even here what one grasps is the *qualitative* configuration of something with specific quantitative dimensions: one sees the discoloration of the marshland water caused by the leakage of the sewage. One reads the problematic situation on its surface, by being a direct witness to the distress: a glance suffices to take in the qualitatively distorted surfaces of the damaged marsh.

The appropriate response to the environmental imperative aims (in Deleuze's phrase) to "liberate the singularities of the surface."[31] For if "the accomplished action [in this case, the detrimental action] is projected on a surface"[32]—there for all to read at a glance—the remedial action must also bear on that same diseased surface. It must somehow re-endow it with distinctive and singular potentialities of health and growth so as to counter the detrimentality of environmental disruption and to rectify it: if not to make a "clean slate" (for such disruption often leaves permanent traces), then to reinstate a significant vestige of ecological health. Just as the apperception of eco-dystrophy arises from a glance cast upon a distressed surface, so the answering action also takes place upon the same surface—upon what Deleuze and Guattari call the "planomenon."[33] The intensity of distress is addressed by the concertedness of the remedial action.

But what exactly is intense about the ecological *via rupta* that induces or instills an environmental imperative? It is a step in the right direction to say that the intensity is qualitative: this is important as a corrective to geomorphic or econometric models of ecological disorder, models that stay within the realm of extensive magnitude. It keeps the situation in the phenomenological register—in the realm of first-person experience where the disruption is first registered and where any imperative for change must first take root. In fact, the alarming character of the disturbed environmental surface often takes the form of being presented with *contrary qualities* on that very surface: for example, in the way in which the blatantly artificial colors of industrial sludge contrast with the mellow marshland into which they have seeped. The metallic colors of the sludge seem to subvert the earth tones of the wet land; they constitute a different spectral scene, one whose lines of force move contrary to that of the natural world. All of this occurs on the sheer surface of what is visible, where the drama, the clash, is manifest.[34]

IX

There is one quite unanticipated effect of this last line of thought: thanks to the intensity registered on surfaces of the environment, there is room, after all and once again, for the face, allowing us to return to our point of departure. This can only happen, however, if the face is no longer considered strictly human, something that is revealed in an existential encounter—in an ethical "relation" that is interhuman only. If the face is to play a role in an ecological ethics, it must be dehumanized. Levinas gestures in this direction when he allows the face to extend from the front of the head to the whole body as well as in his brief discussion of the surfaces of the elemental world.[35] But if it is to be an effective agent of an ethics of the other-than-human, the face must have a place in the environing world as a whole. How can this be? What would it look like?

Here we might borrow an idea from Deleuze and Guattari's *A Thousand Plateaus*, where the authors take the extra step Levinas failed to make. Agreeing with him that the whole body needs to be facialized—"not only the mouth but also the breast, hand, the entire body, even the tool, are 'facialized'"[36]—they add the crucial rider that facialization does not stop at the limits of the body: it includes the full environment, the landscape in which that body is implaced. What they consider a *faciality machine*—that is, "the social production of [the] face"[37]—is such that it "performs the facialization of the entire body *and all its surroundings and objects, and the landscapification of all worlds and milieus.*"[38] The result is what the authors call a "face-landscape," in which landscape is facial and a face landscapelike. Just because the face is no longer human in its primary signifiance—thereby sidestepping the problem of analogy and anthropocentrism—it is able to join up with landscape in a close alliance. Precisely as "deterritorialized," that is, taken out of its humanized role, the face merges with the landscape:

> Now the face has a correlate of great importance: the landscape, which is not just a milieu but a deterritorialized world. There are a number of face-landscape correlations. . . . What face has not called upon the landscapes it amalgamated, sea and hill; what landscape has not evoked the face that would have completed it, providing an unexpected complement for its lines and traits?[39]

Whereas the "head" of human beings refers to other animals and to a shared environment, the face as such is here linked mainly to landscape. And it is in landscape that the face of the place-world shows itself—shows itself to be amenable and settled, or else distressed and disrupted. And we read all this in a glance that detects, or at least suspects, its wellness or illness instantly.[40]

X

I have been pursuing phenomenological prolegomena to an ethics of the environment, keeping in mind that "pro-legomenon" means in its root "before the saying is said" (before the *dire* is *dit* as Levinas might prefer to put it). Before anything is said—either explicitly among interlocutors or implicitly as in the invocation of a categorical imperative—there is the moment of ethical engagement. I began by noting how often and how effectively the glance serves to initiate this first moment of engagement. Its ability to go straight to the heart of the matter, to grasp a situation quickly and yet accurately, to take in the look of the other (who may or may not glance back): all these powers of the glance help us to discern the compelling character of the circumstance—that which calls for responsiveness on my part. Traditional ethical theory has rarely if ever made room for this inaugural moment of the glance, focusing as it has on reason and rules, persons and norms, sanctions and justifications.

Traditional ethical theory has also neglected the environment and its special set of demands and needs. Yet here, too, the glance can be of crucial consequence in alerting human subjects to things that need to be done to address and rectify environmental distress. In this context, the sweeping glance is of particular value: in keeping with the fact that we are literally surrounded by environmental layouts. The comprehensive character of the glance—its gift for *taking in so much in so little time*—is aptly deployed vis-a-vis the environment. Thanks to its characteristic acumen and comprehensiveness, the glance can be considered the leading edge of the ethical; it is in the premonitory position.

I would certainly admit that one is hard pressed to find in the natural environment any exact analogue of the human face. This difficulty persists when one allows for the facialization of landscape: for Deleuze and Guattari, this is only a penultimate step that calls for further deterritorialization, and Levinas allows for it only as an aside when he says suddenly that "the human face is the face of the world itself."[41] Even after taking this final expansive step, one continues to need a compelling source, a "call to action"[42]—or else one will have no strong motive for responding to environmental problems. This call has to come from *somewhere* that is located (albeit not *simply* located) in the place-world.

The compelling point, the sense of oughtness, is something I apprehend by the glance in its vanguard role. This sense is to be apperceived on the surfaces of the environment—surfaces that constitute its accessibility, its very apperceptibility. I endorse Gibson's axiom that "the surface is where most of the action is"[43]—not only the apperceptive action but the ethical action as well. If the tell-tale symptom of environmental disturbance appears anywhere, it must appear on the surface of things—not in some hidden depth (that is the concern of the environmental scientist or the metaphysician, who are in this regard closely allied). It must be there to be seen—*at a glance*. And what do we then see? We see distress, which can be variously construed as incongruity, discordance, contrariness, tension—but above all as *intensity*. Following Kant and Deleuze, I would interpret intensity as qualitative, thus as something we feel as well as apperceive. Differential in character, it presents itself by degrees—building to a point where it not only draws our attention but *demands* it. And when we do attend to it (often by a concerted series of glances), we find something compelling us, telling us, to act so as to alter the disturbed circumstance: to "set it right." In the end, the natural world indeed presents a face to us—but only as belonging to the layout of expressive surfaces inherent in the natural world as a whole. The environment turns a face to us from within its many surfaces: not the infinite and transcendent enigmatic Other's face of such high priority for Levinas but an immanent, intense faciality of its own, one in which we can discern distress without having to make it analogous to human suffering. *That* face is the face of a nonhuman nonsubject—a landscape whose singularity belongs properly to the natural realm. It is the face of the environment calling out to us to address the distress, if not (yet) to cure the disease.

Skeptics will respond: what guarantees that I (or anyone) will respond sensitively to this intensity? What of all those who do not respond, either from self-interest (the logging companies, the paper companies, the chemical companies) or from cynicism or indifference? Does not response to environmental detrimentality require a certain knowledge or sophistication? Is this not a social or political matter rather than an ethical one? Notice that these are all questions that can be posed just as well to the Levinasian model of ethical relation, in which a high level of educated responsiveness is no less presumed. And I would have to give a Levinasian answer as well: even if human subjects fail to pick up the ethical command, even if they are oblivious to its force, this does not mean that they are not *subject to its call to responsible action*. As Levinas remarks:

The tie with the Other is realized only as responsibility, whether this [responsibility] be accepted or refused, whether one know how to assume it or not, or whether one can or cannot do something concrete for the Other. To say: here I am (*me voici*). To do something for the Other. To give [oneself]. . . . The face [of the Other] orders and commands me.[44]

Notice that much the same obtains for other ways of justifying an ethics of the environment: say, the Buddhist doctrine of the interdependency of all natural beings, or Hans Jonas's claim that I am responsible for future generations. I may not be consciously aware of any of these imperatives, much less endorse them, and yet I am *no less under their sway*. True, a certain kind of education or certain benevolent influences from enlightened others will help to make me more aware—and thus more likely to embrace an environmental imperative and to act accordingly. But even if I am naive or unapperceptive, I am still in the presence of intense commands to respond. My failure to do so stems not just from self-interest or indifference or lack of ecological enlightenment but also from a deeper failure, which is not my own alone: the failure to link vision with the lived world around me, due doubtless to the detached Cartesian eye that bespeaks a massive cultural disconnect between human beings and their environments.[45] Then my (and everyone's) glance falls short; it barely notices, if it notices at all; it glances off the ecological surface but fails to take in the intensity on that surface, quickly sliding off the glabrous back of the place-world. This situation is not so much unethical or immoral; it is *a-ethical*: I have missed the message, failed to respond, even though I still stand under the imperative to be responsible. The intensity of the disturbance is there, but I am not able or willing to say *me voici*: here I am for you, I shall make some difference, I shall do something to save your symptomatic surface, something to put you back in the right place, thus to resituate your distressed layout in a more halcyon landscape.

In other words: if there is indeed an ethical relation between human beings, there is also an equally (but differently) ethical relation among all members of the natural environment—to which Levinas's ethical posture remains relevant even if it calls for revision and expansion. In both cases, we stand "encumbered."[46] And if glancing is important in the first case—more important than Levinas allows—it is just as crucial in the second. Glancing makes the difference between indifference and concern. Environmentally uncaring people look away even before they glance; or if they look, they see little if anything of the suffering in the scarified face of the natural world. Unless we can catch the discordance and the pain, the affliction and the damage, we shall be in no position to act and reflect—to do something that makes a real difference to a diseased or traumatized environment. Then we shall finally begin to own up to our unending responsibility to the place-worlds in which we live and move and become what we are in their midst.[47]

Notes

1. Emmanuel Levinas, *Éthique et infini: dialogues avec Philippe Nemo* (Paris: Fayard, 1982), 114 (cited hereafter as EI). He adds that "the relation to the Infinite is not [a form of] knowledge, but of Desire" (EI 97).
2. EI 89. Compare this statement: the Infinite "does not appear, since it is not thematized, at least not originally" (EI 112).
3. See ibid., 89. I am grateful to Peter Atterton of the Philosophy Department, San Diego State University, for drawing my attention to this and related passages on the problematic perception of the face.
4. EI 113. He adds: "It is by this witnessing, whose truth is not that of representation or of perception, that the revelation of the Infinite is produced" (ibid.).
5. Jacques Derrida, *Speech and Phenomena*, trans. David Allison (Evanston: Northwestern University Press, 1967), 104.
6. EI 90, 91. Elsewhere, Levinas ties perception to the tendency to be comprehensive and synoptic: "The experience of morality does not proceed from [eschatological] vision—it consummates this vision; ethics is an optics. But it is a 'vision' without image, bereft of the synoptic and totalizing capability, a relation or an intentionality of a wholly different type" (*Totality and Infinity: An Essay on Exteriority*, trans. A. Lingis [Pittsburgh: Duquesne University Press, 1969], 23; Levinas underlines "consummates." Cited hereafter as TI).
7. EI 91.
8. EI 93. My italics.
9. EI 102. Cf. also Levinas's claim that "the relation with the face can certainly be dominated by perception [indeed, he is conceding that it *is* so dominated], but that which is specifically face is that which cannot be reduced to it" (91).
10. "L'Ontologie est-elle fondamentale?" *La revue de métaphysique et de morale* (1951), 20.
11. Ibid., 22. But Levinas immediately diverts this question into whether the question of whether "art is an activity that lends faces to things," perhaps through "the impersonal allure of rhythm" (ibid.).
12. Ibid.

13. "The living being (*le vivant*) in totality exists as a totality, as if he occupied the center of being and were its source . . . " (Levinas, "Le Moi et la totalité," in *Entre Nous: Essais sur le penser—à-l'autre* [Paris: Grasset, 1991], 23).

14. As Levinas remarks in passing to Nemo: "I analyze the inter-human relation as if, in proximity to the Other—beyond the image I make of the other person [i.e., in perception]—his face, that which is expressive in the Other (and *the whole human body is, in this sense, more or less, face*), were that which orders me to serve him" (EI 104; my italics; Levinas underlines "orders").

15. I am referring here to Husserl's celebrated fifth *Cartesian Meditation*. For all its subtlety, Husserl's model fails to be genuinely bilateral.

16. John Findlay once remarked in conversation that animals—especially dogs—should be regarded as "associate members of the kingdom of ends." This *bon mot* got it half-way right. Animals are associate members of the animal kingdom (as we revealingly call it, echoing Kant's "Kingdom of Ends"). More generally, all natural entities are associate members of the place-worlds to which they commonly belong. (I put "place-world" in the plural here to indicate that a given entity may belong to more than one place-world, as we see in complex natural environments such as rain forests or borderline ecosystems.)

17. J. J. Gibson, *The Ecological Approach to Visual Perception* (Hillsdale, N.J.: Erlbaum, 1986), 307.

18. Ibid. I would add: not just for animals but for all natural things in a given environment, where "environment" (in Gibson's own description) "consists of a medium, substances, and the surfaces that separate the substances from the medium" (ibid.).

19. Ibid. Cf. p. 10: "The literal basis of the terrestrial environment is the ground, *the underlying surface of support* that tends to be on the average flat—that is to say, a plane—and also level, or perpendicular to gravity" (my italics; Gibson underlines "basis").

20. J. J. Gibson, "What is Involved in Surface Perception?" in Gibson, *Reasons for Realism: Selected Essays of James J. Gibson*, ed. E. Reed and R. Jones (Hillsdale, N.J.: Erlbaum, 1982), 111.

21. Ibid., 112.

22. Ibid., 110.

23. "Animals [including human animals]," says Gibson, "see their environment chiefly [as] illuminated surfaces" ("Ecological Optics," in *Reasons for Realism*, 75).

24. Conditions for being indicative are characteristically both more austere—e.g., as in the case of being a bare sign—and more sophisticated: to grasp an indicative sign is to have to understand the larger context within which it functions.

25. This has special relevance for ecological optics, if it is truly the case that the elemental is "nonpossessable" in Levinas's word; if the various elements cannot be possessed as objects, they can at least be held as images in mirrors, framed for view in windows, and depicted on photographs: all of these being surfaces that gather the elemental for display. As Levinas says, "Every relation or possession is situated within the nonpossessable which envelops or contains without being able to be contained or enveloped. We shall call it the elemental" (TI 131). Levinas also emphasizes the indeterminate character of the elemental: TI 132.

26. The disorder may be more subtle, of course—in which case, however, a trained ecologist will then be able to detect it in a glance. This is especially important in the case of early warning signs of environmental distress, say, the perception of the larvae of what will become an insect destructive of trees once it is fully developed. It has been pointed out to me by a veteran ecologist that rather than seeing such educated perception as merely a matter of specialization, it in fact approximates to what many human beings would be capable of were they to live more fully in the natural environment—as was the case for many millenia before the advent of city-based inhabitation (email remark of L. L. Woolbright, Siena College, 2/18/2000).

27. On perceptual faith, see M. Merleau-Ponty, *The Visible and the Invisible*, trans. A. Lingis (Evanston: Northwestern University Press, 1968), 50 ff.; on animal faith, see George Santayana, *Skepticism and Animal Faith* (New York: Scribners, 1923).

28. Here the glance is strangely the counterpart of the earth, which as Levinas says also suffices in its own way: "The earth upon which I find myself and from which I welcome sensible objects or make my way to them suffices for me. The earth which upholds me does so without my troubling myself about knowing what upholds the earth" (TI 137). This last sentence could well be a statement about surfaces, about whose support we also do not often concern ourselves; even the ground to which they ultimately relate is itself, as Gibson avers, a surface of its own.

29. S. Freud, *Introductory Lectures on Psychoanalysis*, trans. J. Strachey, vol. 15 of *The Standard Edition of the Complete Psychological Works* (London: Hogarth, 1975).

30. As Deleuze puts it, "we know intensity only as already developed within an extensity, and as covered over by qualities" (*Difference and Repetition*, trans. P. Patton [New York: Columbia, 1994], 223. Hereafter DR.) See also this statement: "intensity itself is subordinated to the qualities which fill extensity. . . . Intensity is difference, but this dif-

ference tends to deny or to cancel itself out in extensity and underneath quality" (ibid.). I am arguing, however, that in the case of environmental trauma, the qualitative aspect is *not* buried beneath the quantitative dimensions.

31. Deleuze, *The Logic of Sense*, trans. M. Lester with C. Stivale, ed. C. V. Boundas (New York: Columbia University Press, 1990), 141 (cited hereafter as LS).

32. LS 207.

33. G. Deleuze and F. Guattari, *A Thousand Plateaus*, trans. B. Massumi (Minneapolis: University of Minnesota Press, 1987), 70 (cited hereafter as TP): "The plane of consistency, or planomenon, is in no way an undifferentiated aggregate of unformed matters, but neither is it a chaos of formed matters of every kind." At p. 252 the authors assimilate the planomenon to the "Rhizosphere"—hence to a nonarborescent, nonstriated, immanent form of becoming.

34. "From all points of view, whether of quantity, quality, relation, or modality, contraries appear connected at the surface as much as in depth" (LS 175).

35. For this discussion, see TI 130–34.

36. TP 174–75. Cf. also 170, 181. The authors nonetheless do not refer explicitly to Levinas in these passages.

37. TP 181. Because of this social origin of the face, "the face is not a universal" (ibid., 176).

38. TP 181, my italics.

39. TP 172–73. See all of chapter 7, "Year Zero: Faciality," esp. 181, 190.

40. Just as earlier I had to denaturalize the glance—by dephenomenalizing and reducing it—to make it consonant with the human face as conceived by Levinas, so Deleuze and Guattari similarly withdraw the face from its fate as an anatomical head among other features of the natural world. The human head is only relatively different from the heads of other animals. But the face requires a radical withdrawal—thanks to the very traits that Levinas would ascribe to it: its ability to bear and express meaning (its "signifiance") as well as its status as a subject (its "subjectification"): both of which make it incommensurate with all other natural phenomena, enigmatic in relation to them, absolutely deterritorialized. But the face is incongruous with natural phenomena for Levinas because it is transcendent to them—at once ethical and religious, "metaphysical"—whereas for Deleuze and Guattari it is discontinuous with such phenomena because it is a social construct. This is why they insist that its correlate is not the natural world or "milieu" but *landscape*, itself a social construct. With landscape, it forms a close binary pair

called "face-landscape," within which there is not just deterritorialization (relative or absolute) but continual reterritorialization of one term upon the other.

41. "Phenomenon and Enigma," *Collected Philosophical Papers*, trans. A. Lingis (Dordrecht: Nijhof, 1987), 69.

42. This is the title of a section of "Phenomenon and Enigma."

43. *The Ecological Approach to Visual Perception*, 23.

44. EI 101–104. The expression "Here I am" is traced back by Levinas to the Old Testament: "To the voice that calls from the burning bush, Moses answers 'Here I am', but does not dare to lift up his eyes" ("Phenomenon and Enigma," 68).

45. I owe this point to David Michael Levin, in conversation. See his books *The Opening of Vision: Nihilism and the Postmodern Situation* (New York: Routledge, 1988) and *The Philosopher's Gaze: Modernity and the Shadows of Enlightenment* (Berkeley: University of California Press, 1999).

46. "As soon as the Other looks at me (*me regarde*), I am responsible for him, without having to *take* responsibility for him; this responsibility *encumbers* me" (EI 102; his italics).

47. A different version of this chapter has appeared in *Research in Phenomenology*, special issue on Environmental Philosophy, 2001.

CHAPTER 12

What is Eco-Phenomenology?

DAVID WOOD

The Need for a Rapprochement with Naturalism

Phenomenology was born out of resistance to the threat of naturalism. But if phenomenology is to be able to think about Nature, it must either rescue Nature itself from naturalism, or work out a new relationship to what it had perceived as the danger of naturalism. Or both.

The resistance to naturalism is a principled resistance, in various senses. If naturalism means that the phenomena in question are fundamentally governed by causal laws, with the possible addition of functional explanations, and relations of succession, conjunction, and concatenation, resistance takes the form of limiting the scope of such phenomena, or showing that even in those domains in which naturalism might seem wholly appropriate—the realm of what is obviously Nature—naturalism is fatally flawed as a standpoint.

For example, to the extent that perception brings us into intimate relation with the manifold things of this world, and definitively breaks through any sense of phenomenology as an otherworldly idealism, it also becomes clear that phenomenology and naturalism could not simply agree to a territorial division. A phenomenology of perception quickly discovers that it is only as spatially and temporally embodied beings that seeing takes place. Seeing (and hearing and touching) is a phenomenon of the differentiation of the world into discrete bodies, including ourselves, that occupy distinct places at particular times, bodies endowed with a mobility that reflects their needs and desires. These are not just natural facts about the world, but fundamental dimensions of the world, dimensions that structure the very possibility of factuality. And they certainly structure perception, insofar as perception is essentially perspectival, bound to surfaces of visibility, limited by obstruction, and tied powerfully to our embodiment—in our having two eyes, two ears, two hands, and muscles that give us mobility in various dimensions. And that embodiment appears in more complex ways, in our having various somatic and social desires that shape and direct perception, and in the temporal syntheses in which it is engaged. Many of these structures of bodily finitude are invariant for any living creature and could be said to *constitute* perception rather than qualify it. If something like this is true, a certain phenomenology, at least, is both inseparable from our involvement in the world as natural beings, and points to aspects of that involvement that do not seem to be captured by naturalism. Does this mean that we have managed to carve out a space for phenomenology within nature, reinforcing the divorce of intentionality from causality? The key to our position here is that there are dimensions essential to perception which reflect nonaccidental aspects of our natural existence. This means that intentionality is *structured* in a way that *fills out* what is specific about perceptual consciousness, rather than interrupting or contesting the intentional stance. But does this structuration reinforce the distinctness of intentionality (from naturalism), or does it offer a bridge across which a certain conversation could begin?

One might suppose that what phenomenology points to fundamentally is another level of causality, one that is presupposed by the operative causality of everyday phenomena. That other level would be describable through an evolutionary naturalism, one that would explain, for example, how living creatures have acquired the functionally integrated and environmentally responsive bodies that they do indeed possess, and perhaps explain how it is that multiple complex individual living beings developed in the first place, for example, through the incorporation into a single "body" of what began as a group of simpler symbiotically related organisms.[1] Would such an account of a deep causality make phenomenology redundant, or would it actually facilitate an engagement between phenomenology and naturalism?

If eco-phenomenology can give us better access to nature than that represented by the naturalism phenomenology was created to resist, by supplementing intentionality structurally with non- or preintentional characteristics of nature, would not eco-phenomenology be the future of a phenomenology, one which has purged itself of its traumatic gestation in opposition to nature?

Phenomenology could be said to concern itself with what appears in its appearing. But what is at stake here? What is at stake is a recovery of a relation to the *Sache selbst*, one that is covered over by all manner of objectifying illusions—of habit, reflection, naturalism, commodification—whose shared *modus operandi* is the occlusion of the activity of time in an apparently always-already-achieved presence.

Phenomenology opposes itself, then, to a certain kind of naïve naturalism, and to a broader sense of the natural through which the products of human engagement lose any trace of that production. But to recover an engagement with the *Sache selbst* is not at all to return to some pure presence; it is rather to return to a world in which the relation between present experience and the complexity of what is being experienced has always been deeply complex and stratified. Eco-phenomenology is the pursuit of the relationalities of worldly engagement, both human and those of other creatures.[2]

By focusing now on two rich dimensions of such engagement, I would like to develop a sense of a middle ground of relationality, a space neither governed by simple causality nor by simple intentionality, and suggest that in this space phenomenology can recover from the trauma of its birth in opposition to naturalism. These two dimensions we could call the plexity of time and the boundaries of thinghood.[3]

The Plexity of Time

Even though the value of presence has often occluded what is at stake, rather than helped us explore it, it has properly drawn our attention to the centrality of time to experience.[4] While time is central to my sense of phenomenology as essentially oriented to relationality, our experience of time, and the temporality of our experience, can function both as an obstacle to this orientation and also as its central plank. If we think of time as a series of discrete presents, or simply "live in the present," relational complexity is dead. And yet, there is no richer dimension of relationality than time. On the basis of our experience of time and the temporality of our experience, we grasp the continuous identities of things, the coordination of their processual and pulsing rhythms, and many virtual and imaginative ways in which even in the instant we enter a connectedness that transcends the moment. And every form of connection is put into play and contested by the powers of interruption, interference, and breakdown. Phenomenology is indeed descriptive in the sense of trying to get clear about the structures of these relations and disruptions but, heedless of Hegel's warning, such descriptions are also edifying, in alerting us to the illusions of immediacy and in showing us how deep temporal complexity is articulated and how it changes the way we see. Let me say a little more about these four strands: the invisibility of time, the celebration of finitude, the coordination of rhythms, and the interruption and break-down of temporal horizons.

1. *Time as invisible.* It is a commonplace to identify the eternal with the unchanging, and time with change, which would put time and eternity at odds with each other. A clue to how misleading this is can be found in the relation between the visible and the invisible. We typically think of the relation between the visible and the invisible in, broadly speaking, spatial terms. The invisible is either hidden by the visible or occupies some other ethereal realm. But if by the invisible we mean that which does not give itself to a certain kind of immediacy, then we may find the invisible curiously closer to hand than we thought. If, for example, the invisible is to be contrasted to a sense of visibility to which the mere illuminated availability of the thing in front of us is sufficient, then we may find the invisible to be a clue not just to a secret or hidden realm but to a more subtle grasp of visibility itself. And for this, we need to move not to another deeper or more rarefied space but to time.

Suppose I look out the window—what do I see? A tree. There it is. It is there in front of me, as visible as I could want. But what do I see when I see a tree, what does seeing it consist in? If I were an ant climbing up the tree, assuming ants have eyes of some sort, I would be able to "see" the tree. We might argue about whether the ant could really see the tree if it could see only a part of the tree at any one time or if it did not know what a tree "is." It is clear that seeing can be compromised, or at least questioned, by certain kinds of conceptual or perspectival limitations. If this is so, then seeing a tree cannot just consist in it being there, in the light, and I having my eyes open. ("Intuitions without concepts are blind.") But there is a less obvious dimension in which seeing is compromised—that of time. We know that we cannot "hear" music at an instant, but that hearing requires participation in a certain temporality. We have to undergo an experience in time. It would not take long to hear "that there was music playing in the house," but to hear the music "as such," for example to hear what was being played, to hear the piece itself—these each require a temporal engagement. Now of course it is possible that from only three bars I could immediately identify the piece, even have an image of the score flash into mind. If this happened, I would have come to recognize the true temporal extendedness of the object in a snatch, or glimpse. The moment would capture something importantly nonmomentary. And in this, and in many cases where there is in fact no score to be found, the temporal pattern recognized in the moment is one that is essentially repeatable, however distinctive this particular occasion may be. By analogy I am suggesting that the life of the tree, the living tree, the tree of which we glimpse only a limb here, a trunk there, or views from various angles, this temporally extended persisting, growing tree, is invisible. Sometimes we try to capture this extended visibility with the word "watch," as, "last night I watched the match." In watching there is the suggestion of a certain synthetic activity that addresses significantly extended features in the object. Even there, we seem to run against the grain when we try to think of something that essentially unfolds in time as "visible." Something that merely perdures is visible because time does not operate as a dimension of essential unfolding or articulation. So one moment can easily represent any other. But something that grows, develops, transforms itself cannot as easily represent that aspect of itself in any one moment. Think of those photographs of sporting victory that capture the "moment" of accomplishment. The raised arms, the open mouth, the wild eyes mark the moment at which a certain significance has arisen in the course of events.[5] The sign here, the mark of significant accomplishment, transition, or depth, precisely attempts to mark the relation between one particular moment and the temporal horizon of its significance. The sign renders the invisible visible. But it also renders the invisible *as such* invisible, precisely by providing a substitute for it. It is here, for example, that we find the paradoxical success of narrative.

In summary: (a) There is an invisible in the heart of the visible to the extent that the essential temporal articulatedness of things is not itself obviously presented in their immediate temporary appearance. (b) Furthermore, the eventuating ground of things is not itself present, visible, available to us, whether we think of this as an eruptive event (Heidegger) or the product of a contingent conjunction of forces (Foucault). It may, or may not, have ever once been visible. The question here is what can be seen, and this does not admit of a general answer. There are many ways in which "They have eyes but they do not see. . . ."

What phenomenology does is to activate and reactivate the complex articulations and relations of things, restoring through description, through dramatization, a participatory engagement (bodily, imaginative, etc.) with things. A turn to the articulatedness of things, and to their eventuating groundedness, is a return to the conditions of human fulfillment and connectedness, but also to the sources of renewal, transformation, and resistance.

2. *The celebration of finitude.* That time resides as the invisible in the visible opens us to a transformed relation to time. To show this, it would be hard to improve on remarks made in the course of Leishman's introduction to Rilke's *Duino Elegies*:

> The ideal of complete and undivided consciousness, where will and capability, thought and action, vision and realization are

one, is the highest Man can form, and yet so impossible is it for Man to realize this ideal, to become like the Angels, that it is rather a rebuke than an inspiration. What, then, remains for Man? Perhaps, in Pater's phrase, to give the highest possible significance to his moments as they pass; to be continually prepared for those moments when eternity is perceived behind the flux of time, those moments when "the light of sense/ goes out, but with a flash that has revealed/ the invisible world."

You may be surprised by my giving a platform to what sounds like neo-Platonism. But the consequence of the impossibility of the angelic for us humans is the transformation of the most ordinary, whether we see this as an opportunity or, as Leishman does, as an obligation: "[T]he price of these moments of insight is a constant attentiveness and loyalty to all things and relationships, even the humblest and least spectacular, that immediately surround us."

This sense of the infinite in the finite, which is precisely not a spiritual dilution but an intensification of the concrete, can take a number of forms. Repetition, and the awareness of repetition, can be taken to the extreme of intensity that we find in Nietzsche's eternal recurrence. Here connectedness between individual events generates a kind of depth to every moment through which its very singularity is heightened. We can so focus on the immediacy of the present (looking into my lover's eyes) for example, that the passage of time itself seems suspended. Finally, we can come to experience the passage of time as such a constancy that time itself becomes the best candidate for the permanent, what does not change.

If I am right, these various approaches to the infinite in the finite involve a kind of prerepresentational part/whole relation in which the parts are seen to bear within themselves the imprint of the whole, not as a burden but as an intensification. Such a relation captures the kind of complexity with which eco-phenomenology would treat time.

3. *Coordination of rhythms.* To the extent that things bear and embody rhythms, pulses of temporal development, they form part of a manifold and stratified field in which these rhythms interact, interpenetrate, interfere with one another, become locally coordinated and so on. Fireflies come to flash synchronously at the end of an evening, while cicadas carefully space (or time) their periodicities of their emergence from hibernation so as not to overlap and compete. The point here is that through rhythm and periodicity time acquires sufficient autonomous efficacy to generate its own relational differentiation. This example illustrates well the significance of a middle ground. For the coordination of rhythms does

not appear here as the result of the synthetic or constitutive activity of any kind of subject, nor any simple causal mechanism. Clearly there are evolutionary processes behind cicada periodicity. And competitive advantage is clearly tied up with causal mechanisms such as the effect of lack of food on survival rates. What is salient here is that such mechanisms seem to be subservient to the advantages accruing from the eventual rhythmic coordination and differentiation

4. *The interruption and breakdown of temporal horizons.* Lastly, while these first three aspects of temporality build on, if they do not simply respect, the horizonalities of time within which things live, move, and have their being, time is importantly not just about grasping the invisible continuities lurking below the surface of the visible. It is equally about interruption, break down, discontinuity—about the arrival of the unexpected, about the unintended consequence, about the ghosts from another time that still haunt us, about *Nachträglichkeit*, about blindness about the past, about the failure to move forward, about dreaming of impossible futures, and so on. And it is especially in its pursuit of this last of these four aspects of time that eco-phenomenology preserves us against a premature holism, an over-enthusiastic drive to integration. The multiply fractured wholes with which we are acquainted include within them many perfectly completed developments, many acorns that turn into oak trees, and many images, desires, and fantasies of wholeness. Anything, taken singly, can be broken or unexpected or fractured. But not everything can suffer this fate. *We need a model of the whole as something that will inevitably escape our model of it.* Indeed, it could be said that when it comes to nature, time as *physis*, as eruptive event, escapes representation long before it is party to expectations that are not met. It escapes representation by being its presupposition. While I have focused on what we could call temporal relatedness and its breakdowns, it is quite true that there is a kind of primary invisibility in the very upthrust of time as event.

These four strands—the invisibility of time, the celebration of finitude, the coordination of rhythms, and the interruption and breakdown of temporal horizons—offer us, I am suggesting, not just analytical pointers as to how we might think about time, but ways of enriching our temporal experience. This account occupies what I have called a middle ground overlapping the space of intentionality, avoiding both the language of causality and that of ecstatic intentionality. I am sure that an eco-phenomenology could profitably pursue the theoretical elaborations each of them would make explicit, but I will not do this here. The fundamental focus of these remarks has been on their contribution to an enhanced attentiveness to the complexity of natural phenomena and the ease with which that is hidden from view by our ordinary experience.[6]

The Boundaries of Thinghood

It is possible to imagine a world without things, or at least a cosmos of gaseous swirlings and passing clouds. It may be that what we imagine is not possible, that for there to be swirlings, there have to be the cosmic equivalents of coffee cups or bathtubs to contain the swirlings. Nonetheless, we seem to be able to imagine a thingless world. But it is not our world. We could of course imagine a viewpoint on our world in which what we now experience as things would be so speeded up that these things would appear as processes. Extinct volcanoes would be momentary pauses of an ongoing activity, as when a swimmer turns round at the end of the pool. Individual animate organisms would be seen as part of a wider flux of chemical exchanges. Things as we know them would disappear. And as this speeding up would enable us to see things, to make connections that were not previously available, who is to say that it would be a distortion? Do we have any basis for saying that seeing things at this or that speed is more accurate? Well, perhaps we do. If we imagine everything so speeded up that it happened in an instant, it would be impossible to make distinctions at all. It is hard not to see that as an information-deficient environment. And at the opposite extreme, we can imagine such a slow perspective that rivers did not detectably flow, and rays of light seemed to linger forever in the sun's starting blocks. Such perspectives would be distorting because the phenomena of relative change and relative stability would not be available. And as these imaginative experiments are conducted with the memory of such a distinction being indispensable, it is hard not to see these other extreme views as deeply deficient. It might be said that the very slow view really does teach us something deep—that nothing really changes. But that is much less deep a conclusion from a world in which change is not apparent anyway, than from a world of which we might say that *plus ça change mais tout reste le même*. All this is to encourage us to suppose not only that it would be difficult for us (see Kant and Strawson) to make sense of a world of total flux, but that if such a view were to rest on the idea that the temporal frame from which things are viewed is up to us, the flux view is simply a mistake. To make this point the other way round—on the total flux view, there would be nothing very special about May 18, 1980, the day on which Mount St. Helens erupted, compared to the day before or the day after. On the "ordinary" view—which we are defending—there really are events as well as processes, births, deaths, and catastrophes as well as continuities. And these concepts are of an ontological order, not just epistemological. That does not mean that we may not fail to notice them, or to care much. When we crush cicadas under our feet, we may not register the crunch, and if we do, think of it as part of a wider "process" in which only a small percentage of these creatures survive to maturity. But we do know, and most if pressed would acknowledge, that there are individual cicadas, and that crushing them ends their lives, even as it allows that cicada's body to reenter the food cycle by providing nutrients for nematodes.

So, things may come and go. But for them to come and go, they have to be real while they are here, or else they could neither come nor go. Buses come and go, but it would be a strange passenger that refused to get on the bus on the grounds that "buses come and go." Or even more deeply, that this bus will eventually be scrapped. The mechanic working on the bus knows that although the parts will eventually wear out, the connections between the parts is real enough that if one part fails, the bus may not run, and if it is replaced, it will. The surgeon knows the same about his patient. And the poet knows the same about the word she ponders. If she gets that word right, the poem will fly.

Permanence, then, is no test for reality, and many ways in which we think about internal complexity, the part/whole relation, and functional integrity would be impossible unless we admitted the existence of things. It could be replied that these considerations are no less fictional than the original belief in things and that, of course, once we make one error, others will follow. Of course I do not *really* doubt the existence of things, or worry that you need this demonstrated. Nonetheless, good stuff happens when we try to explain why we take *things* seriously. References to mechanics, surgeons, and poets are to people concerned with maintaining or creating complex things, things that can break, or breakdown, or falter, or fail to be realized. Here we have distinguished between machines, organisms, and works of art. Mount St. Helens was a very large lump of rock held together by whatever forces bind crystalline structures together and by gravity (and torn apart by pressure from molten magma). A rock is not a machine or an organism. But even a rock has a certain organized integrity. David did not throw sand in Goliath's eyes; he threw a rock at his forehead. And the rock arrived at his forehead all at the same time, causing serious damage to the skull's capacity to protect the brain, bringing about the collapse of the whole Goliath.

It might be said that nothing of much importance could be true of all these things, from giants to mountains, from buses to poems. Perhaps the differences between them will turn out to be even more interesting, but the point of identifying them all as *things* is to draw attention to something they share, which I have called organized integrity.[7] Obviously this comes in many shapes. Rock composed by aggregation has a less "organized" integrity than rock that, under compression, has formed a large crystal, where the parts have come together in a way that reflects a pattern of organization (as in a snowflake). And to capture the kind of integrity we find in living organisms, we need to speak of self-organization and (dynamically) of growth, self-maintenance, self-protection, and reproduction. Between rocks and rockfish, there are of course many other kinds of organized complexity—such as machines, stock markets, weather systems, and plants. My point in offering here a reprise of the great chain of being is to bring to the fore the idea that things, and the organized integrity they manifest, come in many forms. And that their unity depends, typically, on the relationships between their parts. Now this relationship may be as sensitive to disruption as you like, or as resistant to disruption. A watch mechanism is given a case to keep out dirt that would disrupt its workings in a split second. Gyroscopically driven mechanical systems have the power to maintain their balance in the face of external agitation. What we commonly take to be typical of living systems, however, and some other animal collectivities and human creations, is that they each actively maintain some boundary with what lies "outside" them. Such boundaries are, in part, the products of the very processes that maintain them. Boundaries are the way stations between insides and outsides, the sites of negotiation, of transformation, of sustenance, of protection. Boundaries are real, and yet they are often recessive and ambiguous. Boundaries are not at first things, but they arise in and for certain things, and they may even turn into things. (Think of the Berlin Wall, think of the line we must not cross in a relationship.) But for our purposes, what is especially important is that boundaries are the sites of a special kind of phenomena—limina—and a whole new opening for phenomenology.[8]

We have arrived at this point, the threshold of a new/old continent, by highlighting the reality of things, over against continuous flux, and their possession of a certain organized integrity. We moved on to claim that it is an initially distinctive feature of living things that they maintain this integrity by creating boundaries, which are sites of management of inside-outside relations. This story we are telling is not a biological story. Indeed, to repeat some of the Husserlian hubris, it is engaged in what I would call tentative legislation for any subsequent science. The hubris derives from the thought that there are categories and concepts importantly at work in any science that are not its distinctive property, but also that sciences themselves operate as boundary-generating systems. If so, individual sciences are not in the best position to talk about science as such. At these, part of the role traditionally played by metaphysics[9] is here played by eco-phenomenology's concern with the fabric of time and with the events that occur at boundaries—phenomena that are not the proper purview of any one science. Such a liminology deals not only with the maintenance of boundaries within individual organisms but the ways in which the shape and location of boundaries is transformed during growth, adaptation, and the struggle to survive, in which the breaching of these boundaries is coordinated in the interest of higher groupings (see families, organizations, sex, war), which deals with symbiotic and productive relations of dependency between species, and which deals with the psychic formations necessary both for the maintenance, mobilization, and transformation of such boundaries. All this is not the subject matter of one science, but thinking through these liminological events is something that an eco-phenomenology could protect and encourage.

What would liminology concern itself with? The imperative of boundary maintenance leads to such issues as dependency, cooperation, symbiosis, and synergy. But also rupture, catastrophe, and transformation. All of these are, in an important sense, natural phenomena, phenomena that appear at many different levels in nature. But equally they also suggest something of a concrete logic for nature. And not just what we usually include in "nature."

Between Intentionality and Causality

We have tried so far to show that the gap between naturalism and phenomenology is in an important way dependent on how one thinks of nature. The fundamental principle of phenomenology—that of intentionality—specifically names consciousness as the central actor: "all consciousness is consciousness of something." This is not just a claim about consciousness, but a claim about the kind of relation that consciousness brings into being, which in any usual sense we could call a nonnatural relation. I may be an embodied being, and the object of my awareness may be a tiger or a mountain. But the relation between us—seeing, fearing, hoping, admiring—is not a causal relation, not a physical relation, but an intentional one. When I admire the mountain, the mountain is not affected, and even if rays of light passing from the mountain to me are necessary for this admiration to take place, the admiration is something of a different order. I may be dreaming, say of an imaginary golden mountain, making a causal account of the relation even harder to sustain. And yet the absence of proximate cause does not refute causality. Think of finding a giant rock half-way down a valley. Or seashells in a farmer's field. To understand intentionality to be opposed to causality is important if we associate causality with determinacy, with linearity, and with a certain kind of automatism. But if the realm of causality were to be expanded in a way that overcomes these prejudices, what then?

One obvious way of beginning to bridge the gap between intentionality and causality would be to introduce the idea of information. When I admire the mountain from my window, I add nothing to it and take nothing away. My relation to the mountain may develop—I may decide to climb it. It might kill me through exposure or avalanche. But here at the window, causality is at a minimum. What I receive is information about the mountain, directly, from the mountain, in a way directly caused by the actual shape of the mountain. But I receive this as an information processor, not as an impact of matter on matter. Does this help us to naturalize intentionality? Only a little. When a boot makes an imprint on soft ground, we may say that there is a direct causal dimension—the squishing of clay—but there is an informational dimension, reflected in the precise shape of the imprint. But information can be registered, without it "registering" with the clay. What then is distinctive about human consciousness? The sight of the mountain is information "for" me. Whereas we might say that the imprint of the boot is not information "for" the clay. Two kinds of reasons could be given here. First that the clay has no brain, no capacity for symbolic decoding. We are tempted then to say that because the clay cannot think, cannot reflectively process information, that even if there is something more than mere causality operating, it does not add up, say, to the impact of a footprint on a Robinson Crusoe.[10] But secondly, the clay has no interests, no relation to the world such that what happens out there could matter to it. This second deficiency, the absence of what Ricoeur would call an intentional arc, does not reduce intentionality to causality, but if we accept that this connection to practical agency is central to intentional meaning, it does locate intentionality within an interactive nexus from which causal powers cannot be separated. If I "see" a fruit as succulently delicious, this is intrinsically connected, however many times removed, with my enjoyment of fruit, my capacity to eat, and so on. The fact that I am now allergic to fruit, or that I cannot afford this particular item of fruit, is neither here nor there. The point is that I am the kind of being that eats sweet things, and the structure of my desire reflects that. The same can be said of erotic intentionality and all its transformations and displacements. If this is so, intentionality is firmly lodged within my bodily existence, within the natural world.

It remains to ask how the relation of "ofness" or "aboutness" can be understood naturalistically. We could say this: that intentionality is naturalistically embedded, but is itself an indirect natural relation. It is indirect because it is mediated by such functions as imagination, transformation, delay, and memory, which are often but misleadingly associated with interiority. The frame within which the intentional functions is a complex nonreductive natural setting, in which humans' needs, desires, fears, and hopes reflect different levels of their relation to a natural world. What we call con-sciousness is perhaps only derivatively (but importantly) able to be broken down into consciousness of this or that. Or to put this claim another way, all specifically directed intentional consciousness draws on the manifoldness of our sensory and cognitive capacities. Con-sciousness is a networked awareness, a with-knowing, a knowing that, even as it is separated into different modalities, draws on those others. (Something similar could be said about the relation between individual awareness and the connection this establishes or sustains with others. Through con-sciousness we not only register the significance of things for us, but also connect things together with other things.) Here I would draw attention to the fact that our being able to focus on one particular domain or object is quite compatible with that capacity being in fact dependent on the same being having many other capacities, and there ultimately being an inte-grative basis for this connectedness in our embodied existence. And we must not forget our capacity for productive transformation of the inten-tional order—our capacity for becoming aware of our own awareness, taking our activity as an object of a second-order awareness. I would make two comments here: First, the dependence of focused attention on other nonfocal awarenesses is illustrated in our capacity to see objects as solid, round, and so on. These latter properties are arguably (as Berkeley and Merleau-Ponty have both argued) dependent on our capacities for tactile manipulation, which is imaginatively but only tacitly implicated in our vision. Secondly, I suggest that our capacity for self-consciousness rests firmly on this capacity for demarcating a bounded field, even when that is our own awareness. We can only speculate that there is some cog-nitive crossover from our more primitive capacity to register and defend our own bodily boundaries and systemic integrity, operations that only continue in consciousness what begins at much more primitive levels of life.

In this section, I have tried to indicate various ways in which think-ing about consciousness would take us into thinking about our interre-lated capacities to (a) understand things within fields of relevance (horizons); (b) to bring to bear on one modality of awareness interpreta-tive powers drawn from other dimensions (such as the tactile in the visual); and (c) the ability to reconstitute our awareness as the object of a second-order awareness. I have suggested that in these and other ways consciousness is tied up with the construction, displacement, and trans-formation of fields of significance, and of significance as a field phenom-enon. Merleau-Ponty helps us think through the connection between such phenomena and the idea of a body schema. And I would suggest a more primitive basis for the idea of a body schema in our fundamental need to manage body boundaries. These sorts of connections illustrate how much a certain naturalization of consciousness would require, at the same time, an expansion of our sense of the natural. That, I am arguing, is at last illustrated by (if not grounded on) the existence of things with various degrees of cohesive integrity, which leads, eventually, to ways of managing boundaries. These are natural phenomena that spill over into what we normally think of as distinct questions of meaning, identity, and value.

Deep Ecology

A friend sent me a paper in the late seventies in which he first connected Heidegger to deep ecology, and then charged ecological thinking in general with fascistic tendencies. I do not propose to deal with the politically troubling aspects of *his* argument. But the central worry about ecological thinking, especially its deep version, is worth dissecting. I want to argue that the dividing line between benign and pernicious appropriations of the ecological perspective has to do with these liminological issues of boundary management which eco-phenomenology is in a position to address.

I will draw lightly on Arne Naess and George Sessions's "Eight Points," presented as an outline of deep ecology. Deep ecology is deep in part because of the imperatives it generates from certain claims it makes about the relations between humans and the rest of nature, some of which are already evaluations. The fundamental claims here are that nonhuman life has an intrinsic value independent of its value for humans, that biological diversity promotes the quality of both human and nonhuman life, and that the current human interference in nature is both contrary to the recognition of these values and unsustainable. The fascistic implications thought to arise from these claims would include the claim that one could justify active human population reduction to accommodate the needs of other species, and that more broadly, the rights of individual humans are to be subordinated to those of the species. More generally still, the deep-ecology perspective is presenting itself as a kind of metalegislator of value, dissolving within itself every other dimension or consideration.

The plausibility of such conclusions arises from the understandable belief that if the alternative is an irreversible destruction of nature or an unstoppable escalation in human population growth—such as some sort of catastrophe—then almost any measures might be justified in an emergency. When the house is on fire, you don't reason with the child who wants to finish his Nintendo game; you grab the child and run. (And explain later.) But if the house is merely smoking, or there are reports of its smoking, the situation is less clear. Deep ecology is a crystalized vision of the desperate state we are in. But the need for radical remedies is a reflection of the totalizing aspects of the diagnosis. What I want to suggest, however, is that so-called deep ecology is the product of an *uncontrolled* application of the methodological virtues inherent in the ecological perspective. The central virtue is the recognition of the constitutive quality of relationality. Things are what they are by virtue of their relations to other things. What look like external relations are, if not internal, at least constitutive. Living things eat each other, breath and drink the elements, live in communities, while inanimate things have properties that depend on the properties of other things. Limestone cliffs would not last long in acid rain. Everywhere, it is the interplay of relative forces that produces results, not the absolute forces themselves. What the ecological perspective teaches us is that things with no obvious point to their existence play a role in the life cycles of other beings. It teaches us that the survival of a particular species may depend on the preservation of an environment with very specific features. And it teaches us that the life, death, and flourishing of things is tied up with other factors, conditions, and creatures in ways for which we typically do not have a map, and under variability tolerances we do not know. We can study these things, of course. But as much as ecology is a science, it is also a counsel of caution, precisely because it deals with the interaction of widely disparate kinds of things.

Here we need to contrast a precise science with a field science. A precise science fundamentally idealizes its objects, and in so doing, it can develop highly sophisticated theoretical structures—most notably in mathematics. A field science deals with the interaction of many quite different sorts of things, allowing no consistent method of idealization and inhibiting complex axiological development. Ecology is just such a science. And if we extend "science" more broadly, the same must be said of geography, history, and anthropology. In between, we find physics, chemistry, and biology, and all those sciences that profit from controlling conditions in laboratories. It is a commonplace of physics that a universe in which there are only two bodies requires much less mathematical complexity than that of a universe with three bodies. And once a fourth body is added, all hell breaks loose. Real-life biological environments contain not just huge numbers of bodies but bodies of very different sorts, each of which manages, through various different procedures, its own relation to that environment or to its own niche in that environment. It is curious to realize that although we could not mathematically, or in any other way, really give adequate representation to the complete workings of such a complex system, nonetheless such "systems" do "work." This is not such a mystery, of course. Representation often plays only a small part in the way of the world.[11] But of course another reason such complex systems work is that we usually do not have any precise sense of what it is for them not to work, what outcomes would be failures. Does the outbreak of myxomytosis in Anglesey rabbits signal a failure of the system after foxes have been eradicated, or does it mark a successful transformation of the system? Deep ecology would say that while there may be difficult cases, there are also clear ones: that we know what a dead lake means, and that photographs from space argue that the earth, itself a living being, is dying.

The fundamental thrust of phenomenology is its nonreductive orientation to phenomena. That is what is meant by "Back to the things themselves!" To the extent that deep ecology would permit or encourage the reduction of "things" to the function or role that they play in some higher organization, deep ecology would be opposed to and opposed by phenomenology. I suspect that the ecological perspective more broadly does indeed harbor a tension between finding in "relatedness" a basis of a higher-order synthesis, and recognizing that the kind of relatedness in question will constantly and awkwardly interrupt such syntheses. Take a group of people in a room. We may listen in on their voices and say—"that must be the French soccer team," recognizing them under a collective identity. We may, on the other hand, remember that each of these people has a distinct outlook on the world, that they cannot be collectivized or serialized without an objectifying loss. When we watch them playing on the field, we may conclude that to understand "what is happening," we need a perspective in which we move between these two viewpoints, just as the players themselves, each separately, move in and out of various forms of collective or subgroup consciousness. (One player may be aware of what an opposing player is doing and have a good understanding of where his teammate is moving up to. Another may have a sense of the strategic opportunities created by the different styles of play of each team.) What is clear here can be seen writ large in a living environment in which a multitude of creatures compete and cooperate, eat and feed each other, and whose awareness of one another's presence or existence will vary and fluctuate. If every living being does not merely have a relation to its outside, to what is other than itself, but is constantly managing that relationship economically (risking death for food, balancing individual advantage with collective prosperity, etc.), then however much it may be possible, for certain purposes, to treat such an environment collectively, that treatment will be constantly open to disruption from the intransigence of its parts. Important as it is to see things in relation to one another, and tempting as it then is to see these spaces, fields, playgrounds of life, as wholes, that wholeness is dependent on the con-

tinuing coordination of parts that have, albeit residual, independent interests. At the same time these "things" we call environments, niches, and
the like, are themselves subject to what we might, after Derrida, call the
law of context. And context is an iterative and porous notion. While all
meaning (every creature) is contextual (exists in relation to a sustaining
field), no context is fully saturated, closed, or determinate. Context is
porous for the scientist in that his model of the environment will always
be vulnerable to the incursion of "other factors." But it is porous in itself,
"on the ground" too, in that unusual or unexpected events may always
come into play. And it is porous for living creatures in the sense that the
whole way in which their embodiment anticipates the "world out there"
may turn out not to protect them from injury or death.

The Ends of Nature

It would be a brave scientist who would admit to being an Aristotelian
today. The idea that things have an inherent *telos* seems half way to a
primitive animism. But poor metaphysics may fail to do justice to valuable intuitions. An inherent purpose is a hard thing to find when dissecting a frog; it does not appear alongside heart, legs, and sinews. But nor
does agility, noxious taste, and camouflaged coloration. That a living
organism exhibits a set of integrated functions organized around certain
ends—survival and reproduction—would be harder to deny. It is not so
much that the frog *has* reproduction as its end. Rather the frog—and every
other living being—could better be said to *embody* that end. Frogs may be
said to serve other ends, such as food for the French, or for grass snakes,
or keeping down the population of water spiders. But these are extrinsic
ends. To say that a frog has reproduction as its end is not to suggest that
these are independently definable ends frogs serve. It is simply to say that
the whole of froggy being is organized in such a way that it maximizes the
possibility of its reproduction, species survival. Within that umbrella, we
understand its individual activities—jumping in the air to catch a fly, to
eat, and to grow. Reproduction supplies a hierarchical framework of interpretive intelligibility. Purposiveness is not a part of a frog but a many-lev-
eled characteristic of its behavior, which ultimately makes it the kind of
being it is. At some levels, the frog clearly has purposes in the plural.
Whatever it thinks it is doing, it is actually sitting on the leaf soaking up
the sun or hunting flies. Its behavior is purposive in the sense that there
are ends toward which its behavior is adapted and directed. We may balk
at saying that survival and reproduction are higher-order purposes. It
might be said, instead, that they are just outcomes of the successful

pursuit of other smaller-scale ends, outcomes that have further consequences. The extreme view here would be to say that a living organism is
just a temporarily successful collection of mechanisms that, operating in
proximity, tend to perpetuate themselves—that there really is just mechanism here.[12] In my view the ways in which brains, and to some extent
nerve ganglia, coordinate and even in various ways represent the whole
of a creature to itself (body schemata), the emergence of immune systems,
levels of organized defence for the whole organism, suggest that this view
of a creature simply as a successful collection of parts will not fly. These
three features: hierarchical organization of functions, internal "representation" of the whole, and systemic defense mechanisms operating singly
and together provide a basis for saying that a living creature is not just a
collection of parts but functions, importantly, as a whole. But living creatures then *are* ends, they do not have ends. And of course, this analysis
would make it hard to attribute to a rock the desire to fall to earth. The
elimination of a rock's intrinsic terraphilia should still allow us to
acknowledge, however, the feature we noted above when discussing the
rock with which David smote Goliath—that, perhaps only for a moment,
the rock is an aggregated unity, which can be thrown all at once, or
admired on a desk. Other rocks can be sat on, climbed, worshiped, or protected against quarrying. There are obviously many ways in which
human purposes can enter into the definition of integrity. But the rock
that David threw did not get its integrity from David or Goliath. Rather
David made use of the rock's own integrity by picking it up, placing it in
a sling, and letting it fly.

It would be a foolish and not merely a brave scientist who declared
himself to be an Aristotelian. But just as politics is too important to be left
to generals, so nature is too important to be left to the natural sciences.
There are considerations cutting across the different sciences that can be
productively contemplated together. The particular considerations I am
raising here have to do with the way in which various kinds of things
maintain their integrity, manage boundaries, and relate to their surroundings. Each of these considerations raises ecological (and eco-nomic)
issues, and is best approached through a certain kind of phenomenology.

I recalled earlier the centrality of the distinction between Fact and
Essence for Husserl. But it was Merleau-Ponty who insisted that we
understand essence not in a Platonic way, and not as an objectified representation but, rather, more something like a structure of our Being-in-the-
world, what Merleau-Ponty calls "essence here is not the end, but a
means. *[It is] our effective involvement in the world that has to be understood
and made amenable to conceptualization.*"[13]

Phenomenology: An Open Future

I have discussed the attractions and dangers of deep ecology as a case study of how sensitivity to relationality and interconnectedness can turn into an over-rigid holism. The charge of fascism against deep ecology is understandable, if problematic. The central question has to do with the way in which *closure* operates within deep ecology. And this issue permeates so many contemporary disciplinary debates. The question of closure is the question of economy. In the way that I am construing it, eco-phenomenology, in the double sense of a phenomenological ecology, and an ecological phenomenology, is an important part of our vigilance against a certain kind of closure. The insistence on taking urgent measures like drastic human population reduction to save the planet offers a dramatic case study of the economy of boundary management.

For one of the key questions faced here is the kind of logic we apply to our thinking about the boundary. In so many areas, what we could call *emergency conditions* demand that we decide yes or no, friend or foe, inside or outside the tent, and so on. The reptilian brain is in charge. I assume this is what happens when T-cells in the blood go on patrol, looking for "foreign" material, where there really is an on-off, either/or switch. This mechanism turns out to be too crude when the body's immune system somehow comes to recognize parts of itself as "foreign," and attacks them. Or when it is persuaded not to attack invading cells that mimic the body's own. But this crudeness may be precisely what is normally needed. In contrast to this binary logic, there are more complex responses. "He is not my first choice, but he is someone I can work with." "I'm not really hungry, but you might be able to tempt me." Many boundary disputes get "resolved" by power-sharing agreements, mutual access, dual sovereignty, taking turns, or symbolic contests. There are issues about how we will fairly arrive at a yes/no decision (contests in which all parties accept the rules), as well as about how to resolve disputes in which there is no fully satisfactory answer. And it may be that the norm is that these different logics are always both in play. If Mexico and the United States were to agree to an open border (rather than more heavily defending the border), it might well be that this openness becomes possible precisely as Mexico and the United States become *separately* stronger, politically and economically. The property lines between houses in American suburbs are often marked very loosely on the ground. But this may reflect the fact that everyone has very accurate maps (and there is a highly developed legal system) so that, if necessary, a legal determination can always be made. Where the yes/no border logic is dominant, it often reflects an underdeveloped capacity for thinking—that is, for negotiating complexity—or the recognition that there are forces that would disempower those who think in such a way. Extremists drive even the moderates from the middle ground. What this shows is that a binary logic can operate between binary logic and negotiative thinking. Gresham's law (bad money drives out good) may apply to intellectual life too. If this is so, then phenomenology is a site of resistance to such tendencies. Are we then operating on an oppositional relation to binary thinking? Finally no. There really are emergencies when there is no time for subtlety, where you have to decide—friend or foe. Phenomenology is a resource for the phronesis necessary to distinguish these cases from others.

How does this relate to the question of closure and openness with which we started this section? The strength of deep ecology lies in its taking Hegel's dictum seriously—that the truth lies in the whole. Truth here need not take the form of one comprehensive statement or vision. Even our grasp of individual truths is sharpened when we understand their limitations, conditions, and so on. What is distinctive about deep ecology is its sense that the earth really is a strongly interconnected whole, one in which humans play an important part, but also one in which the part they play is not governed by an adequate grasp of the effects of them playing their part in this way or that. We are pissing in the reservoir and then wondering why the water tastes funny. Deep ecologists are understandably worried about the gap between the collective consequences of our individual actions on the rest of the biosphere and our grasp, whether individual or collective, of the impact we are making. Questions of totality figure in this diagnosis at many levels:

1. We each experience only a part of the earth—our own backyard plus trips, tours, vacations, movies, traveler's tales. If my tree is dying, I notice. But the earth dying, slowly, is not obvious, not something I can see at a glance out of my window. So there is a gap between what I can see and what may really be happening. The glance is ripe for education. Even the possibility of this gap may be something I am unaware of.

2. When I think about *my own* impact on the earth, I think I would find it hard, even if I tried, with my friends, to do *irrecoverable* harm. And to the extent that our consciousnesses of the significance of human action are resolutely individualistic, the collective impact of humans on the earth will fall beneath our radar screens. "Perhaps something should be done, but there is little I can do." Here there is a gap between an individualistic moral sensibility and the aggregated impact of human activity.

3. The deep ecologist not only believes that the earth is an interconnected whole, in which everything affects everything else. He believes that on his model of that interconnectedness, various disaster scenarios loom, and at the very least a series of uncontrollable, irreversible, and undesired outcomes.

4. And these consequences will occur unless very dramatic changes are made very soon. Either masses of people will come to their senses and demand this through normal democratic procedures. Or we need to suspend democratic institutions altogether.

An eco-phenomenological critique of deep ecology would attempt to open up options within its closed economy. The argument that there are circumstances in which democratic societies might suspend democracy is not as totalitarian as it might seem. Every state has emergency powers— to deal with riots, natural disasters, and threats from foreign powers. And of course, democratic institutions can operate as elected dictatorships between elections. Emergency measures, yes/no logics, do make sense where questions of life and death are concerned. The question of whether *the earth is a living being*, however, is not a fact of nature, but inseparable from the very questions about self-preservation, boundary maintenance, and nutrition that lurk at the borders of living things and other natural phenomena, and complex systems.

Conclusion

What then is eco-phenomenology? I have argued that eco-phenomenology, in which are folded both an ecological phenomenology and a phenomenological ecology, offers us a way of developing a middle ground between phenomenology and naturalism, between intentionality and causality. I argue that our grasp of Nature is significantly altered by thinking through four strands of time's plexity—the invisibility of time, the celebration of finitude, the coordination of rhythms, and the interruption and breakdown of temporal horizons. And also by a meditation on the role of boundaries in constituting the varieties of thinghood. Eco-phenomenology takes up in a tentative and exploratory way the traditional phenomenological claim to be able to legislate for the sciences, or at least to think across the boundaries that seem to divide them. In this way, it opens up and develops an access to Nature and the natural that is both independent of the conceptuality of the natural sciences, and of traditional metaphysics.

Notes

Versions of this chapter were presented at the IAEP conference at Penn State, October 2000, and at the Philosophy and Religious Studies department of the University of North Texas, December 2000. I am grateful to those whose comments improved it. A shorter version of this chapter was published in *Research in Phenomenology* 31.

1. See Donna Haraway's discussion in *How Like a Leaf: Interview with Donna Haraway* (with Thyrza Goodeve) (New York: Routledge, 1999).
2. Here we would attempt to think through Heidegger's various formulations of the animal's relation to the world as *weltarm*, or *weltlos*.
3. I have not yet found he word "plexity" in any dictionary, though it appears in various ways on the internet, sometimes in essays in linguistics, and sometimes in the names of websites. It is an attempt to get at the root sense of such words as complexity, implexity, and perplexity. And something of its intended sense can be divined from the SOED entry for *plexus*: "A structure [in the animal body] consisting of a network of fibres of vessels closely interwoven and intercommunicating."
4. Imagination is the central connection between space-boundary questions, and boundary/level transformation.
5. Cf. births, marriages, and deaths, the common thread that joins newspapers to religions.
6. There are paradoxes in the idea of "ordinary experience" that I cannot entirely resolve here. Someone might object, for example, that (surely) ordinary experience is precisely what is most rich. It is just our philosophical representation of it that is impoverishing. There is something right about this. The value of phenomenology, however, rests precisely on its claim to be able to bring out this wealth of subtlety without reductive schematization. The need for phenomenology lies not just in the dangers of such schematization, whether from science or from philosophy. It also responds to the dullness with which we often *live* our ordinary experience, however rich and subtle it may potentially be.
7. I use this phrase in the face of my own misgivings. In my view it marks an indispensable site, even if that is a site of interrogation and dispute.
8. See my paper "Time-Shelters: An Essay in the Poetics of Time," in *Time and the Instant*, ed. Robin Durie and David Webb (Manchester: Clinamen, 2001).
9. I am thinking here of Aristotle's idea that metaphysics, unlike the particular sciences, deals with being qua being.

10. When we speak of "something more than causality," we are trying to address changes in the clay which impact its own capacity to sustain complexity or relationality. Compression of soil can drive out air and water and so transform it from being something that sustains life, to something dead. Or something malleable that can sustain an impression to something hard that cannot. We are not so much escaping from causality here as introducing dimensions of significance which, though tied up with causality, begin to allow us to speak of "for the clay," whether or not it is information that is at stake.

11. This claim needs serious qualification. When a map is drawn showing which parts of the Amazon rainforest are to be clear cut, and what profit will accrue, representation is playing a key role. And capitalism in general, not to mention the information revolution, is driven precisely by representation. Nature seems to be that realm in which representation is not yet fully developed.

12. What is at stake here could hardly be over emphasized. Descartes's opposition to that part of Harvey's theory of the circulation of the blood that posited ventricles in the heart pumping by muscular contraction (rather than as Descartes claimed by rarefaction by a "dark fire" in the heart), was so great that he insisted in a letter to Mersenne in 1639 that "if what he had written about the movement of the heart should turn out to be false, then the whole of his philosophy was worthless." As I understand it, Descartes sees that part of Harvey's *De Motu Cordis* as departing from his own strictly mechanistic understanding of nature. I quote here from Anthony Kenny, *Descartes and His Philosophy* (New York: Random House, 1968), 201–202.

13. "What Is Phenomenology?" preface to *Phenomenology of Perception*, trans. Colin Smith (London: Routledge & Kegan Paul, 1962).

Notes on Contributors

CHARLES S. BROWN is Professor of Philosophy at Emporia State University. His essays have appeared in *Journal of the British Society for Phenomenology, Southwest Philosophical Review, Midwest Quarterly*, and *Dialogue and Universalism*. Two of his essays, one on the dissident movement in postwar Poland, and the other on multiculturalism and the end of Western thinking, have been translated into Polish. He is a former treasurer of the International Society for Universal Dialogue. For four years, he was Director of Emporia State University's Honors Program. He is currently completing a monograph on phenomenology and ecology.

EDWARD S. CASEY is Professor and Chair of Philosophy at State University of New York at Stony Brook, having previously taught at Yale University. In addition to edited collections and numerous articles, his publications include the three-volume series *Imagining, Remembering*, and *Getting Back into Place* (Indiana University Press) and *The Fate of Place: A Philosophical History* (University of California Press). Casey's latest book, *Representing Place: Landscape Paintings and Maps*, has just been published by Minnesota University Press. His current project is entitled "The World at a Glance."

CHRISTIAN DIEHM is completing a dissertation on Levinas and environmental philosophy, "The Gravity of Nature: Other-than-Human Others in the Thought of Emmanuel Levinas." He teaches courses in environmental ethics and deep ecology at Villanova University, and his publications include "Facing Nature: Levinas beyond the Human" and "Arne Naess, Val Plumwood and Deep Ecological Subjectivity: A Contribution to the Deep Ecology-Ecofeminism Debate."

LESTER EMBREE is William F. Dietrich Eminent Scholar in Philosophy at Florida Atlantic University. He has written, translated, and edited books and essays in constitutive phenomenology, philosophy of archeology, and environmental philosophy.

IRENE J. KLAVER is Assistant Professor of Philosophy at the University of North Texas. She is the author of *Ethiek rondom grote grazers* and numerous articles in Dutch and English, including "Silent Wolves: The Howl of the Implicit" (in *Wild Ideas*, ed. D. Rothenberg, 1995) and "The Implicit Practice of Environmental Philosophy" (in *Environmental Philosophy and Environmental Activism*, ed. Marietta and Embree, 1995). Klaver is a member of the Executive Committee of the International Association for Environmental Philosophy and serves on the Editorial Boards of *Environmental Ethics* and *Terra Nova: Nature and Culture*. Her current interests include the relations between environmental philosophy, phenomenology, aesthetics, and feminism.

ERAZIM KOHÁK, Professor Emeritus in the philosophical faculty of Charles University, Prague, Czech Republic, born in Prague, 1933, received his doctorate from Yale University in 1958, taught at Gustavus Adolphus College and at Boston University before returning to Prague in 1991. His writings focus on issues in social and environmental philosophy from the perspective of Husserl's phenomenology and include *Idea and Experience, The Embers and the Stars, The Green Halo*, as well as numerous other books and articles in both Czech and English.

MONIKA LANGER is Associate Professor of Philosophy at the University of Victoria in British Columbia, Canada. She has taught at the University of Toronto, Yale University, the University of Alberta, and Dalhousie University. Principal areas of interest include continental European philosophy, feminist philosophy, social/political issues, and philosophy of literature. She is the author of *Merleau-Ponty's Phenomenology of Perception: A Guide and Commentary*. Her articles have appeared in various books and in such journals as *Philosophy Today, Canadian Journal of Political and Social Theory, Teaching Philosophy, Thesis Eleven*, and *The Trumpeter*. At present, she is writing a book on Nietzsche's *The Gay Science*.

JOHN LLEWELYN has, since first teaching philosophy at the University of New England, Australia, been Reader in Philosophy at the University of Edinburgh, a Visiting Professor of Philosophy at the University of Memphis, and the Arthur J. Schmitt Distinguished Visiting Professor of Philosophy at Loyola University of Chicago. Among his publications are *Beyond*

Metaphysics?, Derrida on the Threshold of Sense, The Middle Voice of Ecological Consciousness, Emmanuel Levinas: The Genealogy of Ethics, The HypoCritical Imagination, and *Appositions—of Jacques Derrida and Emmanuel Levinas.*

DON E. MARIETTA, JR., is Professor Emeritus at Florida Atlantic University, and formerly Adelaide R. Snyder Distinguished Professor of Ethics and Professor of Philosophy at Florida Atlantic University. He is author of *For People and the Planet: Holism and Humanism in Environmental Ethics* (Temple University Press), *Philosophy of Sexuality* (M. E. Sharpe), *Introduction to Ancient Philosophy* (M. E. Sharpe), and journal articles and book chapters, mostly on ethics, primarily environmental ethics. His current interest is the phenomenology of moral judgment.

TED TOADVINE, Chair of Social Sciences at Emporia State University, is co-editor of *Merleau-Ponty's Reading of Husserl* (Kluwer) and *The Merleau-Ponty Reader* (forthcoming with Northwestern) and co-translator of Renaud Barbaras, *The Being of the Phenomena* (forthcoming). He has authored articles and translations in contemporary continental philosophy, especially phenomenology, and ecological philosophy. Currently, he is completing a monograph entitled *Limits of the Flesh: An Essay in Ecological Phenomenology.*

DAVID WOOD is a Professor of Philosophy at Vanderbilt University, and an Honorary Professor of Philosophy at Warwick, England. He has edited some ten books on continental philosophy, and is the author of *Philosophy at the Limit* (1990) and *The Deconstruction of Time* (republished by Northwestern University Press, 2001). He is currently completing four books: *Thinking after Heidegger, Time and Time Again, Things at the Edge of the World,* and a book on philosophy and trees.

MICHAEL E. ZIMMERMAN is Professor of Philosophy at Tulane University. In addition to being author of two books on Heidegger, as well as numerous articles and book chapters, Zimmerman has published *Contesting Earth's Future: Radical Ecology and Postmodernity* and is general editor of *Environmental Ethics: From Animal Rights to Radical Ecology.* Other research and teaching interests include Nietzsche, Buddhism, and philosophical aspects of gender. For seven years, he codirected Tulane's Environmental Studies Program.

Bibliography in Eco-Phenomenology

Although we have limited our selection to works in English, a quick glance at the Philosopher's Index *will show that considerable work in eco-phenomenology is already widely available in other languages. We have also not included classic works of the phenomenological tradition that are relevant to the topic—for example, from the writings of Husserl, Heidegger, Merleau-Ponty, and Levinas. For useful references to such sources, see the notes to the chapters in this volume.*

Abram, David. "Merleau-Ponty and the Voice of the Earth." *Environmental Ethics* 10, no. 2 (Summer 1988): 101–20.

———. "The Mechanical and the Organic: On the Influence of Metaphor in Science." In *Scientists on Gaia*, ed. Stephen Schneider and Penelope Boston. Cambridge: MIT Press, 1991.

———. "The Perceptual Implications of Gaia." *The Ecologist* 15, no. 3 (1985).

———. *The Spell of the Sensuous: Perception and Language in a More-Than-Human World*. New York: Vintage, 1996.

Benso, Sylvia. *The Face of Things: A Different Side of Ethics*. Albany: State University of New York Press Press, 2000.

Berleant, Arnold. *Living in the Landscape: Toward an Aesthetics of Environment*. Lawrence: University Press of Kansas, 1997.

Bernstein, J. M. "Re-enchanting Nature." *Journal of the British Society for Phenomenology* 31, no. 3 (2000): 277–99.

Berthold-Bond, Daniel. "Can There Be a 'Humanistic' Ecology? A Debate between Hegel and Heidegger on the Meaning of Ecological Thinking." *Social Theory and Practice* 20, no. 3 (1994): 279–309.

Bigwood, Carol. *Earth Muse: Feminism, Nature, and Art*. Philadelphia: Temple University Press, 1993.

Borgmann, Albert. *Crossing the Postmodern Divide*. Chicago: University of Chicago Press, 1992.

Braine, David. *The Human Person: Animal and Spirit*. Notre Dame: University of Notre Dame Press, 1992.

Brown, Charles. "Anthropocentrism and Ecocentrism: The Quest for a New Worldview." *The Midwest Quarterly* 36 (Winter 1995).

———. "Humanism and the Voice of Nature: Challenges for a Universal Metaphilosophy." *Dialogue and Universalism* 8, no. 1–2 (1998).

Callicot, J. Baird, and Roger T. Ames, eds. *Nature in Asian Traditions of Thought: Essays in Environmental Philosophy*. Albany: State University of New York Press, 1989.

Carter, Robert E. *Becoming Bamboo: Western and Eastern Explorations of the Meaning of Life*. Montreal: McGill-Queens University Press, 1992.

Casey, Edward S. *Fate of Place: A Philosophical History*. Berkeley: University of California Press, 1997.

———. *Getting Back into Place: Toward a Renewed Understanding of the Place World*. Bloomington: Indiana University Press, 1993.

Casey, Timothy. "The Environmental Roots of Environmental Activism." In *Environmental Philosophy and Environmental Activism*, ed. Don E. Marietta Jr. and Lester Embree, 37–49. Totowa, N.J.: Rowman & Littlefield, 1995.

Cave, George. "Animals, Heidegger, and the Right to Life." *Environmental Ethics* 4 (1982): 249–54.

Clark, David. "On Being 'the Last Kantian in Nazi Germany': Dwelling with Animals after Levinas." In *Animal Acts: Configuring the Human in Western History*, ed. Jennifer Ham and Matthew Senior. New York: Routledge, 1997.

Cohen, Robert, and Alfred Tauber, eds. *Philosophies of Nature: The Human Dimension. Honoring Erazim Kohák*. The Hague: Kluwer Academic Publishers, 1998.

Colony, Tracy. "Dwelling in the Biosphere? Heidegger's Critique of Humanism and Its Relevance for Ecological Thought." *International Studies in Philosophy* 31, no. 1 (1999): 37–45.

Compton, John J. "On the Sense of There Being a Moral Sense of Nature." *Personalist Forum* 2 (1986): 38–55.

———. "Phenomenology and the Philosophy of Nature." *Man and World* 21, no. 1 (1988): 65–89.

Corrington, Robert S. *Nature and Spirit: An Essay in Ecstatic Naturalism*. Bronx: Fordham University Press, 1992.

Dauenhauer, Bernard P. *Elements of Responsible Politics*. Norwell: Kluwer Academic Publishers, 1991.

———. "Heidegger, the Spokesman for the Dweller." *Southern Journal of Philosophy* 15 (1977): 189–99.

Diehm, Christian. "Facing Nature: Levinas beyond the Human." *Philosophy Today* 44, no. 1 (Spring 2000): 51–59.

Dreyfus, Hubert L., and Charles Spinosa. "Highway Bridges and Feasts: Heidegger and Borgmann on How to Affirm Technology." *Man and World* 30, no. 2 (1997): 159–77.

Embree, Lester. "The Constitutional Problematics of Non-Relativity or How to Dump Garbage in Nobody's Backyard." In *Phenomenology and Skepticism: Festschrift for James M. Edie*, ed. Brice R. Wachterman. Evanston: Northwestern University Press, 1996.

———. "An Environmental Phenomenological Examination of Electric Vehicle Technology." In *Technology and Environmental Philosophy*, ed. Marina Banchetti, Lester Embree, and Don Marietta. *Research in Philosophy and Technology* 18 (1999): 115–30.

———. "The Non-Worldly Grounding of Environmentalism." *Pondicherry University Journal of Social Science and Humanities* 1 (2000).

———. "Phenomenology of Action for Ecosystemic Health; or, How to Tend One's Own Garden." In *Environmental Philosophy and Environmental Activism*, ed. Don E. Marietta Jr. and Lester Embree, 51–66. Totowa, N.J.: Rowman & Littlefield, 1995.

———. "The Problem of Representational Adequacy or How to Evidence an Ecosystem." In *The Prism of the Self: Philosophical Essays in Honor of Maurice Natanson*, ed. Steven Galt Crowell. Dordrecht: Kluwer Academic Publishers, 1995.

———. "Problems of the Value of Nature in Phenomenological Perspective; or, What to Do about Snakes in the Grass." In *Phenomenology of Values and Valuing*, ed. James G. Hart and Lester Embree (Dordrecht: Kluwer Academic Publishers, 1997).

Evernden, Neil. *The Natural Alien: Humankind and Environment*. 2d ed. Toronto: University of Toronto Press, 1993.

———. "Nature in Industrial Society." In *Cultural Politics in Contemporary America*, ed. Ian Angus and Sut Jhally, 151–64. New York: Routledge, 1989.

———. *The Social Creation of Nature*. Baltimore: Johns Hopkins University Press, 1992.

Foltz, Bruce V. *Inhabiting the Earth: Heidegger, Environmental Ethics, and the Metaphysics of Nature*. Atlantic Highlands, N.J.: Humanities Press, 1995.

———. "On Heidegger and the Interpretation of Environmental Crisis." *Environmental Ethics* 6, no. 4 (Winter 1984): 323–42.

Foltz, Bruce, and Robert Frodeman. "Inhabiting the Earth: Heidegger, Environmental Ethics, and the Metaphysics of Nature." *Environmental Ethics* 19, no. 2 (1997).

Fox, Warwick. *Toward a Transpersonal Ecology: Developing New Foundations for Environmentalism*. Boston: Shambhala, 1990.

Fuller, Steve. "Sophist Versus Skeptic: Two Paradigms of Intentional Transaction." In *Perspectives on Mind*, ed. Herbert R. Otto, 199–208. Dordrecht: Kluwer Academic Publishers, 1988.

Garrard, Greg. "Heidegger, Heaney and the Problem of Dwelling." In *Writing the Environment: Ecocriticism and Literature*, ed. Richard Kerridge and Neil Sammells. London: Zed Books, 1998.

Glazebrook, Trish. "From *physis* to Nature, *techne* to Technology: Heidegger on Aristotle, Galileo, and Newton." *Southern Journal of Philosophy* 38, no. 1 (2000): 95–118.

Godway, Eleanor M. "The Being which Is Behind Us: Merleau-Ponty and the Question of Nature." *International Studies in Philosophy* 30, no. 1 (1998): 47–56.

Grange, Joseph. "Being, Feeling, and Environment." *Environmental Ethics* 7 (1985): 351–64.

———. "On the Way Towards Foundational Ecology." *Soundings* 60, no. 1 (1977).

Haar, Michel. *The Song of the Earth: Heidegger and the Grounds of the History of Being*. Trans. Reginald Lilly (Bloomington: Indiana University Press, 1993).

Hallman, Max. "Nietzsche's Environmental Ethics." *Environmental Ethics* 13, no. 2 (Winter 1991): 99–125.

Ham, Jennifer. "Taming the Beast: Animality in Wedekind and Nietzsche." In *Animal Acts: Configuring the Human in Western History*, ed. Jennifer Ham and Matthew Senior. New York: Routledge, 1997.

Hart, James, and Lester Embree, eds. *Phenomenology of Values and Valuing*. Dordrecht: Kluwer Academic Publishers, 1997.

Higgs, Eric, Andrew Light, and David Strong, eds. *Technology and the Good Life?* Chicago: University of Chicago Press, 2000.

Holden, Meg. "Phenomenology Versus Pragmatism: Seeking a Restoration Environmental Ethic." *Environmental Ethics* 23, no. 1 (2001): 37–56.

Holland, Nancy J. "Rethinking Ecology in the Western Philosophical Tradition: Heidegger and/on Aristotle." *Continental Philosophy Review* 32 (1999): 409–20.

Holler, Linda D. "In Search of a Whole-System Ethic." *Journal of Religious Ethics* 12 (1984): 219–39.

Howarth, Jane M. *In Praise of Backyards: Towards a Phenomenology of Place*. Lancaster: Department of Philosophy, Lancaster University, 1996.

———. "The Crisis of Ecology: A Phenomenological Perspective." *Environmental Values* 4, no. 1 (1995): 17–30.

Howe, Lawrence W. "Heidegger's Discussion of 'The Thing': A Theme for Deep Ecology." *Between the Species* 9, no. 2 (1993): 93–96.

Ihde, Don. *Technology and the Lifeworld: From Garden to Earth*. Bloomington: Indiana University Press, 1990.

―――. "Whole Earth Measurements: How Many Phenomenologists Does It Take to Detect a 'Greenhouse Effect'?" *Philosophy Today* 41 (1997): 128–34.

Jackson, Arthur F. "Nature and Human Nature in an Existential Perspective." *Contemporary Philosophy* 18, no. 4–5 (1996): 3–6.

James, Simon P. "Thing-Centered Holism in Buddhism, Heidegger, and Deep Ecology." *Environmental Ethics* 22, no. 4 (2000): 359–76.

Jonas, Hans. *The Phenomenon of Life: Toward a Philosophical Biology*. New York: Harper & Row, 1966.

Jung, Hwa Yol. "The Orphic Voice and Ecology." *Environmental Ethics* 3 (1981): 329–40.

Klaver, Irene J. "The Implicit Practice of Environmental Philosophy." In *Environmental Philosophy and Environmental Activism*, ed.y Don E. Marietta Jr. and Lester Embree, 67–78. Totowa, N.J.: Rowman and Littlefield, 1995.

―――. "Silent Wolves: The Howl of the Implicit." In *Wild Ideas*, ed. David Rothenberg. Minneapolis: University of Minnesota Press, 1995.

Kohák, Erazim. "Of Dwelling and Wayfaring." In *The Longing for Home*, ed. Leroy Rouner, 30–46. Notre Dame: Notre Dame University Press, 1977.

―――. *The Embers and the Stars: A Philosophical Inquiry into the Moral Sense of Nature*. Chicago: University of Chicago Press, 1984.

―――. "Forest Lights: Notes on the Conceptualization of the Unconscious." *Journal of Religion and Health* 22, no. 1 (Spring 1983): 49–57.

―――. *The Green Halo: A Bird's Eye View of Ecological Ethics*. Chicago: Open Court, 2000.

―――. "Human Rights and Nature's Rightness." *Lyceum* 2, no. 2 (Fall 1990): 22–36.

―――. *Idea and Experience: Husserl's Project of Phenomenology in Ideen I*. Chicago: University of Chicago Press, 1982; 2d ed., 1985.

―――. "Knowing Good and Evil." *Husserl Studies* 10, no. 1 (Summer 1993): 31–42.

―――. "Of Marmots, Beavers and Architects." In *The Yearbook of the Czech Chamber of Architects*, ed. Petr Bílek, 25–28. Prague: Česká komora architektů, 1999.

―――. "The Phenomenology of Nostalgia." *Terra Nova* 2, no. 1 (December 1996): 6–14.

―――. "Red War, Green Peace." In *Ethics and Environmental Policy*, ed. Frederick Ferré and Peter Hartel, 163–77. Athens: University of Georgia Press, 1994.

———. "Sigmund Freud by Moonlight." *Journal of Religion and Health* 19, no. 4 (Winter 1980): 260–67.

———. "Speaking to Trees." *Critical Review* 6, no. 2–3 (Summer 1993): 371–88.

———. "Transcendental Experience, Everyday Philosophy." In *Transcendental Philosophy and Everyday Experience*, ed. Tom Rockmore and Vladimír Zeman, 43–51. Newark: Humanities Press, 1997.

———. "Transitions: The Ploughman, the Pilgrim and the Distressed Conqueror." *Transitions*, a thematic issue of *The Psychoanalytic Review* 81, no. 1 (Spring 1994): 101–27.

———. "Varieties of Ecological Experience." *Environmental Ethics* 19 (Summer 1997): 153–71.

Kolb, David. "Home on the Range: Planning and Totality." *Research in Phenomenology* 22 (1992): 3–11.

Kress, J. "From Metaphysics to Inhabitation. Review of *Inhabiting the Earth: Heidegger, Environmental Ethics, and the Metaphysics of Nature* by Bruce Foltz." *Research in Phenomenology* 26 (1996).

La Chapelle, Dolores. *Earth Wisdom*. Los Angeles: Guild of Tutors Press, 1978.

Langer, Monika. "Merleau-Ponty and Deep Ecology." In *Ontology and Alterity in Merleau-Ponty*, ed. Galen A. Johnson and Michael B. Smith, 115–29, 192–97. Evanston: Northwestern University Press, 1990.

Leiss, William. "Husserl and the Mastery of Nature." *Telos* 5 (1970): 82–97.

Light, Andrew, and Jonathan M. Smith, eds. *Space, Place, and Environmental Ethics*. Lanham: Rowman & Littlefield, 1997.

Lingis, Alphonso. *The Community of Those Who Have Nothing in Common*. Bloomington: Indiana University Press, 1994.

———. *The Imperative*. Bloomington: Indiana University Press, 1998.

Llewelyn, John. "Am I Obsessed by Bobby? (Humanism of the Other Animal)." In *Re-Reading Levinas*, ed. Robert Bernasconi and Simon Critchley, 234–45. Bloomington: Indiana University Press, 1991.

———. *The Middle Voice of Ecological Conscience: A Chiasmic Reading of Responsibility in the Neighbourhood of Levinas, Heidegger and Others*. New York: St. Martin's, 1991.

———. "Ontological Responsibility and the Poetics of Nature." *Research in Phenomenology* 19 (1989): 3–26.

Macauley, David, ed. *Minding Nature: The Philosophers of Ecology*. New York: Guilford Press, 1996.

Malpas, J. E. *Place and Experience: A Philosophical Topography*. New York: Cambridge University Press, 1999.

Manes, Christopher. "Philosophy and the Environmental Task." *Environmental Ethics* 10 (1988): 75–82.

Marietta Jr., Don E. "The Concept of Objective Value." In *Phenomenology of Values and Valuing*, ed. James G. Hart and Lester Embree. Dordrecht: Kluwer Academic Publishers, 1997.

———. "Decisions Regarding Technology: The Human Factors." In *Technology and Environmental Philosophy*, ed. Marina Banchetti, Lester Embree, and Don Marietta. *Research in Philosophy and Technology* 18 (1999): 57–72.

———. "Environmental Holism and Individuals." *Environmental Ethics* 10 (Fall 1988).

———. "Knowledge and Obligation in Environmental Ethics: A Phenomenological Approach." *Environmental Ethics* 4, no. 2 (Summer 1982): 153–62.

———. *For People and the Planet: Holism and Humanism in Environmental Ethics*. Philadelphia: Temple University Press, 1994.

———. "Phenomenology and Ecofeminism." In *Phenomenology of the Cultural Disciplines*, ed. Mano Daniel and Lester Embree. Dordrecht: Kluwer Academic Publishers, 1994.

———. "World Views and Moral Decisions: A Reply to Tom Regan." *Environmental Ethics* 2 (1980): 369–72.

Marietta Jr., Don E., and Lester Embree, eds. *Environmental Philosophy and Environmental Activism*. Totowa, N.J.: Rowman & Littlefield, 1995.

Marangudakis, Manussos. "Ecology as a Pseudo-Religion?" *Telos* 112 (1998): 107–24.

Maxcy, David J. "Meaning in Nature: Rhetoric, Phenomenology, and the Question of Environmental Value." *Philosophy and Rhetoric* 27, no. 4 (1994): 330–46.

McWhorter, Ladelle, ed. *Heidegger and the Earth: Essays in Environmental Philosophy*. Kirksville, Mo.: Thomas Jefferson University Press, 1992.

Melle, Ullrich. "Ecology." In *Encyclopedia of Phenomenology*, ed. Lester Embree et al., 148–52. Dordrecht: Kluwer Academic Publishers, 1997.

———. "How Deep Is Deep Enough? Ecological Modernization or Farewell to the World-City?" In *Environmental Philosophy and Environmental Activism*, ed. Don E. Marietta Jr. and Lester Embree, 99–123. Totowa, N.J.: Rowman & Littlefield, 1995.

———. "Nature and Spirit." In *Issues in Husserl's Ideas II*, ed. Thomas Nenon and Lester Embree. Dordrecht: Kluwer Academic Publishers, 1996.

———. "Philosophy and Ecological Crisis." In *Phenomenology of the Cultural Disciplines*, ed. Mano Daniel and Lester Embree, 171–91. Dordrecht: Kluwer Academic Publishers, 1994.

Moran, Dermot. "Towards a Philosophy of the Environment." In *Educating for Environmental Awareness*, ed. John Feehan, 45–67. Dublin: University College Dublin Environmental Institute, 1997.

Naess, Arne. *Ecology, Community, and Lifestyle: Outline of an Ecosophy.* Cambridge: Cambridge University Press, 1989.

———. "The World of Concrete Contents." *Inquiry* 28 (1985): 417–28.

Nuyen, A. T. "A Heideggerian Existential Ethics for the Human Environment." *Journal of Value Inquiry* (1991): 359–66.

Oddie, Richard. "The Living Tissue: Environmental Phenomenology and Acoustic Ecology." *Call to Earth* 2, no. 1 (March 2001).

Oelschlaeger, Max. *The Idea of Wilderness.* New Haven: Yale University Press, 1991.

———, ed. *Postmodern Environmental Ethics.* Albany: State University of New York Press, 1995.

Ogawa, Tadashi. "Qi and Phenomenology of Wind." *Continental Philosophy Review* 31, no. 3 (1998): 321–35.

Peperzak, Adriaan. "Levinas on Technology and Nature." *Man and World* 25 (1992): 469–82.

Polk, Danne W. "Gabriel Marcel's Kinship to Ecophilosophy." *Environmental Ethics* 16, no. 2 (1994): 173–86.

Rodick, David. "Poetic Dwelling and Deep Ecology: Bill McKibben and Martin Heidegger on The End of Nature." *Call to Earth* 2, no. 1 (March 2001).

Russon, John. "Embodiment and Responsibility: Merleau-Ponty and the Ontology of Nature." *Man and World* 27, no. 3 (1994): 291–308.

Sakakibara, Tetsuya. "The Relationship between Nature and Spirit in Husserl's Phenomenology Revisited." *Continental Philosophy Review* 31, no. 3 (1998): 255–72.

Sallis, John. *Force of Imagination: The Sense of the Elemental.* Bloomington: Indiana University Press, 2000.

———. "Levinas and the Elemental." *Research in Phenomenology,* 28 (1998): 152–59.

———. *Stone.* Bloomington: Indiana University Press, 1994.

Sanders, John T. "Affordance: An Ecological Approach to First Philosophy." In *Perspectives on Embodiment: The Intersections of Nature and Culture,* ed. Gail Weiss and Honi Fern Haber. New York: Routledge, 1999.

Santoni, Ronald E. "On the Existential Meaning of Violence." *Dialogue and Humanism* 3, no. 4 (1993): 139–50.

Schalow, Frank. "Who Speaks for the Animals? Heidegger and the Question of Animal Welfare." *Environmental Ethics* 22, no. 3 (Fall 2000): 259–72.

Schultz, Robert C., and Donald J. Hughes, eds. *Ecological Consciousness.* Washington: University Press of America, 1981.

Seamon, David, ed. *Dwelling, Seeing, and Designing: Toward a Phenomenological Ecology.* Albany: State University of New York Press, 1993.

Seamon, David, and Robert Mugerauer, eds. *Dwelling, Place, and Environment: Towards a Phenomenology of Person and World.* Dordrecht: Martinus Nijhoff, 1985.

Seamon, David, and Arthur Zajonc, eds. *Goethe's Way of Science: A Phenomenology of Nature.* Albany: State University of New York Press, 1998.

Seidel, George J. "Heidegger: Philosopher for Ecologists?" *Man and World* 4 (1971): 93–99.

Sessions, George. "Spinoza and Jeffers on Man in Nature." *Inquiry* 20 (1977): 481–528.

Sinha, Amita, ed. *Landscape Perception.* London: Academic, 1995.

Steelwater, Eliza. "Mead and Heidegger: Exploring the Ethics and Theory of Space, Place, and Environment." In *Philosophy and Geography I: Space, Place, and Environmental Ethics,* edited by Andrew Light. Lanham: Rowman & Littlefield, 1997.

Steeves, H. Peter, ed. *Animal Others: On Ethics, Ontology, and Animal Life.* New York: State University of New York Press, 1999.

Strong, David. *Crazy Mountains: Learning from Wilderness to Weigh Technology.* Albany: State University of New York Press, 1995.

Taylor, Charles. "Heidegger, Language, and Ecology." In *Heidegger: A Critical Reader,* ed. Hubert Dreyfus and Harrison Hall, 247–69. Cambridge: MIT Press, 1992.

Thiele, Leslie Paul. "Nature and Freedom: A Heideggerian Critique of Biocentric and Sociocentric Environmentalism." *Environmental Ethics* 17 (1995): 171–90.

———. *Timely Meditations: Martin Heidegger and Postmodern Politics.* Princeton: Princeton University Press, 1995.

Toadvine, Ted. "Ecophenomenology in the New Millenium." In *The Reach of Reflection: Issues for Phenomenology's Second Century,* ed. Stephen Galt Crowell and Lester Embree. Boca Raton: Center for Advanced Research in Phenomenology, 2001.

———. "Naturalizing Phenomenology." *Philosophy Today* 43, SPEP Supplement (1999): 124–31.

Tymieniecka, Anna-Teresa, ed. *Phenomenology of Man and the Human Condition.* Dordrecht: Reidel, 1983.

Ulanowicz, Robert E. *Growth and Development: Ecosystems Phenomenology.* New York: Springer-Verlag, 1986.

Van Der Veken, Jan. "Merleau-Ponty and Whitehead on the Concept of Nature." *Interchange* 31, no. 2 (2000): 319–34.

Vogel, Lawrence. "Does Environmental Ethics Need a Metaphysical Grounding?" *Hastings Center Report* 25, no. 7 (1995): 30–39.

West, Richmond. "Can We Really Cope with Creatures? 'Dasein' and Animality in Heidegger." *Contemporary Philosophy* 20, no. 1–2 (1998): 38–44.

Westra, Laura. "Let It Be: Heidegger and Future Generations." *Environmental Ethics* 7, no. 4 (Winter 1985): 341–50.

Zimmerman, Michael. "Beyond 'Humanism': Heidegger's Understanding of Technology." *Listening* 12 (1977): 74–83.

———. *Contesting Earth's Future: Radical Ecology and Postmodernity.* Berkeley and Los Angeles: University of California Press, 1994.

———. "Deep Ecology." In *Encyclopedia of Phenomenology*, ed. Lester Embree et al., 137–41. Dordrecht: Kluwer Academic Publishers, 1997.

———. "Ecofascism: A Threat to American Environmentalism?" In *The Ecological Community*, ed. Roger S. Gottlieb, 229–54. New York: Routledge, 1997.

———. "Feminism, Deep Ecology, and Environmental Ethics." *Environmental Ethics* 9 (Spring 1987).

———. "Heidegger, Buddhism, and Deep Ecology." In *The Cambridge Companion to Heidegger*, ed. Charles Guignon. New York: Cambridge University Press, 1993.

———. *Heidegger's Confrontation with Modernity: Technology, Politics, Art.* Bloomington: Indiana University Press, 1990.

———. "Implications of Heidegger's Thought for Deep Ecology." *The Modern Schoolman* 64 (November 1986): 19–43.

———. "Martin Heidegger: Anti-Naturalistic Critic of Technological Modernity." In *Ecological Thinkers*, ed. David Macauley. New York: Guilford, 1995.

———. "Marx and Heidegger on the Technological Domination of Nature." *Philosophy Today* 23 (1979): 99–112.

———. "Philosophical Reflections on Reform Versus Deep Environmentalism." *The Trumpeter* 3, no. 4 (Fall 1986).

———. "Rethinking the Heidegger-Deep Ecology Relationship." *Environmental Ethics* 15, no. 3 (Fall 1993): 195–224.

———. "Some Important Themes in Current Heidegger Research." *Research in Phenomenology* 7 (1977): 259–81.

———. "Technological Culture and the End of Philosophy." *Research in Philosophy and Technology* 2 (1979): 137–46.

———. "Toward a Heideggerean *Ethos* for Radical Environmentalism." *Environmental Ethics* 5, no. 3 (Summer 1983): 99–131.

Index

Muir, John, 5, 16, 61, 66–68, 71n, 72n
Musil, Robert, 53, 70n

Naess, Arne, 32n, 118n, 125, 134n, 224
Nancy, Jean-Luc, 160, 163, 168n
National Socialism, 22, 85–86, 101n, 166–67
naturalism, xviii, 38–40, 42; Husserl's critique of, xiii, 3, 6–8, 38; phenomenology and, xx, 211–13, 221; scientific, xi
nature: alterity of, 105; dark side of, 105; estrangement from, xx; as historical, 7; as human construct, 80; kinship with, 139–41; lifeworldly, 39; mortality of, 16; nature-as-miracle, 141–43; *physis*, 80, 82–85, 87; problems with conceptions of, 104–5; relation with culture, 110, 156–58, 160; scientific view of, 74; as sentient, 103; teleology of, 28, 140–41, 147, 182, 227–28; "there is" [*il y a*] and, 148–50. *See also* Heidegger: nature in
Newton, Sir Isaac, 54, 93
Nietzsche, Friedrich, xv, 73, 95–96, 103, 106–12, 117, 119n; eternal recurrence, 109, 111, 216; relativity of truth in, 108; *Thus Spoke Zarathustra*, 107–112
nihilism, xv, 75, 81–82, 86–90, 94, 109

objectivity, 4, 8, 13, 22, 25, 26, 40, 54; moral, 9, 11; quantification and, 22
Ockham, William of, 26
Odum, Eugene P., 127
ontology, 116–17, 126–27, 160–61, 164; dualistic, xii, xix, 7, 81, 104–5, 107–9, 115–16; of flesh, 115–16, 147–50, 158; integrative, 112; objectivistic, 122; ontological commitment,128–29, 131–33; phenomenology and, 52, 75–76; as philosophical approach to nature, 73; of the present, 160

panentheism, xv, 95–96
Parmenides, 88
Patočka, Jan, 32n
Pauen, Michael, 98n
Payne Knight, Richard, 53
Peperzak, Adriaan, 183n
perception, 146–47, 211–12; Levinas's critique of, 189–90; perceptual faith, 197. *See also* glance
Peterson, Anna, 98n
phenomenology, x–xii, 25, 52, 57–59, 62, 67, 70, 73, 77, 121, 189, 226; constitution in, 24, 158, 164; constitutive, 37–39, 42–43, 45–48; contributions of, to environmentalism, 106; definition of, 51, 75; description in, 25; eidetic analysis, 23; Husserlian, 164–65; impossible, 140; as liminology, 220–21; moral philosophy and, 5–6; naturalism and, xx, 211–13, 221, 231; ontology and, 52, 75–76; of perception in Levinas, 189–90; as performance, 59–60; reduction, 6, 48 (*see also* epochē); reflection, 131; sedimentation and reactivation, 157–58, 160; self-evidence in, 52; transcendental, 19, 23, 28, 48. *See also* eco-phenomenology; existentialism; intentionality; subjectivity: transcendental
philosophy: academic, x; Anglo-American, 73; Christian, 82, 89 (*see* theology: Christian); continental, 73; ecological, 3, 14 (*see also* ecology: philosophical); environmental, 73, 183; German idealism, 58; moral, 5, 8–10, 65, 73, 125, 191–92; pre-Socratic, 68; traditional, subversion of, 108. *See also* ethics; existentialism; ontology; postmodernism
Plato, 16, 60, 64, 68, 77, 82, 92, 94, 107, 146, 171, 174, 228; neo-Platonism, 216
Plumwood, Val, 118n
postmodernism, 20, 22; postmodern ethics, 73

CPSIA information can be obtained
at www.ICGtesting.com
Printed in the USA
BVHW032120070819
555245BV00031B/5/P